A WHISPER OF ESPIONAGE

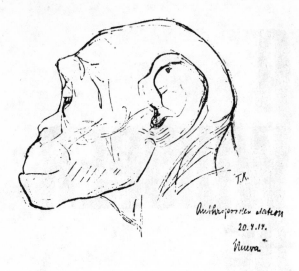

From the frontispiece of *The Mentality of Apes*, German edition, by Wolfgang Köhler. Drawing by Thekla Köhler.

A WHISPER OF ESPIONAGE

Ronald Ley

AVERY PUBLISHING GROUP INC.

Garden City Park, New York

Map of Tenerife reprinted by permission of Faber and Faber Ltd. From *The Canary Islands* by Henry Myhill.

Cover Design: Roy Colmer
In-House Editor: Joanne Abrams
Typesetting: Multifacit Graphics

Library of Congress Cataloging-in-Publication Data

Ley, Ronald.
    A whisper of espionage : Wolfgang Köhler and the apes of Tenerife / Ronald Ley.
        p.   cm.
    Includes index.
    ISBN 0-89529-432-X
    1. Köhler, Wolfgang, 1887–1967. 2. World War, 1914–1918—Secret Service—Germany. 3. Spies—Germany—Biography. 4. Spies—Canary Islands—Tenerife—Biography. 5. Psychologists—Germany—Biography. I. Title.
D639.S8K645   1990
940.4′8743′092—dc20   89-36061
                                                          CIP

Printed in the United States of America

10 9 8 7 6 5 4 3 2 1

Contents

To my daughter, Jessica.

Acknowledgments

Writing a book that tells the story of a search for information about people, places, and events of the past requires a great deal of help from many people in many places. Among those in London, England to whom I give my thanks are: Professor G.C. Drew, University College, University of London; the American Embassy; the Imperial War Museum; Mr. Hiscock, Historical Section of Library and Records Office of the British Foreign Office; J.D. Lawson, Naval Research Branch of Ministry of Defence, Old War Office; Admiral Schünemann, West German naval attaché; E. W. Dunham and Mr. Cox, Public Records Office; and Malcolm Lewis, Media, Limited.

Among those who helped in Tenerife, I wish to give special thanks to Austin and Julia Baillon, friends who opened many doors, not the least important of which were those to their home. Other residents of Tenerife to whom I am indebted are: Molly Abercromby; Anthony Yeoward; Isidoro Luz-Carpenter; Dr. Vincente Pelechano, University of La Laguna; Manuel Florian Ibañez, secretary of the Government of Puerto de la Cruz; Pedro Fernández-Marle; Manuel Abreu-González; Dr. Schotz and Jacob Ahlers, West German Consulate for Tenerife, Santa Cruz; Guillermo Luz-Carpenter; William Clark; Ramón Juega Buide, Meteorological Observatory, Izaña; Tomas Hernández;

Luís Diego Cuscoy, Museo Arqueológico, Santa Cruz; Fernando Molina Herrero, Meteorological Observatory, Izaña; Dr. Christine Jordan; Cecil Bellamy; Pedro Rodríguez García Prieto, Meteorological Observatory, Los Rodeos airport; Sr. Zalote, Meteorological Observatory, Santa Cruz; Francisco Sanchez, University of La Laguna; Susana Groth-Iglesia de Ascañio, Santa Cruz; Carlos Ramón Pérez-Hamilton; Charles Hamilton; and Antonio Martí.

Among those who helped me with my research in West Germany are: Jurgen Rohwer, Bibliothek für Zeitgeschichte, Stuttgart; Dr. Sandhofer, Freiburg Military Archives; Dr. Tholey, University of Frankfurt; Dr. Wolfgang Metzger, University of Münster; the Stadtarchiv Frankfurt; Drs. Kahlenberg, Giessler, and Bobarach, Bundesarchiv Koblenz; Dr. Keipert, Bundesarchiv Bonn; the Max Planck Institute of Munich; Dr. Neuhaus, Berlin Archives of the Max Planck Institute; Dr. Vesper, State Library for Prussian Cultural Possessions, Berlin; Dr. Lowenthal-Hensel, Secret Federal Archives of Berlin. And among those who helped me in East Germany are: Dr. Alfons Sommers and Dr. Günter Wendel, Alexander von Humboldt University; and Archives of the Prussian Academy of Science.

In the United States, the person to whom I am most indebted in matters of research is Richard Solomon, University of Pennsylvania. Dick, the consummate scientist-teacher, was prompt to respond with his help whenever called upon. Other people in the United States to whom I owe my thanks, some of whom made themselves available on the strength of Dick's recommendation, are: Robert Watson, University of New Hampshire; Hans Wallach, Swarthmore College; Henry Gleitman, University of Pennsylvania; Solomon Asch, University of Pennsylvania; Richard Held, Massachusetts Institute of Technology; the Peabody Museum of Harvard University; William Battig, University of Colorado; Michael Wertheimer, University of Colorado; Hans-Lukas Teuber, Massachusetts Institute of Technology; Murphy D. Smith and James McClellan, American Philosophical Society; Jack Dugan, State University of New York at Albany; Archives of the New York Public Library; John Popplestone, Archives of the History of American Psychology, University of Akron, Akron, Ohio; and Warren Roberts, State University of New York at Albany.

When my journey ended and the data were in hand, a number of people helped in the preparation of the manuscript. I wish to give my sincere thanks to Renate and Tom Barker for their generous help in the translation and interpretation of German documents, and to my wife Cindy for her part in the translation and interpretation of Spanish documents and her critical comments from the first draft to the final typescript. In matters of English, I wish to thank Barbara Iselin for her critical reading of early drafts, Joanne Abrams for her careful editing of the final draft, Maribel Gray for typing and keeping track of the many revisions through which the manuscript went, and Rudy Shur for his encouraging words and his belief that I could tell well a story worth telling.

Finally, I wish to thank the administration of the State University of New York at Albany for the sabbatical leave that provided me with the opportunity to undertake my search, and the Research Foundation of the State University of New York, and members of its review committees, for awarding me with two Faculty Research Fellowships. The leave and the fellowships gave me the means for doing the research that needed to be done.

Preface

The complete history of modern psychology cannot be written without reference to the work of Wolfgang Köhler (1887-1967). Although his international reputation was established primarily through his ground-breaking work on cognitive processes in apes and his contributions to the development of Gestalt psychology, the broad scope of his intellectual outlook went considerably beyond the usual range of the experimental psychologist in academe. Köhler was a physicist, physiologist, and philosopher as well as a psychologist. It was in fact a deep interest in philosophy that led to *The Place of Value in a World of Facts*, a book based on his William James Lectures on Philosophy and Psychology given at Harvard University in 1934. It is a tribute to his genius that Köhler was able to incorporate the phenomenological method, the qualitative analysis of experience, into his scientific work and still win high respect from scientists whose views were philosophically opposed to his own.

The first twenty-five years of the twentieth century, the years of Köhler's youth and early adulthood, were an exciting period in modern psychology, a period of promising discoveries and radical departures from the established thinking that marked the beginnings of modern science. It is important to keep in mind that the history of *modern* science is brief. In the nineteenth century, the sciences of physics and chemistry were relatively new, but the enormous successes of the scientific method in generating knowledge captured the imagination of academicians. Physiology was, in its early days, considered to be alarmingly bold because it dared to venture into the sacred realm of living matter in search of basic principles. Successes here led logically to an even bolder step, the application of the scientific method to the study of human experience—psychology.

The significance of Köhler's work is well-known among psychologists, but the impact of his work has not been felt outside of the academic community as much as that of some of his now-famous contemporaries. In order to help the reader appreciate Köhler's place in the chronology of a few important events in the history of modern science and to understand better the intellectual spirit of his times, some scholarly contributions made by some of his contemporaries are noted here.

In 1878, a few years before Köhler's birth, Wilhelm Wundt (1832-1920), the father of modern psychology, founded the first formal laboratory for the experimental study of psychology at the University of Leipzig. In 1904, Wundt, a physician by training, published the English translation of his *Principles of Physiological Psychology;* in 1912, he published the translation of his *Introduction to Psychology.* William James (1842-1910), who, like Wundt, was also trained in medicine, published his *Principles of Psychology* in 1890. Subsequent to this publication, James turned to philosophy, publishing *Pragmatism* in 1907, *The Meaning of Truth* in 1908, and *A Pluralistic Universe* in 1909.

Ivan Pavlov (1849-1936), another physician, received a Nobel Prize in 1904 for his work on the physiology of the digestive glands, and began an extensive program of research on the conditioned response, an outgrowth of a serendipitous discovery connected with his thorough research work on the physiology of salivation. The story of Pavlov's research on the conditioned reflex is told by him in forty lectures published between 1903 and 1928.

Perhaps the best known physician cum psychologist of this period was Sigmund Freud (1856-1939). In 1900, he published a book that many consider to be his greatest work, *Die Traumdeutung,* the book that purported to demonstrate the psychological mechanisms at work in the concealment of the true meaning of dreams. In 1909, Freud came to the United States, where he gave a series of celebrated lectures at Clark University. During the course of two winter sessions of 1915-1917 at the University of Vienna, he gave a series of twenty-eight lectures, which were published in English in 1920 under the title *A General Introduction to Psychoanalysis*. In 1926, Freud returned to the United States, where he gave a series of lectures at the New School for Social Research.

Two German physicists who left indelible marks on the history of science were Max Planck (1858-1947) and Albert Einstein (1879-1955). Planck—who in 1900 introduced the concept of "quanta," which subsequently led to the development of the revolutionary quantum theory of modern physics—received a Nobel Prize in 1918. At about the same time (1902-1909), Einstein evolved the theory of relativity, receiving a Nobel Prize in 1921. Köhler studied physics under Planck as a student at the University of Berlin and was director of the psychology laboratory at the same university during the last eleven years of Einstein's tenure as a professor of physics and director of theoretical physics at the Kaiser Wilhelm Institute in Berlin (1914-1933).

Chief among the American psychologists who followed William James was John Watson (1878-1958), who founded behaviorism in 1913 with the publication of an article entitled "Psychology as the Behaviorist Views It." The thesis of this article was expanded upon in his book *Behavior: An Introduction to Comparative Psychology*, published in 1914. In 1924, Watson published *Behaviorism*, a book based on a series of lectures given at the New School for Social Research a year or two earlier. B.F. Skinner (born 1904) read Watson's *Behaviorism*, as well as H.G. Wells on Pavlov, changed his plans to become a novelist, and entered the graduate school of Harvard University in the fall of 1928 for the purpose of studying psychology.

In 1912, Max Wertheimer (1880-1943), in a report of the seminal research that would give rise to Gestalt psychology, demonstrated that the visual illusion of apparent movement cannot be distinguished from true movement. This illusion, which Wertheimer called the phi phenomenon, underlies the perception of movement in "motion" pictures—the relatively rapid sequential presentation of still pictures each separated by a brief period of darkness. The results of this research challenged the then widely held view that consciousness can be understood through the introspective analysis of experience into sensations. The subjects used in Wertheimer's research were two junior faculty at the Frankfurt Academy, Kurt Koffka (1886-1941) and Wolfgang Köhler. In 1933, Wertheimer, a close personal friend of Albert Einstein, left Germany for the United States, where he became the first chair of the Department of Psychology at the New School for Social Research.

Although the Gestalt school of psychology, which began with the work of Wertheimer, Koffka, and Köhler just prior to the years of World War I, did not grow into a large unified intellectual movement, the influence of its ideas still lives in contemporary psychology. Many principles of cognitive psychology, the dominant field of interest among psychologists today, can be traced directly to the ideas first expressed by Max Wertheimer, Kurt Koffka, and Wolfgang Köhler.

Köhler's work and the rich period of history in which he worked led me to spend part of my 1974-1975 sabbatical leave in Tenerife, an island of the Canary Archipelago, in search of the site of the defunct anthropoid ape research station where Köhler conducted the first experiments demonstrating that apes share with humans the cognitive skills of reasoning and problem solving. In my search, I met Manuel González y García, an eighty-seven-year-old native of Tenerife who had served as Köhler's animal handler and maintenance man at the station throughout its years on the island (1912-1920). The old animal handler recalled amusing anecdotes and interesting stories about his experiences working closely with Köhler. He was delighted to learn that Köhler achieved fame with his book, *The Mentality of Apes*, but was surprised to learn that Köhler had left Germany in 1935 to move to the United States, where in subsequent years he achieved many distinctions including election to the presidency of the American Psychological Association.

When I told Manuel that Köhler had died a few years earlier, he was saddened, and revealed a long-kept secret. He told me that Köhler was a spy for the German military, that the ape research station was a cover for his espionage activities, and that Köhler maintained and operated a concealed radio with which he communicated military intelligence.

This book is an odyssey. It tells the story of my travels in search of evidence that might shed light on the mystery that lay behind the scenes of Köhler's work in Tenerife during the years of World War I. Like many journeys of exploration, mine was to lead me in many directions beyond my original destination. As I searched for the facts about Köhler's life and times on that small island off the African coast, I was to gain an unexpected view of the private Köhler—of Köhler the husband, the father, and the man. And, as is so often the case in exploratory journeys, I was to gain a fresh view of myself.

Foreword

Most of those who have had a course in elementary psychology have heard of Wolfgang Köhler's *Mentality of Apes*, and most psychologists will recall that the studies were carried out by Köhler when he was marooned on the Island of Tenerife off the west coast of Africa during the First World War. I well remember the excitement that was created when he lectured to American university audiences in the late 1920s and showed the films of his chimpanzees' demonstrating their problem-solving abilities by stacking boxes or by using sticks to retrieve bananas that were out of reach. "Insight" became part of the current vocabulary of psychology.

It was not until a half-century later that one psychologist, Ronald Ley, the author of this book, thought to raise the questions that were neither raised nor answered in Köhler's book. The initial question that haunted him was "Could the site of the defunct research station still be located?" Once he decided to answer this question, further questions pressed for answers. Why was it founded? How did a German research station happen to be located on this Spanish island? Why was young Köhler, inexperienced in animal psychology, selected to head it? Why did he leave suddenly in 1920, and move the chimpanzees to Germany?

What began as a specific search to be conducted as a project during a sabbatical year in 1975, ended for Ley, an established experimental psychologist, as an odyssey that required numerous trips over the next three years. These took him to England and the Continent (as well as return trips to Tenerife) for meetings with those still alive who had recollections going back to the years of 1912 to 1920, when the Research Station was in existence, and to archive sources that would be informative about the times and particularly about Köhler.

Ley proved to be an indefatigable sleuth, following every lead, and any lover of detective fiction will be intrigued by this story, revealed through notes that he took, his comparisons of one report with another to find agreements and inconsistencies in his search for an understanding of what really happened, and, eventually, his thoughts on what all that he learned told him about Köhler, the man. He treats Köhler throughout with respect, and despite some unexpected revelations about him as they relate to the intelligence apparatus of Germany at the time, this is in no sense a muckraking account to discredit Köhler's achievements as a psychological scientist, a theorist, and one of the founders of Gestalt psychology.

Preparing the book itself took another decade in which to fit all the pieces together. In his investigations, Ley learned many of the lessons that true historians have to learn. For example, while the interpretative aspects of history call for attempting to understand historical events in their context, the most difficult task may be to find where reliable information has been preserved, and then to visit and sift through the located archival sources. Ley's persistence has led to this remarkable and revealing story of Wolfgang Köhler.

To establish the context of the research at Tenerife, Ley had to know about the later years of the endeavors of the government of Kaiser Wilhelm II, and to discover why Tenerife, on the Atlantic shipping lanes from North to South, was important to the British, whose ships were being sunk by the German submarines in the neighboring waters. The Germans were somehow being assisted from Tenerife, even though it was a Spanish island, and Spain was neutral. All this, of interest to historians as much as to psychologists, became relevant to the understanding of the roles of Köhler, and why he departed suddenly in 1920.

As a result of this study, which began to answer straightforward questions about the location of the research station, we now know a great deal more than heretofore about Köhler the man, who talked little about his private life. Included among the informants were the surviving children of his first marriage—his marriage to the wife who helped him in Tenerife, and there gave birth to three of their five children. She was the artist who drew a frontispiece for the German edition of his book (not reproduced in the English version). Some details of that picture bore on the hypotheses that Ley was exploring. Köhler was not much of a father and saw almost nothing of these children after his divorce. He had one daughter during his second marriage. His wife of this marriage survived him, and her recollections are part of this story, telling also that he was not a family man.

The excitement of the odyssey began when Ley met the man who had maintained the facilities of the Research Station and taken care of the animals throughout the station's existence. After meeting him, a prolonged search began for the detailed context that was required to understand all that was missing in *The Mentality of Apes.*

As I started reading the book, expecting to skip ahead a bit just to catch the flavor, I found myself so fascinated that I read every word. Its thoroughness and abundant detail, instead of being tedious, leads you to wonder what revelation will come next, and every encounter is fresh and full of the suspense associated with the best of detective stories, with the added advantage that these are real people recounting events in the real world of geography and history.

I believe that any reader who begins this book will be fascinated, as I was—whether or not he or she has any special interest in Wolfgang Köhler. If, however, the reader is a student of psychology, the account will have the added interest of a story about one of the most distinguished psychologists of the twentieth century.

Ernest R. Hilgard
Stanford University

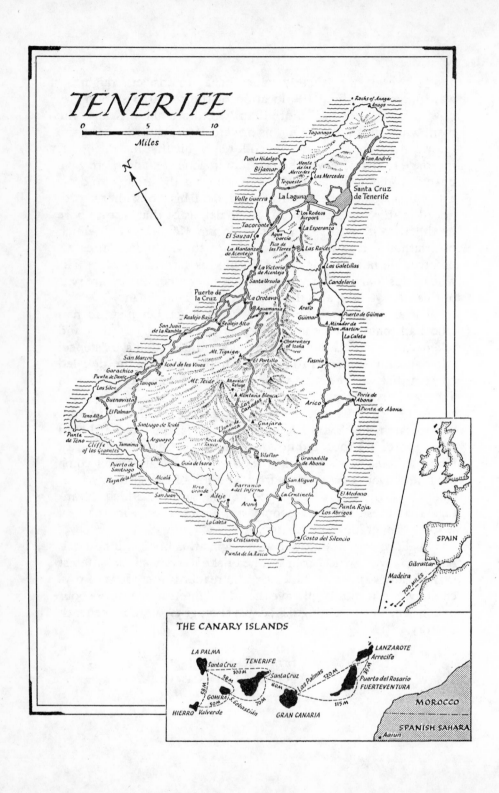

1.

There Are No Apes in Tenerife

The airplane gained only a few thousand feet after taking off from Las Palmas before it began banking into a gentle westward turn for its sixty-mile trip toward the northeastern tip of Tenerife, the shank end of the ham-shaped island. From a window seat on the port side of the jet, I had a good view of the island's most outstanding feature, the snow-capped volcanic peak of Mount Teide, which reaches over twelve thousand feet. Teide and the Cañadas Mountains that partly surround it lie in the western part of the island, in the center of the butt portion of the ham.

I was on the last leg of a long trip that had begun on the afternoon of the previous day, January 11, 1975, in Albany, New York. Although I was in a cranky, weary mood from too little sleep and too much time in the dry air of a pressurized jet, the rising of the sun reminded me that I was on sabbatical leave from the university. With this thought, my mood, like the sky, brightened rapidly.

I had spent the first semester of my leave writing up the results of several experiments my students and I had conducted during the past couple of years, and my plan for the second semester was to visit universities in England and call on other experimental psychologists who were doing research on the psychology of learning and memory. I'm not sure why I decided to visit Tenerife before going to London. Most of my friends assumed that I was looking for a warm place to spend a few weeks in midwinter. While sitting in the sun is not my idea of a good time, they weren't entirely wrong, because my decision to visit Tenerife was made on one of the first cold nights of autumn as I sat in my study consulting an atlas opened to a Mercator projection of the world. The region I studied was the tropics.

I placed my index finger on the Tropic of Cancer and my thumb on the Tropic of Capricorn, and moved my hand eastward from the Western Hemisphere across the Atlantic Ocean. When my index finger reached the northwestern coast of Africa, it pointed to the Canary Islands. The island of Tenerife, prominent among the seven that constitute the archipelago, brought forth a rush of associations connected with the late Wolfgang Köhler and his book *The Mentality of Apes*, which reports the research he conducted on the island during World War I. Psychologists, especially experimental psychologists, are familiar with Köhler's work because it was the first scientific research on anthropoid apes that purported to present experimentally derived evidence to support the theory that animals lower on the evolutionary scale share with humans the cognitive processes of reasoning and problem solving. Historically, Köhler's experiments are at the roots of the present-day controversy over whether or not there are left any sharp distinctions (language and the concept of self) between humans and the great apes, the tailless, semierect anthropoids.

Most people who have taken at least one course in psychology remember Köhler, along with fellow German psychologists Max Wertheimer and Kurt Koffka, as a founder of Gestalt psychology. (Köhler emigrated to the United States in 1935 and became president of the American Psychological Association in 1959.) Fewer remember that his research on apes—the research that established his international reputation in the field of science—was carried out in Tenerife. And even fewer know that Köhler conducted his famous experiments during the years of World War I. In spite of the fact that Köhler's research received a great deal of recognition and was the first of its kind, I had never read or heard of any research from the station after Köhler's return to Germany in 1920. My curiosity was aroused. What had happened to the ape station? Might it not make an interesting historical note to locate the site of the station and try to trace events after Köhler's departure?

The possibility of uncovering information that might make a small contribution to the history of science was perhaps sufficient intellectual justification for my trip, but it wasn't the whole story. On the cold autumn night when I first studied the islands of the Canary archipelago, I became aware of thoughts and feelings long dormant. I had first read Köhler's *The Mentality of Apes* years earlier, during my senior year in college. The experiments reported by Köhler were interesting enough in their own right, but the African coastal island setting of the ape research station added a dramatic dimension. I wondered what it might have been like at the station during Köhler's days there.

And now, here I was, more than twenty years later, sitting in an airplane that was beginning to make its approach to the island of Tenerife, where I would satisfy my curiosity and uncover the details of a story I had not dreamed of.

* * *

As the jet drew close to the island, I was surprised to see how brown it appeared. In my imagination, islands off the coast of Africa where scientists study apes are covered with lush, green, vine-entangled tropical vegetation, not brown earth and rust-colored mountains. My disappointment was overcome by my amusement at the realization that the traveler's expectations are colored more by the popular media than by lessons in geography. I was well aware of the variation in climatic conditions throughout the vast continent of Africa, but somehow the knowledge that apes were studied in Tenerife had given me the impression that the island would resemble the terrain of the equatorial region of the continent. The impression was bolstered by dozens of movies about Africa, almost all of which either were filmed in jungles or pretended to have been filmed in jungles. From what I could tell of the island from the air, there were few vines to be swung on in Tenerife.

After a short time, my plane passed over the coastal city of Santa Cruz, and began the final turn toward the long runway of the airport of Los Rodeos.

A few hours later I was settled in a cozy apartment of a recently constructed building located in the eastern tip of Puerto de la Cruz. From the front of my sixth-floor location, I had a good view of the sea and of the city, and from the rear I could clearly see the shallow caves that dotted the sides of the cliff, upon which rested the tiny town of La Paz.

*   *   *

I spent the next several days exploring my surroundings. From the research I had done prior to my departure, I knew that Puerto de la Cruz was no longer the small village it had been during World War I, nor was it any longer an important commercial port. The primary industry of Puerto today is tourism, an industry that began to flourish in the 1950s and continues to grow. It was partly for this reason that I had gone to Puerto; it was the only city in Tenerife about which my travel agent had any information. Although there are old buildings and picturesque narrow winding streets to remind you of the quaint Spanish village that Puerto once was, the dominant motif of Puerto today is one of tall resort hotels, complete with all the accompanying facilities demanded by European tourists in search of a warm climate and a sunny beach.

In January, the height of the tourist season, the sidewalks of Puerto are crowded with visitors, most of whom come from Spain, Great Britain, Germany, and Scandinavia. Although the tall waves of the Atlantic Ocean, which break dramatically off the black lava sand of the Martiánez Beach, are quite cold, a surprising number of hardy tourists swim and surf in them. The Avenida de Colón, a broad street just above the beach and adjacent to the promenade that follows the coastline, is crowded most of the day with tour buses, taxicabs, and shiny new rental cars. The general scene is similar to that of other resorts in warm climates throughout the world. However, Puerto is only one city of the island, and although it is an important one, a description of Puerto tells nothing about the rest of Tenerife, an island that I came to learn has more diversification of natural beauty than any I had ever visited.

* * *

I decided to begin my search for the site of Wolfgang Köhler's anthropoid ape station in the port of Santa Cruz, the major commercial city of the island and the capital of the Province of Tenerife. (The Canary Islands are divided into two provinces. The western Province of Tenerife is composed of the islands of Tenerife, La Palma, Gomera, and Hierro, while the eastern Province of Las Palmas is composed of the islands of Gran Canaria, Fuertaventura, and Lanzarote.) My reason for beginning there was based on research I had done in Puerto de la Cruz concerning sources of relevant information on the island. My plan was to make inquiries at the Municipal Museum of Anthropology and Archaeology, the Municipal Library, and the Zoological Gardens. Earlier I had purchased a map of the city, located the places I planned to visit, and then calculated the route that would most efficiently connect me with each of the places I sought. After the long bus ride up the ridge of mountains to La Laguna, the old capital of the archipelago, and down the other side of the mountains to Santa Cruz, I discovered that both the museum and the library were closed—it was Sunday.

I left the museum, which is located on the busy waterfront overlooking the harbor where Admiral Nelson lost his arm in an unsuccessful campaign against the Spanish, and headed north in the direction of the zoo. There was little traffic on Sunday on the downtown streets of Santa Cruz, a modern commercial city of about 300,000 permanent residents. Santa Cruz is very different from Puerto. Whereas Puerto is dedicated to tourism, Santa Cruz gives the appearance of a serious, hard-working community.

When I reached the charming municipal park where the zoo is located, I was pleased to learn that it was not closed, but disappointed in what I found. The Zoological Gardens were situated on a fraction of an acre and consisted of a few colorful birds, some common barnyard animals, and a few monkeys. The attendant on duty confirmed that these were the only zoological gardens in Santa Cruz. I wasn't surprised that he knew nothing

about Wolfgang Köhler or the research station, but I was surprised to learn that apes are not native to Tenerife and never
have been. I had assumed that the primary reason for establishing the ape station in Tenerife was the island's handy supply of
apes. If this was not the case, I wondered why the ape research
station had been established there.

After lunch and a short walk along the waterfront, I boarded
the bus for the bumpy trip back to Puerto. As I rode through the
town of La Laguna, I noticed the campus of the university.
Surely there must be a psychologist on the staff who had some
interest in the history of experimental research. I decided to visit
there first thing Monday morning.

*   *   *

When I arrived at the old campus of the University of La Laguna,
I went to the office of Dr. Vincente Pelechano, chairman of the
Psychology Department. After I told Pelechano about my interest in Köhler and the ape station, he explained that he also was
interested in the history of the station, that he had studied at the
Max Planck Institute of Psychiatry in Munich after he took his
Ph.D. at the University of Madrid, and that he was in the process of trying to locate the site of the station. He said that he did
not know the exact site, but he did know that it was located
either in Puerto de la Cruz or some place nearby. He added that
in view of the enormous development of Puerto, it was likely that
the buildings Köhler used no longer existed. After all, it was
almost sixty years ago that Köhler had left Tenerife. Pelechano
explained that he had been at the University of La Laguna for
only one year and had not had the opportunity to do very much
research on the history of the station.

I asked Pelechano if he knew of anyone who might have
direct knowledge of the station. He said he did not. Although he
agreed that there probably were people living today who had
been in Puerto during the years of the station, he said that it
might be difficult to locate them because many old people had
been forced to relocate as a result of expanding tourism. I was
disappointed to hear this, but the information that the station

was located near the very place I was staying more than offset this minor disappointment.

* * *

On my return to Puerto, I made plans to visit the city hall and search for municipal officials who might be able to direct me to documents pertaining to the station or to people who might have some recollection of the station. In *The Mentality of Apes*, Köhler mentions that "seven of the animals belonged to the old branch of the anthropoid station which the Prussian Academy of Science maintained in Tenerife from 1912 to 1920." Since this implies that the German government had indirectly sponsored the station, it seemed even more likely that records indicating the purchase or leasing of land for the station should be on file at the city hall. Now that I knew the general location of the station, I felt confident that I would find the site.

The knowledge that the station was nearby subtly changed my perception of Puerto. As I walked from the bus terminal to my apartment, I seemed to notice more of the details of what remained of the quaint village, and less of the bold backdrop of the modern tourist city—a reversal of figure and ground. When I arrived at the street of my apartment house, I looked at the caves in the cliff above my building and found my thoughts shifting from speculation about whether or not the caves may have been inhabited by Guanches (the aboriginal inhabitants of Tenerife) to speculation about whether Köhler may have looked at the same caves and wondered if Guanches had inhabited them.

* * *

It wasn't until Thursday that I was able to visit the city hall. I was delighted to find that the offices of the municipal government were located in an old section of the city, a short distance from the port. I asked to see the secretary of the government of Puerto, Manuel Florian Ibañez, and in spite of his busy schedule, the secretary graciously welcomed me and offered his assistance. Although he had no firsthand knowledge of the ape station, he had heard of it and remembered that a relative of a man who had worked for Köhler lived in Puerto and was employed at a place not far from the city hall. Don Manuel called an assistant, who escorted me to the man's place of employment and introduced me to Marco González Arbelo, the grandson of Köhler's animal handler. After I told Señor González Arbelo about my interest in obtaining information pertaining to the ape station, he told me that he knew little about it, that the man I should consult was his grandfather, Manuel González y García, the man who had served as Köhler's animal handler. He gave me his grandfather's address.

I went directly to Señor González y García's home, where his niece informed me that he was out and was not expected to return before six o'clock that evening. Since I was eager to talk to the man, I asked his niece where he was and whether it would be possible to see him before he returned home. She explained that her uncle worked each day from about eight in the morning until six in the evening at the Hotel Tigaiga. After doing some quick arithmetic, I began to wonder whether we were talking about the same man. She assured me that her uncle, who was eighty-seven years old, was the man who had worked at the ape station throughout the years of Köhler's stay in Tenerife. I thanked her for her help, and as I turned to leave she mentioned that her uncle was partially retired, that he worked only a half-day on Saturdays.

2.

Manuel de los Machangos

The Hotel Tigaiga is located in the Parque del Taoro, a picturesque and neatly manicured plateau on a large hill that lies about a half-mile from the coastline of Puerto. The hotel, which is relatively small and quite elegant, caters primarily to German tourists. The clerk at the desk called a bellhop, who took me to a small maintenance building behind the gardens adjacent to the hotel. Inside, Manuel González y García had a shop where he built wooden bird cages for guests of the hotel. Manuel, a short, stocky man with thick hands that bore testimony to a long life of manual labor, was busily at work on a cage when I arrived. I introduced myself, explained how I had located him, and told him about my interest in Köhler and the ape station. He smiled warmly and expressed his pleasure in having me call on him; he told me that he would be happy to talk to me and answer my questions, but cautioned that he was an old man, and that it had been many years since he worked for Köhler.

In answer to the question of what happened to the station, Manuel told me that Köhler and his wife and children returned to Germany when World War I ended. He couldn't remember the exact date of their departure, but he did remember that they left very abruptly. It was virtually without notice that Köhler and

9

his family suddenly packed their personal belongings and left. The animals were sent to Germany soon after Köhler's departure. A Mr. (what sounded like) "Acobales" was responsible for things after Köhler left Tenerife, but it was he (Manuel) who put the animals in crates, accompanied them to a ship in Santa Cruz, and instructed members of the crew on the animals' feeding and care during the voyage to Germany. He said that Köhler and Mr. "Acobales" wanted him to go to Germany with the animals, but he refused because he did not wish to leave his family. He did not know why Köhler left or why the station was closed, but added simply that "the war ended."

In answer to the question of where Köhler lived and where he kept the animals, Manuel said that it was here in Puerto, on a farm: "It belonged to Señor Isidoro Luz, but he sold it to some English People, Yeowards." Manuel thought they were still the owners, and added, "There is a school, with their name, that they gave to Tenerife." I told him that I would like to visit the farm, and he said that he would be happy to take me there. He said that the house on the farm was the same one in which Köhler had lived.

I made arrangements to meet with Manuel at the hotel on the following Monday, but continued our conversation by asking him how he came to get his job with Köhler. He told me that he began taking care of the animals before Köhler arrived in Tenerife. According to Manuel, the animals were shipped from the Cameroons to the old port of Puerto de la Cruz and were being maintained in their shipping crates in the courtyard of the old Hotel Martiánez during the two weeks before Manuel first encountered them. He was twenty-five years old at the time, and had just finished his military duty with the Spanish Army. An employee of the hotel who had been given the task of taking care of the animals was fearful of them and unwilling to get close enough to feed them properly and otherwise maintain them. Manuel, who was not afraid of the animals, volunteered for the job and was hired. When Köhler arrived in December 1913 with his wife and two infant children, he was pleased with Manuel's work and asked him to stay on and help him at the animal compound at La Costa, at the farm where Köhler was to live and work during his first four years in Tenerife.

Manuel accepted Köhler's offer and worked closely with him during the entire time that Köhler was on the island. The job was such an exceptionally well-paying one for that time—ten pesetas per day, when manual laborers were earning about two pesetas—that Manuel was able to support four families on his earnings: his own (a wife and two children), his mother's, his sister's, and a friend's (a man named Sarten, who had nine children). From Manuel's description of his duties, it appeared that he deserved his salary. In addition to taking care of the animals, Manuel was responsible for the general maintenance of the facilities at the compound, and for delivering food and water from the town of Puerto to the farm. Köhler bought a burro for him to ride to and from his home in Puerto, a few miles away. The workday began in early morning and lasted until about ten at night. As he reminisced about the past, Manuel said, with emphasis, that he did much for Köhler. He implied that he did more than his duties called for, though the implication was not a complaint of a man overworked but rather a statement of fact by a man who took pride in a job well done.

In an attempt to probe Manuel's memory, I asked him if he recalled Sultan, an exceptionally intelligent ape that played a very important part in a number of experiments Köhler reported in his book. Manuel laughed heartily as he repeated the name: "Sultan! The male. He was fierce!" He pointed to a finger as he told me that Sultan once bit him there and that he lost the nail as a consequence. He said he was so angry that he hit Sultan in the mouth with a rock and knocked a few of his teeth out. But apparently Sultan wasn't the only fierce ape. Manuel rolled up one of his sleeves and one of his trouser legs and showed me scars left from another occasion, when several of the animals attacked him at the same time. He said that Sultan was not the worst one, that Grande was the most aggressive of the seven apes.

Manuel related an incident in which Mrs. Köhler was badly bitten by La Rana, a chimp with froglike legs. According to Manuel, Mrs. Köhler frequently went into the compound with him and that when she did, La Rana would often jump into her arms and embrace her. On the occasion of the attack, Mrs. Köhler had been carrying La Rana in her arms for several minutes. As she attempted to take the animal from her arms and place it on the ground, La Rana bit Mrs. Köhler on the arm and on the breast. This was the last time Mrs. Köhler went into the compound. Manuel qualified the story by saying that for the most part the animals were harmless if left alone, that they would not attack unless provoked.

As Manuel thought back through the years, he recalled an amusing incident in which the animals escaped from the compound and could not be found. Köhler was very worried about the damage the apes could do to the houses of the neighboring workmen, not to mention the panic that might result if the apes wandered into town. (The local inhabitants were quite fearful of the animals, which they called "machangos," a Canary Island word that means "animals with ugly faces.") The two men searched the fields and the banana tree groves that surrounded the compound, but they could not find the animals. The area of the farm in which the compound was located was only a few hundred yards from the edge of a tall cliff that rose straight from the sea, about two hundred feet below. Manuel decided to look there for the animals. When he arrived, he saw the seven of them sitting in a row looking out over the ocean.

Manuel dabbed his eyes with his handkerchief as he laughed at his story. He said that when Sultan saw him, the ape began running back in the direction of the compound, with the others following. Manuel gave chase, and hit each ape with a stick as it entered the compound. He explained that it was important to punish the animals immediately, and that he had to use a stick to beat them because they would bite him if he used his hands. On one occasion they had ripped his shirt off while he was punishing one of them; nonetheless, he never showed fear. He felt that if he had, he would have lost control. In the end, they came to fear his stick. When he took the stick from his belt and made a threatening gesture, the animals would urinate. (If Köhler ever observed what appears to have been a conditioned emotional response, he did not report it in his book.)

In spite of the difficulties in caring for the animals, it was clear that Manuel thought back on them with fondness and amusement. He told me how Sultan used to help him feed the other animals. When Manuel came into the compound with a bunch of bananas, Sultan would join him, and Manuel would give the bunch to Sultan to hold. Then, on the oral command,

"Two each," Sultan would walk about the compound and dole out two bananas to each of the other apes. Manuel smiled and shook his head in a gesture of astonishment at Sultan's feats of intellect.

I asked Manuel how Köhler felt about the animals. He said that he thought Köhler liked them, but that he didn't enter the compound very often, and that he never entered it alone. From Manuel's description, it seemed that Köhler made his observations from outside the bars of the wire-mesh-roofed compound.

Manuel also mentioned that individual cages were made for each of the animals so that only one or any combination of the animals could occupy the large common quarters of the one thousand-square-foot compound, the mesh roof of which was suspended from twenty-foot poles in the center of the compound to the six-and-a-half-foot fences that formed its walls. The individual wooden holding cages were placed in a row and rested against one of the four walls. Manuel recalled an experiment in which Köhler instructed him to hang a small bunch of bananas from the top of the mesh roof. Within the compound there were some wooden boxes and some sticks. If the animals tried to get to the bananas by climbing the walls, which they did, Manuel was instructed to discourage this route. The animals then dragged the boxes to the center of the compound and piled them up in an attempt to form a staircase on which to stand and thus reach the bananas. Manuel described the basic format of the experiments that Köhler reported in a chapter on "Building" in *The Mentality of Apes.*

When I told Manuel about Köhler's book and the fame that his experiments with the apes had brought him, Manuel seemed surprised. He asked me if Köhler was still alive. I told him that Köhler had died in 1967 in the United States, where he lived from the time that he left Germany in 1935, that Köhler had become a famous psychologist, and that part of his fame was the result of the work that he had done in Tenerife.

Manuel was saddened by the news of Köhler's death. Although it had been more than fifty years since he last saw Köhler, and although the sharpness of his memory for specific details may have dulled through the years, his fondness for Köhler and for the years they spent together seemed to be unaffected by the passage of time. In response to the news of

Köhler's death, he said: "He was as young as I." Tears came to his eyes as he said this.

He told me that Köhler cured his daughter of "suffocation of the throat" (asthma?) by treating her with cold baths, and that Köhler treated many other people in the community as well, but that he was harassed by a British physician who tried to stop him from practicing medicine. Spanish authorities visited Köhler concerning this matter, but nothing came of it because Köhler never charged a fee. Manuel added that Köhler was well liked by the local people, and that he was very friendly with the Spanish government.

According to Manuel, two chimpanzees, given to Köhler as a gift from King Alfonso, were sent from Africa aboard a Spanish ship, which anchored in Las Palmas. Manuel said that Köhler gave him five hundred pesetas to rent a boat for the trip to Las Palmas to pick up the animals. He said that Köhler could not go because he was afraid of being captured by the British, that Köhler and his wife and children rarely left the compound because of the British.

Since the Canary Islands are a part of Spain and Spain was neutral throughout the war, I did not understand why Köhler was afraid of the British. Manuel explained that the British believed that Köhler was a spy and that the ape research station was a cover for his espionage activities. He said that some of the local people also suspected that Köhler was a German agent, but that he never betrayed Köhler's secret.

At first, I though that I had misunderstood what he said. I asked him what the secret was. Manuel told me, sotto voce, that Köhler was a spy—that he had a concealed radio, which he operated from the roof of his house. He added quickly that he had never told anyone about this.

Manuel's story made little sense to me at the time, because I did not understand immediately how Tenerife could be of any military significance to Germany. From what I remembered of the history of World War I, the war was fought in Europe, the major fronts being in France, Russia, and parts of southeastern Europe. When I asked Manuel for more specific information concerning Köhler's activities during the war, he responded that

Köhler spent his time observing the animals; he made it clear that he did not wish to talk more about Köhler's activities as an agent of the German military. He seemed a little troubled by what he had said, so I didn't press him for more information then. If what he had said was true, it is understandable that he may have experienced a conflict. On the one hand, he wished to cooperate with me and tell all he remembered about his years with Köhler. On the other hand, agents of the German military operating within Spain were in violation of the law, and Manuel didn't want to tarnish the reputation of a man for whom he felt great fondness and respect.

I asked Manuel if he remembered any more stories about the animals. His eyes scanned back and forth for a few moments before he recalled an experiment in which Sultan was allowed to watch from his cage while Manuel painted a door. After a short time, Manuel departed the compound but left the paint and brush next to the partly painted door. When Sultan was released from his cage, he went to the door, picked up the brush, and began painting the door, imitating exactly what Manuel had been doing.

I laughed with Manuel at this story, and decided that this might be a good time to terminate the interview. I thanked him for meeting with me and confirmed the time and date of our next meeting, when he would take me to La Costa and to El Ciprés, the two places where Köhler lived and worked during his years in Tenerife. As I was about to leave, Manuel said, "I did much for them [the Köhlers]." And with a conspiratorial hand-over-mouth gesture, he whispered: "He was not at fault. He had a good companion. When people asked me, I knew nothing."

Then Manuel told again, very briefly, the story of how he picked up the chimps from the Spanish ship in Las Palmas. It may have been a long time since he had last thought about his days with Köhler, and perhaps an even longer time since he had talked to anyone as interested as I in hearing what he had to tell. Perhaps my sincere interest in his recollections was motivation enough for him to recount all that he remembered. I hoped that our conversation would jog his memory so that he might have more to add when I met him next.

* * *

After leaving the Hotel Tigaiga, I thought for a long time about the meeting with Manuel, especially his remarks concerning Köhler's work as a spy. Was it possible that the important scientific contribution made by Köhler through his research in Tenerife was merely an offshoot of a mission whose primary purpose was to serve German military interests? If it was, what, precisely, was the military function of the station?

It occurred to me that Manuel's age may have affected more than just his memory for details of past events. But if his story was an invention of his imagination, what prompted it, and why was he reluctant to tell the story? Manuel appeared to be a simple, honest, hard-working man. He was born in Orotava, a town just a few miles from Puerto de la Cruz, and had never been farther from home than the island of La Palma, where he went on one occasion to visit his son. For the past thirty years he had worked at the Hotel Tigaiga, where, even though now retired, he was still provided with a place to work and thereby supplement his pension with the sales of his bird cages.

It was obvious that Manuel felt considerable fondness for Köhler. He took pride in the work he had done and described his large salary as a windfall. From what I knew of him, there was nothing to suggest a man who made up fanciful stories, nor was there any preconception on my part that might have led to questions that prompted him to make up stories.

There was no question in my mind that Manuel's claim to have worked with Köhler was authentic. Not only did he recollect the names of several of the apes and tell anecdotes involving the animals, but he also gave me a postcard sent to him by Köhler, postmarked Berlin, February 21, 1921. The following is a translation of the message, handwritten in Spanish by Köhler:

Berlin 18 February 1921

My wife and I send you our most sincere thanks for your most gracious letter and for the magnificent seeds that we have recently received. I only wish we had the climate and the sun so favorable for the flowers as they were at La Costa and El Ciprés. Surely you must still have an active interest in the chimpanzees. Imagine our happi-

ness when in the beginning of January we had no doubt
that Chego was pregnant. But the end was bad, because
a few weeks later she gave birth to a tiny dead [stillborn]
chimpanzee and she herself died a few hours later; we
don't actually know the cause in spite of the fact that
most illustrious physicians of Berlin performed the au-
topsy. Surely Sultan is no longer a child. You wouldn't
recognize him for his strength and furious rage. It turns
out that now Rana also is pregnant, you can imagine that
we wish her better fortune and luck in childbirth. And
how are you liking things at the Hotel Martiánez? Re-
gards to the Beutel's. I have been made chief of the
major institute of psychology in Germany. It's very good,
but much more work than ever I had in Tenerife. Besides,
I miss the sea, the sun, and the natural joy of Tenerifians.
My wife is not with me because in Berlin there are no
accommodations for families, and only once in a while
do I see her and the children in the little town where they
live.

I am always happy with the notices you send me.

Your friend,
Dr. Wolfgang Köhler

The card attested to Manuel's authenticity and indicated as
well that Manuel's relationship with Köhler was a friendly one,
one that went beyond the bounds of a typical employer-em-
ployee contract. This was to be expected if Manuel worked as
closely with Köhler as he said he had. The general tone of the
card supported Manuel's claim, and nothing that Köhler mentioned contradicted anything that Manuel had said.

As I reread the card, an item that caught my attention was
Köhler's statement that he had been made "chief of the major
institute of psychology in Germany." He was obviously referring
here to his appointment as the head of the Psychology Laboratory at the University of Berlin. I remembered that he held this
post until the time that he left Germany in 1935 to relocate in the
United States, but I did not remember that he was appointed to
this post so soon after his return to Germany from Tenerife. I
consulted Edwin Boring's *History of Experimental Psychology*, a
book that I knew to contain a biographical sketch of Köhler, and

found a statement corroborating the news that Köhler had sent to Manuel.

> Köhler stayed at Teneriffe [*sic*] until 1920, returned to Germany, served as acting director of the Berlin laboratory for a year, received the appointment to succeed G.E. Müller at Göttingen on Müller's retirement in 1921, and then actually did succeed Stumpf at Berlin on his retirement in 1922. Why did Köhler get the chief post at Germany's most important university?

Why *did* Köhler get the chief post at Germany's most important university? Boring states that Köhler's meteoric rise from *Dozent* (an untenured rank roughly equivalent to that of an instructor/assistant professor) at the newly established and undistinguished University of Frankfurt in 1913 to professor and director of the psychology department at the prestigious University of Berlin in 1922 (acting director in 1920) can be partly attributed to the publication of his *Die physischen Gestalten in Ruhe und im stationären Zustand* in 1920.

In 1920, when Köhler was appointed acting director at Berlin, he was thirty-three years old and had never held an academic appointment as a professor. During his six years in Tenerife, he was out of touch with German academic circles, or at least so it seemed at the time. As anyone familiar with the academic world knows, the quality of one's work, no matter how important the work may be, seldom leads automatically to high-level appointments. In his biographical sketch of Köhler, Boring alluded to this fact in a statement following his question of how Köhler got the chief post at Germany's most important university: "Such matters are never determined in a simple manner." To what extent did Köhler's work in Tenerife contribute to the sudden rise in his career?

As I thought about the meeting with Manuel, I was reminded of the fact that there were no apes in the Canary Islands, and that Köhler's animals had come from the Cameroons, a section of equatorial Africa that Germany acquired during the latter part of the nineteenth century and held until World War I. Why, then, was the ape station established on a Spanish island several thousand miles from the German colony that was the natural habitat of the animals, the place best suited for the health of the animals and where an abundant supply of animals was readily available? If serious illness or an epidemic wiped out Köhler's relatively small collection of animals, he could not replace them very readily. (As it was, two of his animals did die soon after they arrived in Tenerife.) Köhler was not a physician, and although he may have provided medical help for the local inhabitants, as Manuel claimed, he was not trained to care for serious illness in the animals. For that matter, to my knowledge, Köhler had no previous experience doing research with apes or any other animal prior to his stay in Tenerife (his doctoral dissertation and post-doctoral research at Frankfurt had been in psychoacoustics), nor did he pursue a program of animal research after Tenerife. As Boring pointed out: "Köhler was always a physicist in his thinking, indebted for stimulus in his student days at Berlin to Max Planck rather than to Stumpf [the German psychologist who served as Köhler's dissertation advisor]."

Perhaps the health of the animals and the accessibility to additional animals were factors that were overridden by the inconvenience of traveling the extra distance from the Canary Islands to the Cameroons. But if this was the case, why wasn't the station established in Germany? All the experiments reported by Köhler were conducted within the confines of a caged compound; they could have been conducted indoors as easily as outdoors. Furthermore, although the climate of Tenerife is generally mild throughout the year, with little variation from season to season, the climate is not tropical; there are cold spells during the winter months that are frequently accompanied by long periods of rain, especially on the northern coast, the region in which Köhler was situated.

In view of the considerable financial investment involved in establishing the station (transportation and living expenses for Köhler and his family, costs of purchasing the animals and transporting them several thousand miles, costs of building the animal compound, costs of maintaining the animals and the compound, etc.), it would seem that someone with a background in zoology and experience in working with animals would have been a more suitable candidate for the position of director of the ape station. I was reminded, too, that Köhler, who was twenty-six years old when he assumed the responsibilities of the director of the station, had been working closely with Max Wertheimer and Kurt Koffka on the formulation of the basic tenets of Gestalt psychology at the time that he accepted the post in Tenerife. When Köhler returned to Germany, he resumed his work on the formulation of the principles of Gestalt psychology and pursued this line of research for the remainder of his career. Although his research with apes was interpreted as support for Gestalt theory, the research was not a crucible of the theory; it was in fact tangential, and was infrequently cited by Köhler in his subsequent research—research that centered on testing hypotheses derived from the theory. I wondered why he decided to leave the company of Wertheimer and Koffka and the highly promising work they were doing in Frankfurt to take a post on the remote island of Tenerife. Köhler's research prior to leaving for Tenerife was very well received, and he was already establishing himself in the German scientific community. Although the research in Tenerife ultimately established his reputation internationally, his decision to take the post in Tenerife would appear to have been a gamble.

*   *   *

In preparation for the next meeting with Manuel, I decided to reread *The Mentality of Apes*. Although the book makes no direct references to Manuel by name, there are several references to "the keeper." The preface is quite brief; there are no acknowledgments, and the book is undedicated. Nothing in the book gives a hint as to the everyday activities at the station or to general aspects of life on the island at that time.

I was somewhat surprised to find on page seven the statement that "practically all the observations were made in the first six months of 1914." This implies not only that the project was rather limited in scope, but that it was essentially complete before the outbreak of World War I. The book, which consists almost entirely of an elaboration of these observations, attests to Köhler's outstanding skill as a keen observer of very subtle forms of behavior; but the conclusion is less than four and a half pages long, and there are only about twenty references to published research. In view of the difficulties Köhler must have experienced in obtaining scientific publications, especially during the war, it is quite understandable that his citation of collateral material is meager. And although the conclusion is brief, there can be no denial of the fact that the experiments were brilliantly conceived and that the substance of Köhler's observations was excellent. However, I think it is a fair estimation that the preparation of the manuscript took less time than the collection of the data. It must be remembered that Köhler was free from the many time-consuming activities with which a university professor is confronted: teaching, preparing lectures, advising students, consulting, serving on committees, etc.

Thus, it appears that Köhler had a considerable amount of unencumbered time during his stay in Tenerife. It must also be remembered that Köhler was free from the distractions of day-to-day city living; the cultural offerings of Puerto de la Cruz in 1914 were a far cry from those of Berlin and Frankfurt, the two large and active cities where Köhler had lived during his adolescence and young adulthood. These years in Germany were exciting years as well; this was when Germany was beginning to realize its vast potential for industrial and economic growth, when it was vying for world power through a foreign policy of colonial expansion.

* * *

On Monday, January 27, I hired a Seat sedan and drove to the Hotel Tigaiga at the appointed time. Manuel, who was waiting, was dressed for the occasion in a dark jacket, clean dress shirt, and beret, in contrast to the work shirt and straw hat he had worn when I met him for the first time. He joined me in the Seat and gave directions that led to a narrow dirt road a few miles from the hotel. A short distance, perhaps two hundred to three hundred yards, from the paved road he instructed me to stop the car and park it next to a tall stone wall, the top of which was lined with large pieces of broken glass embedded in concrete. As we left the car and walked to the iron gate in the wall, Manuel explained that this was El Ciprés, the house where Köhler and his family lived from 1917 until the time of their departure for Germany.

A minute or two after we rang the bell, a young Spanish girl came to the gate. Manuel told her who we were and explained our purpose for visiting. The girl, who was a servant for the German family that was leasing the house, explained that the residents of the house were out for the afternoon, but that she would not object to our going through the house, provided we did not stay too long. We agreed, and she opened the gate to the path, which led to a surprisingly large and luxurious old house built in the Spanish colonial tradition of the nineteenth century. I was astounded by the opulence of the house and of the garden that surrounded it. The elevation of the terrain was such that even though the house was two stories high, it could not be seen from the road, nor could any portions of the garden be seen from outside the wall. The splendor of the house and garden could be appreciated only by the residents and their guests.

Manuel took me to a terrace on the north side of the house, which provided a splendid view of the town of Puerto de la Cruz and the sea beyond it, and an equally splendid view of Mount Teide, which on this afternoon was free from any cloud cover. The beauty of the house, the garden, and the view gave the visitor an inkling of the kind of environment that only the very rich know and live in. Beyond the glass-topped walls that enclosed the house and garden on all sides, there were hundreds of acres of banana plantations filled with thousands of trees whose broad green leaves moved like wind-rippled water of a calm sea.

From the northeast corner of the spacious terrace, Manuel leaned against the low stone wall that enclosed it and pointed to an area of the garden about ten feet below. He explained that this had been fenced in, and that it was the place where the animals were housed during Köhler's stay at El Ciprés. We walked from the terrace to the garden area where he said the animals had been kept, but we found no remains of the compound that had been located beneath the large leafy tree that now shaded this corner of the garden. Manuel described where the fence had been located and explained how a wall of the house had served as one side of the compound. He said that El Ciprés was very different from La Costa, and that Köhler spent less time with the animals here than he had at his first house.

I asked Manuel why Köhler had moved from La Costa to El Ciprés. He told me that Köhler was forced to move when the Yeoward Company, a British fruit exporting company that culti- vated bananas in the Orotava Valley, bought the farm and house where Köhler was living. Manuel added that the British bought it because they wanted to move Köhler out and thus disrupt his work.

When I told Manuel that I did not understand why the British wanted Köhler to move from La Costa, Manuel seemed a bit flustered, and said simply that the British were constantly harassing Köhler. Manuel added that dozens of British ships encircled the island throughout the years of the war. He told me that soldiers of the Spanish National Guard visited Köhler to search his home almost every week, that their visits had been prompted by the British consul, who maintained that Köhler was secretly operating a radio through which he communicated with Germany. Manuel laughed as he explained that friends of his would alert him in advance that the Spanish patrol was going to inspect Köhler's premises in search of his radio. Manuel would then tell Köhler, and Köhler, in turn, would conceal his radio and order servants to prepare food and coffee for the men of the patrol so that it would be ready for them when they arrived. He said that the soldiers usually sat in the kitchen and chatted as Köhler entertained them. According to Manuel, the visits by the patrol were always cordial. Although Spain was officially neutral throughout World War I, Manuel claimed that the Spanish Army had great respect for the German Army, and that their sympathies were with Germany, not England.

The maid invited us to tour the interior of the house. The large, high-ceilinged rooms were furnished in an elegant style consistent with the impressive exterior of the house. Manuel said that although there had been some changes in the house since the time that Köhler lived there, the house was essentially the same as it had been. There may be some question of whether or not Köhler lived in jeopardy while at El Ciprés, but there can be no question that he lived in comfort.

*   *   *

After we left El Ciprés, we drove for a few miles to La Paz, a small town on the top of the cliff that borders the eastern tip of Puerto de la Cruz, then through the town to a narrow dirt road at its eastern end. Less than a mile from the town we came to another narrow dirt road, which intersected our road at right angles. A turn to the left for about two hundred yards led to the edge of a cliff overlooking the sea; a turn to the right for about two hundred yards led to the house that had been Köhler's residence from the time he arrived in Tenerife in December 1913, until the time he moved to El Ciprés in 1917. It was here at La Costa that Köhler conducted the experiments that he reported in *The Mentality of Apes.*

At the intersection of the road that led to the house, a chain suspended between two posts prevented uninvited visitors from driving on the road. I parked the car, and we set off on foot up a gentle slope through a banana plantation in the direction of a single tall palm tree that marked the location of the house—a square, yellow, two-story stucco structure that lay in the center of a complex of small sheds and shelters. Manuel explained that Köhler and his family had lived in the large building, and that the smaller buildings were used as barns for the shelter of live-stock and the storage of animal feed and farm implements, and as living quarters for the men who worked the plantation. A few chickens and two barking mongrel dogs greeted us as we approached. Manuel called a greeting through the open door of the house and roused a middle-aged woman who identified herself as the mother of the family who rented the house from the Yeoward Company, the owner of the house and the surrounding plantation. We explained our reason for wishing to look about the house, and she responded by politely giving us permission to look freely at anything that was of interest to us.

Manuel took me to an area of the banana plantation that lay about fifty feet diagonally across the road from the northeast corner of the house, and identified the area as the site of the animal compound. Manuel pointed to a low stone wall, and explained that this marked one of the four fenced walls of the compound. He described the general construction of the compound and pointed to the approximate locations of the tall posts from which the iron-mesh roof had been suspended. Except for the increased growth and density of the banana plants, he said that the farm and its buildings looked exactly the way they had when Köhler lived there. He led me to a garden adjacent to the house and told me that this was a favorite playground for the children. He remarked that the children were barefooted almost all of the time, that Köhler felt that this was a healthy habit that aided the strength and development of the children's feet and legs.

I asked Manuel if the children went to school. He stated emphatically that they did not, that Köhler, his wife, and the children rarely left the farm. He repeated again that Köhler was afraid of the British, who kept him under surveillance at both La Costa and El Ciprés. By way of evidence to support Köhler's concern, Manuel mentioned that two Germans who had been living in the mountains had been captured by the Spanish military and had their radio confiscated. Although he did not connect these men and this incident directly with Köhler, the suggestion was clearly made that there was good reason for Köhler to be concerned. He said that Köhler was very interested in keeping abreast of events in the war in Europe, and that Manuel was frequently sent in search of German newspapers that contained stories about the war. He also recalled that Köhler sent him to Santa Cruz a number of times for news about German submarines that had been sighted in the area.

As I stood with Manuel next to the house where Köhler had lived, and looked at the large, white, fleecy clouds that floated above the sea, it was easy to imagine how it might have been in 1914. Suddenly, the questions raised by Manuel's story seemed something more than just abstract historical issues; I realized that my feelings had become stronger than those of a dispassionate scientist searching for facts. I was excited. I was experiencing the excitement of discovery, the excitement so common in childhood when every rock holds the promise of new delights just for the turning, and every new path holds the promise of adventure just for the following.

* * *

Later that night, as I sat on the terrace of my apartment and looked out over the sea to the distant cliffs of La Costa, I thought about the events of the past few days, and of the serendipitous discovery I had made. It wasn't long, however, before my pleasant reverie was interrupted by a remote association that gave rise to what had become a nagging, irritating, inescapable train of thought that centered on the university, my research, and my future.

Since leaving graduate school, I had single-mindedly pursued an academic career. I had established a laboratory for the experimental study of memory and other psychological processes; I had engaged a coterie of graduate students who collaborated with me in a long-range program of research; I had obtained a number of modest grants and fellowships to help support my research; I had presented papers regularly at important conventions of appropriate professional organizations; I had published much of my research in prestigious journals; I had chaired a fair number of doctoral dissertation committees of students who had conducted research with me. All told, I had established my credentials as a competent scientist.

Although I had attained the goals I had set at the end of graduate school, this fact didn't leave me with a fulfilling sense of accomplishment. I experienced some pride in my achievements, but I was left feeling flat. Virtually all lines of work, even the most creative fields of endeavor, entail a certain amount of routine. But it was more than the ennui of day-to-day tasks that I was feeling; it had to do with the anticipation of a future that held no promise of the excitement that comes with new challenges.

During the year before my sabbatical leave was to begin, my uneasiness had grown. I found it increasingly difficult to make plans and to concentrate; I was plagued by the muse of distraction. Even pastimes that I had for years enjoyed seemed a waste of time. My zest for almost everything diminished. For the first time in my life, my thoughts about the future included retirement. Was it depression? Was it "burn-out"? Was it "mid-life crisis"? I wasn't sure of the answers, but there was no denying the anxiety these questions raised.

As I tried to analyze my inner turmoil, it became clear that whatever else was happening in my life, my interest in investigating the well-mined field of memory had begun to wane. Changing to a new line of research, however, would be no simple matter. The issue of whether I should continue my study of memory or venture into a new field preyed on my mind. Closeness to the problem made the decision, which I knew to be a critical one, difficult. In other times, I had known what I wanted to do, or, perhaps, what I needed to do. But for the past year, I hadn't felt a true sense of direction.

Now, as good fortune would have it, I was experiencing an exhilaration that I had not felt for so long. Had Köhler been a spy? Clearly, I could not simply ignore the question. It was too intriguing, too tempting. Through chance, I had been presented with a challenge. Could I take the skills learned as a scientist and use them as a detective might to explore something new and different, something that was of immediate interest to me, something that had not been explored by anyone else?

As I considered the possibility of performing such an investigation, I remembered a line from one of B.F. Skinner's essays: *"When you run onto something interesting, drop everything else and study it."* Why not? A unique opportunity had presented itself at a moment when I was uncertain about the direction of my future research and free of responsibilities at the university. Why not change my plans? Why not seize this chance to look into the past, into the youthful years of a man who had helped to shape the course of modern psychology?

Somehow, the increased physical distance between me and the university reduced the magnitude of my conflict, and with each passing day I seemed to spend less time ruminating about the future and more time enjoying the present. I knew that I was simply postponing the inevitable decision, but maybe a postponement was just what I needed. Perhaps by stepping back from my problem, I would improve my perspective and ultimately reach a sounder decision. What I wanted to do—what my gut feelings told me to do—was investigate Manuel's story.

Thus I began my odyssey in search of the past—not the past of significant events about which history is written, nor the past of events on which biography is based, but the past of events that reconstruct a brief period in an individual's life. I would try to learn all there was to learn about Wolfgang Köhler and his life on the island of Tenerife.

3.

London: The Game's Afoot

y plans were vague—not by design, but by the limitations of my knowledge of the methods of historical research. I knew well how to conduct experiments in psychology, but this wouldn't help me very much with the problem of how to test my hypothesis that Wolfgang Köhler had been an agent of the German military during the years of World War I.

Unlike experimental research, historical research does not provide for precise operational definitions of variables, for the quantification of the measurement of variables, for controls that allow for the manipulation of independent variables while changes in dependent variables are observed, for replication, etc. There are, however, some basic principles that appear to be common to virtually all scholarly pursuits; among them are the objective recording of data, the acceptance of the rules of logic and evidence, and the application of a rule of reason in the interpretation of data.

Aside from considerations of how best to approach my subject, there were the practical limitations of what I could reasonably expect to do given my resources and limited time. In matters of practical concerns, B.F. Skinner is a font of wisdom. I remembered that his second informal principle of scientific practice states: "Some ways of doing research are easier than others." Since I was already scheduled on a flight to London, where my original sabbatical leave plan was to commence, I decided to begin my investigation of Köhler's past there. It was essential that I gain a general understanding of naval warfare in the Atlantic Ocean and a specific understanding of both the nature and significance of the role that the Canary Islands played in World War I. Certainly this information would be available in London.

* * *

It was March when I settled in a garden flat in Hyde Park. Westbourne Terrace was a good location, situated midway between the Lancaster Gate and Paddington underground stations, and only a few blocks from Kensington Gardens. Although I had been to London before and was familiar with many of the museums and important historical sites, I was not familiar with sources of archival documents and other historical information.

Before I left the United States, I had been in touch with Professor G.C. Drew, head of the Department of Psychology at University College, University of London. If Drew couldn't help me directly, I felt that he might be able to refer me to people who could. I called his office and made an appointment to see him.

The day before the appointment, I called on the American Embassy to ask for assistance. After I identified myself and explained the reason for my visit, I was told that my request would be forwarded to a member of the staff who would call me in a few days to advise me on what help the embassy could offer.

* * *

The next morning, I took the underground from Paddington to the Euston Square Station, and walked a short block south to the campus of University College and the buildings on Jower Street, which housed the Department of Psychology.

In my meeting with Professor Drew, I told him about my trip to Tenerife and my conversations with Manuel. Drew was interested in my story and told me that he had met Köhler in 1934 or 1935, when Köhler and his wife visited England and Köhler gave a colloquium at University College. Drew said that he did not remember many details of the meeting, but that two events stood out in his memory. One was the fact that Köhler was quite jittery before he gave his talk, that he nervously shredded handkerchieves during the period just before he was scheduled to speak. The other was that Köhler did not talk at all about his research in Tenerife, and when questioned about this research during the period following his talk, refused to discuss it. Drew said that he and other members of the audience were disappointed by Köhler's refusal to comment on his research at the ape station, because there was a great deal of interest in it at that time. In view of the fact that Köhler's book, *The Mentality of Apes*, had done so much to establish his reputation, Drew thought that Köhler's reluctance was rather unusual.

Professor Drew suggested that I visit the Reference Library of the Imperial War Museum; he believed that if there were military operations in the Canary Islands during World War I, I would find a historical record of them there.

* * *

On Monday morning, I took the underground to the Lambeth North Station, just a short distance from the Imperial War Museum. It was necessary to obtain permission for the use of the Reference Library from the director, and since the director was not immediately available, I had the opportunity to tour part of the museum and view some of the extraordinary relics of war that it contains.

My interests centered primarily on the models of ships and submarines of World War I. I was reminded that the German warships of this period were steamships fueled by coal, and that the submarines were powered by diesel engines when afloat and by electric motors when submerged. They seemed primitive by comparison with the ships and submarines of today, not because of their appearance so much as their functional capabilities. The German surface cruisers' range was limited by the frequent need to refuel; steam boilers consumed enormous quantities of coal, so large that warships traveling at full speed required refueling in less than a week. Since the ability to move quickly is the primary tactical defense against a larger force, the very life of a ship depended upon readily available sources of fuel in or near zones of operation. To this end, colliers (coal-carrying ships operating out of land-based sources of coal) were secretly dispatched to rendezvous with warships for the purpose of supplying them with fuel.

Although German submarines were powered by relatively efficient diesel engines, their range was limited by their capacities for carrying fuel. World War I was the first war in which the submarine was tested on a large scale. Germany's surface fleet was second to Britain's in size, but its submarine fleet, composed of ships that ranged in size from 200 to 2,100 tons, became second to none. Compared with modern submarines, those of World War I were little more than surface ships capable of submerging. Beneath the water, the submarine's electric motors propelled it at a speed considerably slower than either diesel-powered or steam-powered warships; thus, it could not pursue. Its tactical advantage was to surprise the enemy through its concealment. And although the submarine was fairly fast on the surface, its limited fuel capacity and firing power did not make it a match for a surface cruiser. Furthermore, the electric motors that powered the submarine beneath the water were run off large storage batteries that had to be charged frequently by the piston engines when the submarine was on the surface. An additional limitation of the submarine's underwater capability was the fact that the air needed to sustain the crew was obtained from tanks of compressed air that had to be filled at frequent intervals when the submarine surfaced. Thus, the effective life of the submarine, as well as that of the steamship, depended heavily on secure and reliable sources of fuel in or near its zone of operation.

The German military was, of course, well aware of the logistical problems of the submarine. Evidence that the German military solved these problems is provided by statistics that show that the German U-boat (*Unterseeboot*, or "under-the-sea boat") fleet of World War I is credited with having destroyed over 15 million tons of Allied ships, the total value of which, including cargo, came to $8 billion (United States currency in 1918). During a forty-week period from March 4 to December 2, 1917, German U-boats sank 925 British ships, for a weekly average of more than 23 ships. The peak came during the week of April

16–22, when 55 British ships were sunk, for an average of almost 8 ships per day!

* * *

After my meeting with the director of the library, I was granted permission to use its collection and advised on sources of information that might be helpful. The first and most significant book consulted was Julian S. Corbett's *History of the Great War Based on Official Documents: Naval Operations*, Volume I. Corbett's account of the early months of World War I (August through December 1914) makes it clear that the Canary Islands, although provinces of neutral Spain, were involved in naval military operations from the earliest days of the war. Aside from proximal coastal waters, Britain's concern centered on the mid-Atlantic areas, through which passed trade routes from the Mediterranean, the Cape of Good Hope, and South America. (As the war progressed, Britain's concern spread to the North Atlantic, where ships from the United States sailed.)

The mid-Atlantic area contains four groups of islands that run north to south: the Azores, which lie about 800 miles west of Cape Finisterre, the westernmost point of the Spanish mainland; Madeira, which lies about 400 miles west of Casablanca; the Cape Verde Islands, which lie about 1,000 miles due south of the Azores and about 300 miles west of Dakar, Senegal; and the Canary Islands, which lie about 300 miles due south of Madeira and about 100 miles west of the Spanish Sahara coastline. All of the islands, except for the Canaries, belong to Portugal. In subsequent sections of Corbett's account, it is made clear that the Canary Islands and other parts of Spain were especially important to Germany as potential sources of fuel and intelligence, because while Portugal, although officially neutral until 1916, was openly sympathetic to Britain and the Allies, Spain was not.

The primary function of a navy is to maintain and protect those sea lanes that constitute the trade routes to its country. Although both Germany and Britain would depend upon the importation of materials from abroad to support their military efforts on the Continent, Britain's dependence would be greater. The importance of the naval zone of operations in the Atlantic along the west coast of Africa is made clear in Corbett's summary of the priorities and the strategies of the British high command, and in his report of the events surrounding the sinking of the German cruiser *Kaiser Wilhelm der Grosse* by the British Navy about 100 miles south of the Canaries on August 26, 1914.

In October of 1914, events took place in the Canary Islands and their adjacent waters clearly indicating that the German military, in collaboration with officials of the Spanish government, was using the islands as a source of fuel and intelligence. These events are reported by Corbett in his account of the activities of the German cruisers *Karlsruhe* (commanded by Captain Eric Köhler, unrelated, as far as I know, to Wolfgang Köhler) and *Crefeld:*

> Here, as elsewhere, the successful protection of our trade rested in a great measure on our power of cutting off communication with the enemy's cruisers. This we had not been able to do entirely, for, as the Admiral found out, a private wireless installation was being constantly used by German and Austrian consular officers to send cipher messages relating to shipping. No such privilege for consulates was generally recognized, and in this case there was no need for it, since the cable connections were excellent. Cipher wireless messages, indeed, could serve no special purpose except for communicating secret intelligence and orders to ships at sea. One intercepted by the Victorian on September 6 was actually sent to and acknowledged by Captain Köhler of the Karlsruhe. On these grounds, at the Admiral's instigation, our Foreign Office made representations to Madrid. The Spanish Government was at first reluctant to take action, pointing out that the privilege was permitted to both sides. But, as the Admiral objected, the privilege was of no use to us while it practically furnished the Germans with a means of communication which was otherwise out of their power. For this reason what was being permitted amounted to unneutral service. After some negotiations the Spanish Government admitted the justice of our contention, and, thanks to Admiral de Robeck's persistence, cipher wireless messages were altogether forbidden.

On the basis of my newly acquired knowledge of British and German naval operations in and about the Canary Islands during the early months of World War I, I confirmed what I suspected was the work of German agents in the islands. The broad overall purpose would be, of course, to act as adjuncts to the German Navy. The specific work probably involved the acquisition of fuel and supplies for all ships, including submarines; the maintenance of communications with ships for the purpose of delivering fuel, supplies, and information concerning the location and destination of British and other Allied ships; the acquisition of local information concerning the sailing schedules of British and other Allied ships; the communication of acquired local information to German intelligence headquarters in Nauen (the town west of Berlin that served as the coordinating center for German military intelligence); the transmission of radio messages from Nauen to German ships and to other relay stations in the German-African network; and the maintenance of a friendly and cooperative relationship between Germany and the Spanish government.

Whatever other functions agents performed, chief among them was communications. The complex logistical problems of naval warfare required close coordination and the accurate and reliable transmission of intelligence. The British, who were well aware of this, set out in the earliest days of the war to destroy Germany's Atlantic radio communications system, a system that spanned from South Africa all the way to Nauen. Britain's insistence that Spain was violating its neutrality by allowing private German wireless stations to broadcast points clearly to the singular importance of radio communication.

4.

Help From the American Embassy

A day or two after my research at the Imperial War Museum, I received a message from the American Embassy, advising me to consult with Mr. Hiscock at the Historical Section of the Library and Records Office of the British Foreign Office, and to call Admiral W. Schünemann, defense and naval attaché at the Embassy of the Federal Republic of Germany. I telephoned Admiral Schünemann. He said that he would act as my liaison between London and the proper authorities in West Germany if I would give him a written summary of my research and my research interests. I agreed, and we planned a meeting at his office for Monday afternoon, April 7. I then called Mr. Hiscock and made an appointment to see him that afternoon.

* * *

During my meeting with Mr. Hiscock, I learned that all of the German military records, dating from World War II to considerably before World War I, had been captured during the closing days of World War II. The records were moved from Germany to England, and during the early postwar years were cataloged and microfilmed by a team of archivists from the University of Michigan and Oxford University. Mr. Hiscock said that the records were quite complete, except that they did not contain information pertaining to personnel—that these records were not among those captured. He suggested that I get in touch with Mr. J.D. Lawson, archivist of the Naval Research Branch of the Ministry of Defence, that Mr. Lawson was best suited to help me obtain relevant information.

* * *

I called Mr. Lawson the next day, and made an appointment to see him on Friday morning, April 4, at his office in the old War Office on Whitehall. I was eager to meet him and excited by the prospect of seeing the interior of the building, the center of Allied military operations during World War II. This was the place where the Allied staff under General Dwight D. Eisenhower, supreme commander of Allied Expeditionary Forces, planned the invasion of Europe and the military operations that followed.

* * *

The next day, Mr. Lawson and I spent the morning discussing my ever-increasing interest in the history of World War I. Lawson invited me to lunch at the building's dining hall, and we continued our talk through the early afternoon. He told me that he knew Admiral Schünemann and advised me to be perfectly candid with him, as Admiral Schünemann could be quite helpful.

Prior to our meeting, Lawson had consulted the index to the captured German military records, the records that Hiscock had told me about. He gave me the reference numbers of volumes that covered German military operations in the Canary Islands during World War I.

Lawson suggested that I visit the Public Records Office in London, that British Admiralty Records were available there. When I told him that I would be interested in studying these records, he immediately called the Public Records Office and put me in touch with a Mr. Evans. After I explained the reason for my interest in the Admiralty Records, Evans said that I was welcome to use them provided I could supply him with a letter of recommendation. Lawson agreed to write the letter and told me to stop at his office on the following Monday to pick it up. When I left the meeting with Lawson, I was delighted with the kind help and consideration he had given me, but I did not know then how important his help would prove to be.

* * *

On Monday afternoon, April 7, I stopped at the old War Office to pick up the letter of recommendation from Mr. Lawson before going to Admiral Schünemann's office in a commercial building on Knightsbridge, a short section of road just south of Hyde Park, across from the Barracks. Consulting the wall directory in the ground floor foyer, I found no mention of Admiral Schüne-mann or of the West German Embassy. I inquired of the British doorman and was told that Admiral Schünemann's offices were on the second floor. However, when I consulted the directory again, I noted that it simply indicated that the second floor was occupied. It did not say by whom.

When the elevator doors opened on the second floor, I faced a rather formidable unlabeled steel door on the opposite wall of a small waiting room. An intercom telephone was mounted on the wall to the right of the door. I put the phone to my ear and, after a few moments, a female voice with a German accent asked me to identify myself and state my business. I did, and a few moments later a young man opened the door, greeted me, asked for my summary, invited me to sit in a chair next to the telephone in the waiting room, and informed me that Admiral Schünemann was a little late but would be free to see me shortly. I sat down, and when I looked to my left, I noticed another steel door, this one with a peephole that probably provided a view of the entire area in which I sat—the area of the waiting room and the doors to the elevator.

After about ten minutes, the young man who had greeted me returned to the door and invited me to come in. He led me to an office within the suite and introduced me to Admiral Schüne-mann, the West German naval attaché. We had coffee and chat-

ted for a while before discussing my research interests. I admired
a large photograph of a four-masted square-rigged sailing
schooner, which Admiral Schünemann identified as a training
ship used by the German Navy before World War II.

As we chatted, I became keenly sensitive to the important
function of the obligatory small talk in which people engage
following formal introductions. The brief conversation provides
each party with the opportunity to evaluate the other and to
make decisions about the discussion of more important issues. I
liked Admiral Schünemann. There was something about him
that reminded me of Miniver Cheevy—the character in Edwin
Arlington Robinson's poem who felt more a part of bygone times
than he did of his own time. Maybe Schünemann did not ''miss
the medieval grace of iron clothing,'' but he did openly express
his regret that the days of Renaissance men had passed, and he
did state, with a touch of envy, that Köhler may have been the
last of them. I hadn't thought of Köhler as a Renaissance man,
but then I knew relatively little about him at this time. I wondered how much Admiral Schünemann knew.

The admiral indicated his satisfaction with my elaboration of
the summary I had written, and assured me that he would forward the summary to a leading German naval historian for evaluation and assistance. At the end of our meeting, he stood
straight and tall as he told me, in an efficient military manner,
that I would have a reply concerning my request in a week's
time. I believed him.

5.

The British Foreign Office Files

On Tuesday morning, April 8, I took the underground from the Lancaster Gate Station to Chancery Lane and walked to the Public Records Office. There, I presented Lawson's letter of recommendation to Mr. E.W. Dunham, who in turn provided me with a Reader's Ticket, a document that granted me permission to use the archives. Mr. Dunham introduced me to Mr. Cox, who took me to the index of the Admiralty Office files.

Cox doubted that there would be documents of interest to me among the Admiralty files, because British Naval Intelligence agencies carefully review all Admiralty documents before sending them to the archives, and remove any that might compromise their operations or agents. Cox added that he thought it would be fruitless to try to obtain documents from Naval Intelligence, and that if I did not find anything in the Admiralty Records index, my best bet might be to study the recently released (1967) Foreign Office files at the Land Records Building.

Cox was right; a check of the index of the Admiralty records for the years of World War I produced nothing. Hence, I walked to the nearby Land Records Building, where I was instructed in the use of the card index for the Foreign Office files for the years pertaining to World War I. After I mastered the document-retrieval system and adjusted to the somewhat Spartan working conditions (it seemed as though the temperature in the damp, dark building was rarely above 60 degrees Fahrenheit), I spent the next two weeks searching for documents that might provide information about what was going on in the Canary Islands during World War I, information more specific than that given by Corbett, details about relevant events and the people involved in them.

Unfortunately, there were a number of documents cited in the card index for which I could not find a corresponding file. I learned that while the Foreign Office staff composed the card index at the time the documents were originally filed, Naval Intelligence worked in conjunction with the archivists in selecting those files that would be available at the Public Records Office and those that would either remain secret or be destroyed. Thus, many documents listed in the index were not available.

As I leafed through the documents of the first set of files retrieved, I was fascinated by them, not only by the information they contained, but by the medium itself. I had in my hands the very same documents that were routinely handled by the staff of the British Foreign Office during the era of World War I. I knew intellectually that documents such as these are the raw data of history, but I had never experienced the sense of immediacy with the past as I did when I felt the texture of the paper and studied the antique typeface and handwritten notes that they contained. In a city as immutable as London, the chilly building and the simply appointed room in which I sat may well have been exactly as they were in those days when the documents were written. The documents I read were very much alive. Suddenly, I felt close to the past I had sought when I first decided to search for the truth about Wolfgang Köhler.

1913

Two 1913 documents indicated Britain's recognition of the military importance of the Canary Islands as a source of fuel and intelligence. Both documents were written by A.L. Taylor, the

British consul for St. Vincent, Portugal. One document, dated January 11, 1913, referred to a "report on the workings of St. Vincent naval intelligence centre during 1912" and contained an enclosure entitled "Summary of Intelligence Received," a list of German ships, the dates of their arrivals and/or departures during 1912, their destinations, the mode of communication of information (cable or post), and the source of information.

The other document, a letter dated January 11, 1913, was addressed to the Right Honorable Sir Edward Grey, British foreign secretary from 1905 to 1916, a man who expressed concern over Germany's colonial-expansionist efforts in north Africa. Taylor's letter to Grey summarized his evaluation of mid-Atlantic ports relevant to British trade routes between Britain and South America, the Cape of Good Hope (South Africa), and the West Coast of Africa, and pointed out the military importance of the Canary Islands to Britain, thus explaining, indirectly, why Germany, also, would be interested in the Canaries. According to Taylor: "The Canaries sit astride of the Trade Routes both to South America and to the Cape and West Coast of Africa, while St. Vincent only commands the former route; thus all intelligence of shipping on the latter route must reach St. Vincent through the Canaries."

Taylor also mentioned that St. Vincent, the cape at the southwestern tip of Portugal, did not yet have a wireless radio station. The absence of a wireless telegraphy station in St. Vincent illustrates the primitive stage of radio communication just a year before the beginning of World War I. It was only a short time earlier, in 1901, that Guglielmo Marconi had succeeded in transmitting the letter "S" across the North Atlantic from Great Britain to Newfoundland; and it was only 1904 when Sir John Fleming developed the first vacuum electron tube, which made possible the electronic detection of radio waves and thus facilitated the development of radio telephony—the transmission of music and speech. The consequences of communication via radio were just beginning to be realized in the years immediately prior to World War I. It was in fact ship-to-shore communication that provided the impetus for the development of the radio during the early days of its history. Large ships were outfitted with radios and well-trained radio technicians. Early radios were fairly simple in their design and construction, but the quality of components was poor, and thus it was essential that a person knowledgeable in the basic principles of electricity and the technology of the radio be on hand if reliable transmission and reception were critical.

1914

The card index for 1914, the first year of the war, led to a Foreign Office file that contained documents concerning the establishment of German wireless stations in the Canary Islands—one in Tenerife, and one in Las Palmas. The earliest document, dated August 26, 1914, just twenty-two days after Great Britain entered the war, was a directive to the Foreign Office from the Intelligence Division of the British Admiralty War Staff. This directive revealed that a Mr. V.B.D. Cooper, a British engineer who had been ''superintending the construction of a new water works,'' reported seeing a ''German observatory about 9000 feet up at the Peak at Teneriffe [*sic*]'' in which a wireless station was believed to have been established. Mr. Cooper indicated that he had firsthand knowledge of materiel recently purchased by the observatory, and that it included ''a three-phase dynamo, transformers, and a battery of cells''—electrical equipment necessary for the construction of a radio transmitter.

In response to this directive, the Foreign Office sent a telegram the same day (August 26, 11:15 p.m.) to John Croker, the British consul in Tenerife, requesting that he investigate Cooper's allegations. On August 28, at 11:00 a.m., Croker replied via telegram that he had requested the British vice consul at Orotava to inquire into the matter.

Croker's mention of ''Orotava'' referred either to the town of Orotava, situated just a few miles south of Puerto de la Cruz, or to Puerto Orotava, the name of the village that came to be known as Puerto de la Cruz. In either case, the vice consul was requested to inquire because he was situated closer to the ''peak'' than Santa Cruz, the principal city of Tenerife, the capital of the province, and Croker's residence.

At 2:45 p.m. of the same day, Croker sent a second telegram to the Foreign Office stating that the governor of the Province of Tenerife ''assures me that there is absolutely no truth in report regarding wireless telegraphy station or operation on the Peak of Teneriffe [*sic*]. Small party of Germans using observatory for scientific research under Spanish military supervision.''

In a third telegram to the Foreign Office, dated August 31, 1914, Croker suggested that the assurance of the governor of the province may not have been sufficient to assuage all doubt; Croker asked whether he should send an ''Englishman possessing knowledge of wireless telegraphy up to the Peak to make secret investigation.''

According to a letter from the Foreign Office dated September 4, copies of Croker's telegrams were sent to the secretary of the Admiralty. The files did not contain a response to the letter, but on September 8, the Foreign Office sent a telegram to Sir A. Hardinge, the British ambassador to Spain, to inform him that coded wireless messages from Las Palmas, designated for the German cruiser *Karlsruhe*, had been intercepted. The telegram instructed Hardinge to make a formal complaint to the Spanish government, adding that: ''It is of the utmost importance that the Atlantic islands should be absolutely denied to the enemy for intelligence purposes, and the Spanish Government can hardly desire that this abuse of Spanish neutrality by German intelligence agents should continue.''

The file ended with this telegram, but according to Corbett, the ambassador's representations to Madrid were successful. This meant that the Spanish government no longer *condoned* the sending of wireless messages by German agents; but did it *stop* them? Subsequent documents made it clear that Britain could not work successfully through formal channels to force the Spanish government to act on its behalf, and resorted instead to the use of informal channels of counterintelligence agents. This would explain why, according to Manuel, Köhler was afraid of the British but not the Spanish.

The exchange of letters and telegrams concerning the wireless station in the mountains reminded me that Manuel had said that two Germans living in the mountains had been captured by the Spanish military and had had their radio confiscated. If the governor of the Province of Tenerife was incorrect in his appraisal, the two incidents may have been the same.

It is interesting to note that the governor's investigation was a fast one. The first telegram to Croker was sent at 11:15 p.m. on

August 26. This means that Croker probably did not receive it
until the morning of August 27. In his first telegram of August
28, the telegram sent at 11:00 a.m., Croker informed the Foreign
Office that the governor "now orders investigation." If we take
Croker at his word, the governor's investigation was completed
sometime before 2:45 p.m. on the same day, the time Croker
sent his second telegram of August 28. If this was the case, the
governor's investigation took less than four hours! Even if the
governor had been consulted on August 27, the earliest day
Croker could have received the first telegram, and had begun the
investigation on the same day, there would not have been much
time for a thorough investigation, an investigation that, according to Croker, led the governor to assure him that "there is
absolutely no truth . . . regarding wireless telegraphy station . . .
on the Peak of Teneriffe [italics mine]."

  If a wireless station in the mountains had been found, there
could be no criticism of a brief investigation, but in view of the
negative findings, a brief investigation is open to reasonable
criticism. After all, if German agents were knowingly engaged in
a covert operation, they would not readily admit to it, especially
if questioned by representatives of the Spanish governor. Furthermore, if the Germans in the mountains were operating a
radio, it seems self-evident that they would certainly try to conceal it from the Spanish military. And if the Spanish military did
make investigation, their neutral status would make them less
zealous than, for instance, the British military. How thorough an
investigation could they have made in such a brief time?

                              1915

One of the earliest documents indicating Britain's concern about
German submarines operating in the waters off the Canary Is-
lands was a letter to the Admiralty, dated July 30, in which the
Foreign Office told of its proposal to alert British consuls in the
Canary, Madeira, Azores, and Cape Verde islands to the threat
of enemy submarines.

  The response from the Admiralty, dated August 25, supported the Foreign Office proposal and recommended a Mr.
Ralph Hirst to serve as an intelligence agent in the Canary Is-

lands. "This gentleman speaks Spanish and Portuguese fluently, has been trained in wireless telegraphy and has recently been in a shipping office in Chile. He is 27 years old and is accustomed to rough boat work in the Amazon River."

1916

Most of the topics in the card index for 1916 that were relevant to the Canary Islands dealt with German submarines. One of the interesting exceptions was a letter to Consul Croker from Victor Pérez, a Spanish businessman residing in Tenerife, who expressed his fear of a possible German zeppelin raid on the island. Pérez's letter of April 5, 1916, was forwarded to Ambassador Hardinge in Madrid by Croker, and then forwarded to the Foreign Office by Hardinge. The idea that a zeppelin raid might be planned for Tenerife may sound a bit preposterous in view of today's knowledge of the history of the zeppelin, but in April of 1916, the potential destructive capacity of the zeppelin as a machine of war was not well understood. The zeppelin was the atomic bomb of its day, and the terror that it wreaked was not completely without foundation.

Zeppelin raids on the English coast and London during 1915 and 1916, in which these 300- to 600-foot airships dropped 5,806 bombs, resulted in the deaths of 557 people. Although this is a small number by contemporary standards of warfare, it was a large enough number in 1916—a time when the bombing of civilians was unheard of—to create considerable anxiety among the civilian population. It must be borne in mind that the zeppelin raids on London were the first of their kind. In the past, the threat of enemy artillery on civilian populations was limited by the range of the guns, the proximity of which was known or fairly accurately estimated. This was the first time that airborne weapons of war could be transported from distant locations to the heart of civilian populations far from the battle fronts. The British civilians were the first to experience the anxiety of the threat of bombs dropped from the sky, the anxiety of the impersonal destruction of unheralded missiles, the anxiety that all of us now suffer.

In 1915 there was no radar to warn of the forthcoming bombers; civilians were helpless to escape from or defend against bombs falling from the sky. In 1915 there were no effective antiaircraft guns, nor were there effective pursuit airplanes; there was widespread fear that the zeppelin might destroy the major cities of Britain and France. It was not until the end of 1916 that fighter planes armed with machine guns were able to defeat soundly the zeppelins and thus curtail their raids and reduce their threat.

Although Pérez's letter may have been inaccurate in evaluating the possibility of a zeppelin raid on Tenerife, the letter did contain interesting information regarding the activity and interests of certain Germans in Tenerife, chief among them Professor Dr. G. Pannwitz who, ''on behalf of the German Government of whom he is one of the most dangerous and unscrupulous agents . . . appeared in Tenerife posing as an Apostle of science and wanting to convert this Island into a world famed Sanatorium. . . .'' According to Pérez, Pannwitz and Professor Hergesell, ''the scientific advisor of Count Zeppelin,'' obtained a grant of land in the plateau of the Cañadas Mountains surrounding the peak of Tenerife, presumably to establish an altitude station and an observatory, ''but which in reality was undoubtedly destined for a most wonderfully situated and strategically protected station for Zeppelins and air ships. . . . It should be stated here that one of the portable houses that Pannwitz and Hergesell erected on the site of their concession was a personal gift from the Kaiser himself who provided it with its full equipment. . . .'' Pérez added that the portable houses were occupied by ''a German scientific commission, which happened to be in Tenerife when the war broke out, and has remained living in the south of the Island. . . .''

Pérez concluded his letter by warning that a German zeppelin invasion of Tenerife would ''threaten all the English lines of communication which pass by the Canaries.'' Such a conclusion is difficult to understand unless he meant to imply that submarine bases would be established following the zeppelin invasion. The range of the zeppelin was considerable, and its speed of 50 to 60 miles per hour was faster than any warships of its time, but the 8,000 pounds of bombs it carried could not be dropped with very much accuracy on a moving target such as a warship. It wasn't until December 7, 1941, and the destruction of a sizeable portion of the United States Navy at Pearl Harbor, that the vulnerability of warships to attacks from the air was fully realized.

The most interesting points of Pérez's letter were his statements and comments concerning the interest in Tenerife on the part of so many Germans. If Pérez's conclusion that a zeppelin raid on Tenerife posed a threat was false, was there any substance to his statements and comments about German interest in the island? Did Pannwitz obtain "a most dangerous grant of land in the high and unique plateau called the Cañadas"? And if so, for what purpose? Were the portable houses that Pannwitz and Hergesell erected on the site of their concession a personal gift from the Kaiser? And was it the Kaiser who equipped them? Was the "German scientific commission, which happened to be in Tenerife when the war broke out" the same group of Germans alleged to have operated a wireless telegraph station in Tenerife during the early months of the war? Were they the same ones about whom Manuel had told me? Were they connected with Köhler?

* * *

Britain's growing concern with the ever-increasing devastation caused by German submarines was clearly evident in the Foreign Office files for 1916. There was little or no defense against the submarine at that time. In an attempt to diminish the activity of German submarines, Britain increased its efforts to eliminate or, more realistically, reduce the major sources of fuel and supplies for the U-boat. Since Britain controlled the surface of the sea, German submarines operating in the mid-Atlantic were forced to depend primarily on land-based fuel depots. Spain and its islands, the Balearic Islands in the Mediterranean Sea and the Canaries in the Atlantic Ocean, were the major locations of these depots.

The sinking of Allied ships in the waters of the Canary Islands was documented in a letter of December 7, 1916, from Fernando Vázquez, the Portuguese consul in Las Palmas, to Sir Lancelot Carnegie, the minister of foreign affairs of Portugal.

Carnegie, in turn, forwarded the letter, and three other letters from Vázquez, to Arthur J. Balfour, the man who left his post as first lord of the admiralty to replace Sir Edward Grey following Grey's resignation as Britain's foreign office secretary.

According to Vázquez, the first ship to be attacked by submarines in the coastal waters of the Canary Islands was the Dutch steamer *Kedivi*. Vázquez reported that "two submarines, the larger of the two being about 250 to 300 feet long and ... provided with a wireless apparatus," intercepted the *Kedivi* about eight miles south of Melenara, a town on the southern coast of the island of Gran Canaria. As was frequently the case in the early days of submarine warfare, deck guns, rather than the less accurate and more expensive torpedoes, were used to sink the unarmed vessel under siege. As was also the case in these early days, the smaller of the two submarines courteously towed "three boats with the 43 members of the *Kedivi's* crew to near the Maspalomas lighthouse." All of this took place while another Dutch steamer, the *Rindjani*, was held at bay and prevented from assisting the crew of the *Kedivi*. The *Rindjani* had to stand by and "look on at the shelling which caused terror in the women and children she had on board as passengers."

Following the sinking of the *Kedivi*, a boarding party from one of the German U-boats searched the *Rindjani* before allowing it to continue.

The second ship to be sunk by German submarines off the coastal waters of the Canaries was the Greek steamer *Spyros*, which was bound for the British port of Hull. According to Vázquez, this attack took place in the same vicinity as the first one, about twenty miles south of Melenara. And as in the case of the first attack, a submarine towed the twenty-nine members of the *Spyros's* crew to within about eight miles of the Maspalomas lighthouse, where they were picked up by a launch and a tugboat sent from shore to rescue them.

The details of this second sinking contained information suggesting that military intelligence delivered by means of wireless radio was very likely a contributing factor in the attack. According to Vázquez, a German officer from the submarine that boarded the *Spyros* told the master of the *Spyros* that he had "full knowledge of her departure from Dakar" and had apparently been awaiting her arrival at the point of interception. "The officer from the submarine told the master of the Greek steamer that they had orders to sink every vessel bound for allied ports. Some 30 miles to the south of the *Spyros* another Greek steamer was expected to pass and it is supposed that she met the same fate as the *Spyros*. The captain of the latter attempted to warn the other steamer by wireless but being discovered by the German officer he was prevented.''

Several German merchant ships that happened to be anchored in ports of the Canary Islands on the day that Britain declared war were prevented from leaving their anchorages by the British Navy. A second letter from Vázquez to Carnegie, dated December 8, 1916, described communications between the German ships interned at Las Palmas and German submarines. In this instance, the communication was alleged to have taken place at night by means of signal lights. Vázquez also reported his source of information concerning the movement of German submarines: "An individual who was formerly a Portuguese but who is now a Spanish subject, Alexandro dos Santos . . . and who is in the confidence of the German crews, served as bearer of correspondence for the Germans who were in Fernando Po, and vice versa, declared that a fleet of submarines would proceed to the Azores.''

The third letter from Vázquez, dated December 8, explained how German submarines obtained fuel and supplies from ships of neutral countries by intercepting the ships at sea, boarding them, taking the desired supplies, and then paying for the supplies at such a high rate that the ships found it profitable to store supplies for the purpose of selling them to the submarines. One of the ships mentioned by Vázquez was the American barque *James Whall*. It seems that when the *James Whall* arrived in Las Palmas, the American master "told someone that a submarine had boarded him" and forced him to sell eighteen tins of benzene for one thousand dollars. A few weeks later, the *Whall* returned to port "alleging that she had been compelled to put in owing to stress of weather and that she had been boarded by the submarine U.9. . . . In my opinion the *Whall* came here to get provisions for the submarine, which she handed over in exchange for good payment, she pretended a storm and now she will return for more provisions and doubtless after some days

will put into another port under some alleged cause, after having
met the U. 9 or some other submarine.''

The fourth letter, also dated December 8, reported on the
relative ease with which German seamen from submarines could
move about the island of Gran Canaria. According to Vázquez,
the *El Kab*, a German steamer forced to remain at its anchorage
in the bay at Las Palmas, served as an infirmary for sick members
of submarine crews. He also reported an incident in which four
sailors from a German submarine went ashore at Marfeia, a
village on the east coast of Gran Canaria. According to the
report, the four German submariners drank a few beers at a local
store before buying a sizeable quantity of expensive beer, which
they took back to their ship. Vázquez used this incident to illus-
trate the fact that any kind of provisions, including benzene and
petroleum, could be obtained easily by the crews of German submarines.

Comments on Vázquez's letters by members of the Foreign
Office staff indicated further the frustration and futility that the
British government experienced in its attempts to prevent the
Spanish government from violating its neutrality. One staff
member lamented that the ''Spanish authorities at Las Palmas
are scandalously pro-German or utterly slack; probably both,''
and recommended that the Foreign Office ''collect the information in the possession of the French and Portuguese relating to
unneutral proceedings at Las Palmas and make joint representations to the Spanish government.''

In response, a second Foreign Office staff member stated: ''I
believe a Vice-Consul specially appointed for intelligence purposes is shortly going to Las Palmas and his reports will probably
give us ground for strong protest at Madrid. Even, however, if
Sir A. Hardinge could be prevailed upon to make a strong protest I doubt whether the Spanish government would do anything. I am afraid mere words would not produce much effect on
them.''

The British Navy had control of the surface of the seas in
1916, but control of the surface had almost no effect on German
submarine warfare, warfare that raised havoc with thousands of
Allied merchant ships carrying vital materiel via the mid-Atlantic
trade routes to military forces on the Continent, warfare readily

supported by German agents on the mainland of Spain and on its islands.

An additional fact that confirmed the casual operation of German submarines in the waters of the Canaries was contained in a telegram of December 7, 1916, from Vice Consul Staniforth to the Foreign Office. According to Staniforth, the governor of the Canary Islands had informed him that on December 6 at 1:00 p.m., the whole population of Valle Santiago, Gomera had seen a submarine heading toward the southern end of the island. Staniforth added that there were three submarines "reliably reported operating in these waters."

* * *

The last item for 1916 directly relevant to German activities in Tenerife was a memorandum of December 22, from the Section de Controle of the French War Office in Paris. The memorandum informed the British Foreign Office that there were "stores of oil at Santa Cruz," and that it was believed that the Canary Islands were a "centre for German activities, correspondence and espionage."

1917-1918

During 1917 and 1918, the last two years of the war, the situation in Tenerife and the other islands of the Canaries appeared not to have changed in any radical way: German submarines operated relatively freely in the waters of the islands; the British government became more aware of the activities of German agents in mainland Spain and the Canaries, but was not effective in curbing them; and evidence of corruption among Spanish officials by German agents reached scandalous proportions.

One file in particular rather neatly described Britain's problem of trying to curtail the use of Spanish ports as supply depots for German submarines. The first of three documents in the file was a letter dated March 13, 1918, from Lieutenant Commander A.E. Whalley, a British naval intelligence officer in Tenerife, to Admiral Grant, the British naval officer in charge of operations at Gibraltar. In this letter, Whalley reported that he had met with a French Secret Service agent in Las Palmas who told him that German submarines were sighted regularly by residents of the island of Hierro. According to the French agent, about twice a week, a small 800-ton submarine was seen transferring supplies to larger submarines. The German group on shore, which presumably managed the supply operation, was reported to be well organized.

The second document in the file, covering the last four months of 1917 and the first two months of 1918, was an annotated summary of the use by German submarines of Spanish ports as supply depots, fuel depots, intelligence centers, personnel replacement depots, and rest and possibly recreation centers.

The third document in the file was a draft of a letter dated May 13, 1918, from the Foreign Office to the Admiralty with the notation that a copy should be sent to the British Embassy in Madrid. This letter made it clear that Britain's tolerance for the frustration it experienced in its unsuccessful attempts to curb Spain's informal support of Germany's submarine warfare was near its limit. The letter recommended that the British Navy extend its aggression against German submarines into Spanish waters, if necessary.

Balfour's decision in May 1918 to order the British Navy to invade Spanish coastal waters in pursuit of German submarines and warships may seem a bit drastic, but events that soon followed made it clear that the magnitude of violations of Spain's neutrality by Spanish officials justified the decision. An article that appeared in the *London Times*, datelined Madrid, June 7, broke the news in England that Señor Manuel Bravo Portillo, the chief of police in Barcelona, was in jail on charges that he was employed as an espionage agent by the German government. The article further stated that information which he supplied led to the sinking of Spanish merchant ships by German submarines:

> It has been the constant complaint of well-informed Spaniards, especially those who dwell near the coast, that the German submarines which destroy the Spanish mercantile marine with so contemptuous a disregard of Spanish neutrality are aided in their task by confederates

on shore—not only Germans and Spaniards in their pay, but occasionally also, by the local authorities; that the Germans and their friends have organized a complete system of espionage from Ayamonte, at the Portuguese frontier, on the south-west, to Palamos, on the north-east, and that *the Canaries and the Balearic Islands are particularly busy centres of submarine activity* [italics mine]
. . . .

> *A colored poster has recently been circulated showing that nearly a quarter of the Spanish mercantile marine has been destroyed and over 50 Spanish sailors killed by German submarines* [italics mine]. . . .

It is said that . . . Señor Portillo procured the torpedoing of three ships—the *Villa de Soller*, the *Mercedes*, and the *Vita*—within a few days, and that for such services he received a good salary from the German consulate.

Subsequent correspondence to the British Foreign Office from Mr. C.S. Smith, the British consulate general in Barcelona, provided more details about the Bravo Portillo scandal, a scandal that finally forced the Spanish government to admit that its existing penal code was not adequate to insure that both native and foreign residents of Spain would respect Spain's neutrality. In light of the increased sinkings of Spanish merchant ships by German submarines, public sentiment among Spaniards was strongly against Bravo Portillo. The Spanish public may have been divided in its attitudes towards Britain and Germany, but they were united in their indignation toward a Spanish official who was contributing to the deaths of fellow countrymen.

The reaction of the Spanish government to the Bravo Portillo scandal was the Spanish Parliament's swift passage of an Espionage Bill on July 26. As is so often the case in the hasty passage of emergency legislation, the remedy that the new law provided contained a sequela potentially equal to or worse than the ill. The new law of the land gave the government censorship powers that could be used to prohibit the publication of all news of the war and any comment on it, however moderate or reasonable. The irony was that the new law would have prohibited the publication of the newspaper story that led to the exposure of Bravo Portillo and his subsequent arrest and indictment! Since it was Germany that required espionage in Spain to maintain its submarine warfare, the upshot of the new law was to help Germany and hinder the Allies. However, the potentially harmful effect of the law was never fully realized; the war ended less than four months after its passage.

Meanwhile, in Tenerife, during those final months when it appeared that the stalemate which marked the long years of the war might be broken, there appears to have been considerable activity on the part of German businessmen to attempt to obtain farm lands. The Foreign Office files contained letters from Elder and Fyffes Company, Hamilton Company, New Zealand Shipping Company, and Yeoward Company—British business firms in Tenerife—warning of an impending takeover of the islands by German business interests. The letters emphasized the strategic importance of the Canaries to the British government and the necessity to deny use of the islands to Germany in the event of a future war. The letters further suggested that Germany might already be engaged in preparations for a renewed military attempt to achieve the goals of its colonial expansionist policies— goals it had tried and failed to achieve in the course of the war.

* * *

World War I ended November 11, 1918, with the signing of the armistice at Compiëgne, France. Although the Allies were credited with a victory and Germany with a defeat, there was no decisive battle that marked the turning point in the war. At the time of the armistice, Germany still occupied territory from France to the Crimea; the depletion of resources necessary to sustain the war and the revolution were the primary factors that forced Germany to surrender.

The information obtained from the Foreign Office files provided a rich picture of the background in which Köhler lived and worked during the years of the war. My personal knowledge of the role of the Canary Islands in World War I had greatly increased since those days in Tenerife when I talked with Manuel.

The importance of this new-found understanding cannot be overemphasized, because it made me sensitive to a problem in historical research that has a counterpart in psychological research. In psychology, it is called anthropomorphic subjectivism, and is the error of attributing to animals those attitudes or values held by the observer. In history, it is the assumption that people in the past knew and felt what is known and felt today.

For example, while the technology of the early twentieth century seems outdated to the present-day reader, it produced machines that must have left peasants like Manuel awe-struck. What did he think when he first heard telephonic communication—voices of people hundreds of miles away produced by a mysterious box powered by the equally arcane force of electricity? How did Manuel and his neighbors react to ships that could carry powerful weapons and sail beneath the sea? What anxieties did Manuel feel when he learned that enormous gas-filled aircraft could fly miles overhead and drop bombs capable of destroying his town in a matter of seconds? What a contrast there was between Manuel, the poorly educated *campesino* whose knowledge of the world was based on his immediate sense of matters concrete, and Köhler, the Renaissance man who was au courant on abstract matters of theoretical science as well as the technology of his time.

Although I knew Manuel as a man in the world of the present, the Foreign Office files opened my eyes to a view of Manuel as a man in the past. Perhaps it was the concreteness of the documents I read, original documents of the period that they described, that helped me to become sensitive to the importance of maintaining an objective view of the past and wary of evaluating events in the past from the perspective of knowledge gained in the present. However, it was also important that I not lose sight of the constancy of human emotion, a factor that cuts across cultures and through time. Just as Köhler had studied the psychobiological behavior of his apes in captivity, it was necessary that I study Köhler as a human being, as well as a captive of his time and place.

6.

Stuttgart and Freiburg

S several days before completing my research at the Public Records Office, I received a letter from Admiral Schünemann containing a copy of a letter from Dr. Jurgen Rohwer, a naval historian at the Bibliothek für Zeitgeschichte (Library of Modern History) in Stuttgart, West Germany.

Rohwer prefaced his response to my request for information concerning Köhler by stating that the issue was a complex one that could not be dealt with in a short time and with the means available to him. It was his opinion, however, that in 1913, when Köhler went to Tenerife, a submarine war was not anticipated by Germany. He said that as far as he could determine at the time of his writing, there were only about twelve submarines in the zone of the Azores from June 1917 until the summer of 1918, and that they only partly entered the waters of the Canary Islands.

This bit of information rather surprised me. According to the Portuguese consul in Las Palmas, there were a considerable number of witnesses to the submarine sinkings of the Dutch *Kedivi* and the Greek *Spyros* off the shores of the island of Gran Canaria in 1916. Furthermore, the governor of the Canary Islands had stated that *German submarines were seen by the entire population of Valle Santiago off the island of Gomera in 1916.*

59

Although Rohwer's letter was pessimistic, the discrepancy between his report of German submarines in the Canaries and the information I had obtained from the Foreign Office files had the effect of encouraging rather than discouraging me in my search for the facts. Consequently, I accepted Rohwer's invitation to pursue my investigation further.

*   *   *

On Monday, April 28, I called Professor Rohwer and made an appointment to see him at his office Wednesday morning. I also called Dr. Ploog, the director of the Department of Psychiatry at the Max Planck Institute in Munich, who told me that his knowledge of Köhler was limited to Köhler's published work. He recommended, however, that I consult Professor Hans-Lukas Teuber, chairman of the psychology department of the Massachusetts Institute of Technology. It was Ploog's understanding that Teuber had been close to Köhler during Köhler's years in the United States, and that it was Teuber who was in possession of Köhler's personal files.

*   *   *

On Wednesday morning, I met Professor Rohwer and reviewed the events I had summarized in my letter. Rohwer indicated again the conservative attitude that he had made clear in his skeptical response. He mentioned, however, that a source of potentially valuable information might be the German military records stored in the archives in nearby Freiburg. He then dismissed this suggestion rather quickly because the retrieval system was somewhat complicated, and it would, therefore, require considerable time to obtain the volumes containing files that might pertain to German military activities in the Canary Islands—if in fact there were any German military activities there.

I asked Rohwer whether these were the same military records captured by the Allies during the last year of World War II. He said they were. I then produced the list of index numbers given to me by Mr. Lawson, the naval archivist at the old War Office Building in London. When Rohwer read the list, his interest mounted. The list not only contained index numbers to the German military records, but also contained descriptive titles of the information contained in the volumes, titles that made it clear that German military operations were established in the Canary Islands throughout the years of World War I, titles that stated explicitly that there were *Etappes* (espionage bases) in Tenerife and Las Palmas. Rohwer called the director of the Freiburg military archives and arranged a meeting for that same day.

* * *

It was mid-afternoon when I arrived at the military archives and met Dr. Sandhofer, the director. Sandhofer asked for my list of index numbers and took me to a reading room where I was told to wait while the documents were retrieved.

By the time the dozen or so dusty volumes were delivered, it was late afternoon and there was little time in which to study the documents contained in them. However, it was clear from just a cursory examination that covert German military operations were carried out in the Canary Islands throughout the years of World War I. The strong concern expressed by the British over German agents in the Canaries was justified.

I returned the next day and discovered that the bulk of the documents was not interpretable—the documents were handwritten in an obsolete style of cursive writing that has not been in common use since about the time of World War I. The director of the archives assured me that there would be no problem in forwarding copies of the documents for transcription, but added in passing that military personnel records were not part of the documents in the Freiburg archives, that these records were in the Bundesarchiv in Koblenz. Thus, if Köhler had been a member of the German military, his name should be listed among the documents in the Koblenz archives, but not necessarily in the military records in Freiburg.

* * *

Shortly before leaving London for Germany, I had received two letters that pressed me to return to the United States. One was from my assistant, who informed me that the data-collection phase of an experiment conducted during my leave was completed and required my attention; the other was from a graduate student who had completed the research for his doctoral dissertation and had prepared an initial draft of his thesis. Since it would be several months before the files from Freiburg would be available, I decided to postpone visits to Koblenz, Frankfurt, Munich, and Tenerife until after I tended to matters in the United States.

* * *

On the flight from Zurich to New York, my thoughts centered on the events of the past several months. Since I had to take care of business at the university, I wondered how I could use my spare time to advance my research on Köhler. I tried to think of people in the United States who might either know something about Köhler's years on the island of Tenerife or be able to give me leads to people who might know something about Köhler's work during the years of World War I. I made a list of several people to whom I would write and outlined the format of a query letter on that part of Köhler's past that was of interest to me.

If sufficient time were available, I considered looking for archival documents in the United States such as those at the Akron, Ohio Archives of the History of American Psychology, but decided that information contained in such places was not likely to refer to events so early in Köhler's career. Köhler did not emigrate to the United States until 1935, and his international reputation was not established until after his stay in Tenerife. It seemed to me that my time might be best spent trying to locate people who could give me firsthand information about Köhler, rather than searching for documents that held little more than a remote chance of telling me about the very early years of his career.

7.

Sources of Information in the United States

One of the first persons to whom I wrote after my return was Mary Henle, a professor of psychology on the faculty of the New School for Social Research. On the basis of my association with Mary during the years I taught at the Graduate Faculty of the New School, I knew that she had worked closely with Köhler from shortly after the time he first accepted a post at Swarthmore College until the time of his death. It was just a few years earlier (1971) that Mary had edited *The Selected Papers of Wolfgang Köhler*, a collection of Köhler's writings that span his career from 1913 to 1967. *Selected Papers* contains a broad assortment of Köhler's works—works that deal with topics such as philosophy of science, cognitive processes, animal psychology, physiology of the brain, anthropology, and human values. The book is a monument to Köhler, a tribute to the breadth of his intellectual efforts, and Mary makes her admiration of Köhler clear in the brief biographical sketch that follows the preface of the book.

As a man, Wolgang Köhler possessed the same simplicity—the elegant and sophisticated simplicity—the same directness, the same dignity that his thinking did. He had a quality that gave every human contact a special character: everyone with a Köhler story to tell—colleague, friend, laboratory technician, student—cherished it as a treasured possession. Despite his many honors, he remained modest. He enjoyed life—and he enriched it by his work and by his personality.

As I later learned, no one knew Köhler well, but among my colleagues in psychology, Mary Henle knew him best. In my letter to her, I said that I had located the site of the anthropoid ape station in Tenerife, and because of its historical significance, I was interested in learning about the events that led to its establishment. I also told her I was "seeking background material relevant to the more mundane aspects of living on a banana plantation on a somewhat remote island during the course of World War I." I asked to meet with her to discuss what she knew about Köhler's time in Tenerife. I told her that "I hope to learn more about the personal side of Köhler and his family, as well as details concerning the history of the establishment of the anthropoid station." But I did not tell her about Manuel, or about my research in England and Germany. My feelings were that Mary's strong dedication to the perpetuation of the memory of Köhler as a model of perfection might inhibit her from revealing anything about Köhler that was inconsistent with the model she had created. This is not to say that I did not share her respect for Köhler's intellectual accomplishments; I did. But it is to say that I was interested in a complete, uncensored account of Köhler's career, an account that would reveal Köhler the man, rather than Köhler the god.

Dr. Henle responded promptly, but said that she knew nothing about the details of Köhler's life in Tenerife. She did mention that Hans-Lukas Teuber, the son of Köhler's predecessor in Tenerife, might know something about it. Mary also told me that she would send a copy of my letter and hers to Mrs. Köhler, but that she doubted that Mrs. Köhler could add much.

I was disappointed and a bit surprised to learn that Mary knew nothing about Tenerife. Köhler's work there was the single most important event in establishing his professional reputation, and yet Mary, who had known Köhler on a personal as well as professional basis, said she knew nothing about Köhler's years in Tenerife.

I was not surprised to learn that Hans-Lukas Teuber was the son of E. Teuber, Köhler's predecessor in Tenerife (I had already written Teuber), but I was surprised to learn that Köhler's widow was alive, and even more surprised that Mary should doubt that Mrs. Köhler could tell me anything. I wrote a second letter and asked for Mrs. Köhler's address.

In Professor Henle's reply, she explained that Mrs. Köhler knew nothing about Tenerife because she did not meet Wolfgang until after his return to Germany from Tenerife, that it was an earlier Mrs. Köhler, now dead, who was in Tenerife. Mary said that at the time of her writing, Mrs. Köhler was vacationing in the Black Forest region of Germany, and that for this reason, as well as the fact that Mrs. Köhler would not be of any help, Mary saw no need to send her address to me.

It seemed odd that Köhler should never have discussed his years in Tenerife with his second wife, even though he had been married to another woman during those years. Thus, I decided to write to Mary again and to be very direct in my request for specific, basic, factual information that would help to locate people who might know something about Köhler's years in Tenerife. The following excerpts are from my letter of June 19:

. . . What do you know about the first Mrs. Köhler? Can you tell me her maiden name, birthdate, birthplace, year of death, cause of death, place of death, etc.? Were she and Professor Köhler living together at the time of her death? If not, how long had they been separated before her death? How many children did she have? Who are they? Any information you could give would be greatly appreciated.

I'm also interested in the second Mrs. Köhler. What is her maiden name, birthdate, birthplace, etc.? When were she and Professor Köhler married? How many children did she and Professor Köhler have? Who are they? Where are they?

. . . In spite of the fact that the second Mrs. Köhler wasn't on Tenerife with Professor Köhler, I would still be interested in meeting her or corresponding with her for the purpose of finding as much as I can about what Professor Köhler told her concerning his stay in Tenerife.

Incidentally, I wrote Teuber a second letter a couple of weeks ago and have not received a reply to date. If you are in touch with him, I would appreciate a word on my behalf. I told him in my letters that I would be on hand to see him at his convenience.

I hope you can give me some information or leads on the first Mrs. Köhler. Thanks again for your very kind help.

In a prompt response to my letter, Professor Henle indicated that she felt that my questions would not yield answers of any scholarly interest. She told me that she knew nothing about the first Mrs. Köhler, and as far as the second Mrs. Köhler was concerned, Mary felt that Wolfgang told her about his work with the apes, but not about details of day-to-day living in Tenerife. Mary added that Mrs. Köhler was not young and had not been well; she suggested that I not try to get in touch with her.

I wrote to Dr. Henle again to explain my reasons for asking the questions I did. In her reply she did not give me the information I requested, but she did tell me why she would not give me Mrs. Köhler's address: Dr. Henle asked me if I wouldn't be concerned about a friend who had a recent heart attack. I would, of course. And if Mrs. Köhler's condition was so delicate that questions about her late husband's past might worsen it, I would be the last person to ask the questions. However, the fact that Mrs. Köhler was at that time vacationing in Europe made me wonder about the delicacy of her health. Nonetheless, I decided not to pursue the issue further at that time.

At about the same time I wrote my first letters to Henle and Teuber, I also wrote letters to Richard Solomon, a professor of psychology at the University of Pennsylvania who is well acquainted with many of the older members of the American psychological establishment; and to Robert Watson, a former editor of the *Journal of the History of the Behavioral Sciences*, who was, in May, at the time of my writing, completing the last year of his tenure as a professor of psychology at the University of New Hampshire. Solomon, who had not known Köhler well, suggested I get in touch with Professor Hans Wallach at Swarthmore College, and Professor William Smith at Dartmouth College. I followed his suggestions, writing to Wallach and Smith on May 28.

Wallach, who responded promptly, said that he regretted very much that he could not help me with my work on the anthropoid station, that Köhler may have talked to him about his life there, but if he had, Wallach had forgotten it. He added that he had heard that Mrs. Köhler was spending the summer in Germany, but that he did not have her address. He suggested that I might be able to get it from Professor Mary Henle at the Graduate Faculty of the New School. Smith, who did not respond until January of the following year, recommended that I get in touch with Mary Henle, that she was very close to Mrs. Köhler. Professor Watson wrote to me on May 13 and informed me that Mary Henle was an executor of Köhler's literary estate. It seemed as though all roads led to Mary Henle, and Mary Henle was a dead end.

Although I had little success in obtaining help in the United States, on the basis of my success in winning the cooperation of people in Tenerife, England, and Germany, I looked forward to resuming research in Europe and Africa. When word arrived that I had been granted permission to study documents at the Bundesarchiv in Koblenz, I made the necessary travel arrangements and departed from New York on the evening of July 14.

8.

Frankfurt, Koblenz, and Bebenhausen

My flight arrived in Frankfurt early the next morning. Frankfurt is a very large industrial city with little left of the old-world charm that existed before World War II. The ride from the airport to the center of the city was a fast one. It was still early morning when I settled down in a small hotel located a short distance from the railroad station.

The next morning I went to the library of the University of Frankfurt, where I sought a dossier or other information concerning Köhler's tenure at the university. Except for the dates of his appointment, the library had no information on him.

I walked from the modern building that housed the library to an old brownstone building that had "Goethe Universität" embossed above the main entrance at its center. The Institute of Psychology was still housed in the same place it was during the days when Max Wertheimer, with the assistance of Köhler and Kurt Koffka, conducted his research on the phi phenomenon, the illusion of movement created by the rapid onset and offset of successive static lights not too distant from one another. The director of the institute was not on hand, nor were many of the faculty—they were on vacation; classes were not in session. I was fortunate, however, in locating Dr. Tholey, a young member of the staff who held the position of Dozent, a recent recipient of a doctoral degree who serves a research and teaching apprenticeship for several years in preparation for a professorial appointment. It is customary for the Dozent to do a postdoctoral dissertation. To this extent, the role of Dozent is close to that of a postdoctoral fellow. Köhler was a Dozent during his days at Frankfurt (1909–1913); it was during this time that he conducted research on audition, served as a subject in Wertheimer's research on the phi phenomenon, and participated in lengthy discussions with Wertheimer and Koffka concerning scientific and philosophical issues that led to the formation of the basic tenets of Gestalt psychology.

After I introduced myself and told Tholey about my interest in the early years of Köhler's career, he welcomed me enthusiastically. He then took me on a tour of the institute's facilities, and showed me the room that served as Wertheimer's office. From the window of this second-floor room, Tholey pointed to a courtyard below where he said Wertheimer, Köhler, and Koffka spent many hours in deep discussion concerning the ideas they would later write about. According to Tholey, this spot more than any other can be identified as the birthplace of Gestalt psychology.

Tholey showed me a piece of equipment that he said was constructed by Köhler for use in his postdoctoral research on psychoacoustics. I did not understand fully what the function of the equipment was, but I was impressed with the intricacy of the apparatus and with the careful and professional design and construction. Tholey agreed wholeheartedly that the equipment demonstrated considerable mechanical and engineering skill on Köhler's part, that Köhler had an exceptional talent for constructing equipment.

I asked Tholey if he had ever heard anything about Köhler's days in Tenerife, or about Köhler's years in Berlin after his return to Germany. He said that he did not know very much about Köhler, except that he did think it rather odd that Köhler should have been appointed director of the Psychology Institute at the University of Berlin at such a young age and so soon after his return to Germany. Perhaps Tholey was projecting some of his personal anxiety about receiving a professorial appointment, but Köhler's appointment was almost unprecedented in German academic circles, albeit Albert Einstein was also appointed to a professorship at the University of Berlin at the age of thirty-five.

Tholey told me that the person in Germany who knew Köhler during his years at the University of Berlin was Professor Wolfgang Metzger, the director of the Institute of Psychology at the University of Münster, who served as Köhler's assistant when Metzger was a student at Berlin. Tholey recommended strongly that I get in touch with Metzger. He told me that it was unlikely that Metzger would be in Münster, that I should try to reach him in Bebenhausen, a small village south of Stuttgart, where he and his wife had a country residence.

* * *

The next day I went to the Stadtarchiv, where I was told that Köhler had not lived in Frankfurt during his years at Goethe University, that there was no social security file or other record of his residence in Frankfurt for the years from 1909 to 1913. There was, however, a file for a Wolfgang "Koehler" in the town of Neu-Isenburg, a small town in the suburbs of Frankfurt, but I was told that it would be necessary for me to go there to obtain information from their records. Although "Koehler" is an alternative spelling for "Köhler," the risk of wasting several days tracking down a file that might not be the one I was seeking seemed too great, especially since I now knew about Metzger and was eager to locate him and find out what he knew about Köhler. I decided, therefore, to go to Koblenz and try to reach Metzger while I searched for documents at the archives.

* * *

On Thursday, I took the train from Frankfurt to Mainz and a Rhine River excursion boat from Mainz to Koblenz. The Rhine from Mainz to Koblenz is probably the most picturesque, most widely known, and most heavily traveled route in Germany. It was my good luck that on this particular day the air was crisp and clear, and the sky was a brilliant blue, filled with occasional large, white, fleecy clouds that ever so slowly changed shape as they floated overhead. It was a perfect day for a boat ride along the tall, steep, vineyard-covered slopes of the river, slopes whose rich fields were broken at fairly regular intervals by the ruins of medieval castles situated at strategic spots to guard the waterway.

Koblenz, a moderately small city at the junction of the Mosel and Rhine rivers, still possesses some of the old-world charm one associates with the Germany of a hundred years ago, the Germany that exists in the minds of the many millions of Americans whose ancestors emigrated from Germany in the middle of the nineteenth century. I arrived in mid-afternoon and went directly to the Bundesarchiv where I met Dr. Kahlenberg, the director of the archives, and his assistant, Dr. Giessler.

After I explained my research interests, Kahlenberg suggested that a fruitful line of inquiry might be to trace the source of funding for Köhler's ape station. He doubted that the Prussian Academy of Science would directly underwrite a research project carried out by a young scientist, because the academy sponsored only senior research scholars whose reputations were well established. It was more likely that a project such as Köhler's was funded by the Kaiser Wilhelm Gesellschaft, an agency begun in 1911 for the purpose of providing the German government with indirect means of establishing scientific research projects in those parts of the world that fell within the scope of Germany's foreign policy, a policy aimed at economic expansion.

Scientific expeditions and programs of assistance to underdeveloped nations were sometimes used as a means for obtaining the friendship and cooperation of foreign countries that might be of economic value to Germany. The kinds of projects sponsored by the German government before World War I were not unlike those sponsored by the United States in recent times, projects that provided the means for placing intelligence agents in foreign countries of interest to the United States. It was then the agents' job to obtain information and attempt to influence the nation in question to work in a direction that would best meet the goals of the United States government. This is not to say that expeditions of this type were not legitimate scientific projects—they probably were. The implication was that the expeditions might not have been financed if they had not also provided the potential for serving the government's foreign policy. Thus, decisions on the funding of research projects may have depended on the location of a proposed project rather than the scientific merit of the project. Alternatively, the nature of a project and its location may have been to some extent determined by funding priorities established by the government, in much the same way that the United States government shapes the nature and location of research by allocating large sums of money for specific types of research projects. Ambitious young scientists must often focus their research efforts on fundable projects rather than projects that hold the greatest amount of intrinsic interest for them. This fact of life may not be apparent to people outside of the scientific enterprise, but a portion of scientific research is not a labor of love.

Kahlenberg seemed amused when I told him that apes were not indigenous to the Canary Islands, that the animals used in Köehler's experiments had to be transported several thousand miles from other parts of Africa. He agreed that it did seem strange that an anthropoid ape research station was established in a foreign country a considerable distance from the source of the animals at a time (1913) when Germany had a colony in the Cameroons, a natural habitat of apes. If scientific research on apes was the sole purpose of the station, why wasn't it located in the German Cameroons, where a plentiful supply of apes was on hand, rather than in Tenerife, where there were no apes? Furthermore, all of Köhler's experiments were conducted within the confines of a caged compound, a compound similar to those found in large zoos; none of the experiments involved observations of the animals in a natural setting. The type of research conducted by Köhler could have been carried out in Germany, thus precluding the expense and inconvenience of transporting Köhler and his family to Tenerife, or to the Cameroons. Kahlenberg felt that it was quite possible that the ape station in Tenerife had been government-funded.

Kahlenberg's interest mounted when I told him that prior to Köhler's years in Tenerife, he had no experience doing experimental research with animals, at least no published research. Between 1909, the year Köhler graduated from the University of Berlin, until 1913, the year he left for Tenerife, Köhler published twelve articles, none of which dealt with apes or any other animals.

As I thought about his list of published works, which consists of six books, a little over a hundred articles, and forty-eight reviews, I couldn't remember any research on animals except for the studies that came out of Tenerife. Animal psychology per se was obviously not an area of keen interest to Köhler. His research on apes was an outgrowth of a theoretical position that supported the existence of cognitive processes in animals, a position that opposed the mechanistic trial-and-error theory favored by American psychologist Edward L. Thorndike. But marshalling evidence in favor of a cognitive interpretation of *animal* behavior (*The Mentality of Apes*) had little immediate relevance to Köhler's primary concerns, the development of Gestalt psychology and phenomenology (the qualitative analysis of human experience), concerns that occupied his thinking throughout his career, from his early years at Frankfurt with Wertheimer and Koffka until the time of his death in 1967.

Köhler's work with the apes in Tenerife was brilliant; it made a significant contribution to the field of psychology—but a very modest one to Gestalt psychology. After Tenerife, his published works contained scarce reference to his research with the great apes.

Why did the Prussian Academy of Science select a young man, twenty-six years of age, with relatively little experience conducting experimental research and no experience conducting research with animals, to be the director of an anthropoid ape station on a distant foreign island off the coast of Africa, far from the German Cameroons, the source of the apes? In view of Germany's colonial expansionist foreign policy in 1913, and in view of her great concern with increasing her already enormous military power, it did not seem inconceivable that the anthropoid ape station had been located in Spanish Tenerife with an eye towards possible service to the German government.

The German military records from Freiburg revealed that a German espionage base was located in Tenerife. The British Foreign Office files revealed that members of a German scientific expedition in Tenerife were forbidden by the Spanish government to visit their observatory in the Cañadas Mountains because they were suspected of operating a concealed wireless radio there for the purpose of relaying military intelligence that would assist the German Navy. I wondered whether Köhler and the members of the scientific expedition in the Cañadas were connected. Surely they must have known one another.

As for the military personnel records, Kahlenberg said that he did not have them, that it was his understanding that army personnel records had been destroyed and were not part of the military records captured by the Allies shortly before the end of World War II. He did indicate, however, that military draft records were available in Koblenz, and that at age twenty-six, being married and the father of children would not have exempted Köhler. Kahlenberg instructed Giessler to check this out. Kahlenberg also instructed Giessler to check out files for records of German citizens living abroad. After the outbreak of the war, every German citizen in a foreign country was required to report to the nearest German Consulate. Kahlenberg assured me that twenty-six-year-old German males were very much in demand in 1914! He was certain that young German men living abroad would have been instructed to return to Germany immediately after the outbreak of the war.

We consulted the German *Who's Who* for the 1920s and did not find an entry for Wolfgang Köhler; but we did find one for Wilhelm Köhler, an older brother, born in 1884 in Reval, Estonia, who was employed as a museum director and university professor in the town of Weimar. The biographical sketch indicated that Köhler's father was Dr. Franz Koehler, a high school principal in Reval, and his mother was Wilhelmine, née Girgensohn. According to Kahlenberg, there were a number of German communities, which, perhaps because they were in foreign countries, were more nationalistic than comparable communities of Germans living in Germany—that is, comparable middle-class German businessmen and their families. Kahlenberg said that the people of these German communities along the Baltic isolated themselves from the natives of their countries of residence and maintained their German culture. This, of course, required a German educational system complete with German teachers. Köhler's father was a part of this educational system, the principal of a German high school in a German community in Reval, Estonia. Ironically, a biographical entry for Wolfgang Köhler does not appear in the German *Who's Who* until 1935, the year Köhler left his post at the University of Berlin and moved permanently to the United States.

It was not until the morning of the next day that Giessler and I were able to go through the index files to search out the numbers of documents that might be of interest. Giessler said he would retrieve the documents that afternoon and have them ready for me on Monday. Before I left Koblenz to return to Frankfurt for the weekend, Kahlenberg told me that a record of the establishment of the ape station should be among the Foreign Office files in Bonn.

* * *

I had been unable to reach Metzger when I called from Koblenz, but on Friday evening when I called from Frankfurt, I reached him in Bebenhausen. He was very interested in talking with me and invited me to visit him the following day.

On Saturday morning, I took a train from Frankfurt to Stuttgart, and a bus from Stuttgart to Bebenhausen, a village that fits nicely the American image of nineteenth century Germany, a village so small and so cozy that I could have located Metzger in a matter of minutes, even if I hadn't known his address.

Professor Metzger and his wife, who is also a psychologist, were very pleased to talk to someone about the old days in Berlin. As a student at the University of Berlin, Metzger attended Köhler's lectures from 1923 until 1926, worked as Köhler's assistant from 1927 to 1931, and later served as Wertheimer's assistant at the University of Frankfurt from 1931 to 1933. In 1933, Wertheimer escaped from Nazi Germany for the United States, where he made his home until his death in 1943. Although Metzger was Köhler's assistant for two years, he was not able to tell me anything about Köhler's days in Tenerife that I did not already know; it was clear that Köhler did not talk very much about his days in Tenerife. For that matter, I got the impression that Köhler did not talk very much about anything, except, perhaps, psychology.

Mrs. Metzger mentioned that although Köhler was born in Reval, Estonia, where he spent his very early years, his family moved to Wolfenbüttel, a small town near Hanover, where Köhler grew up. We chatted about Köhler's early appointment as director of the Psychology Institute at the University of Berlin. I told Metzger that Edwin Boring, the author of the *History of Experimental Psychology,* thought it unusual that Köhler should have been appointed to such a high post so early in his career. Metzger agreed that Köhler was very young for such an appointment, but added quickly that Köhler was an *exceptional* young man.

I asked Metzger what he knew about Köhler's first wife. He told me that she and Köhler had four or five children, that sometime around 1923 to 1925 they were divorced, and that after the divorce Köhler never again had anything to do with the children. Although it was a difficult time in his life, Köhler never talked about it; but he did begin to show signs of strain—a tremor in his hands that he had all the time. The worse he felt, the more his hands trembled. When Köhler, who was very severe with his students and assistants, arrived at the institute in the morning, his assistants would check to see how much he was trembling so as to get a "barometer reading" of Köhler's mood. I told Metzger that Professor Drew at the University of London had told me that Köhler was very jittery just before he was scheduled to give a talk. Metzger said that this was true, that Köhler suffered *Lampenfieber* (stage fright), that he never allowed his assistants or anyone else besides the students in his class to attend his lectures.

According to Metzger, Köhler was very secretive; he did not wish to have anything about his private life known to others. On one occasion, an incident that occurred when Metzger worked as Köhler's assistant, Köhler asked him to get several books from the library. By the time Metzger had retrieved the books, Köhler had left his office and gone home. Since Metzger thought that Köhler urgently needed the books, he took them to Köhler's house and dropped them off. The next day, Köhler told Metzger in a very harsh manner that he should never again visit his home!

Metzger said that after the divorce, Köhler married a Swedish woman who was a student at the University of Berlin. She and Köhler had a daughter, Karin. Mrs. Metzger added that Köhler disliked small children, that during the early years of his second marriage, his daughter Karin was placed for a period in a foundling home. I didn't question her further about this matter, but I thought it a somewhat extreme and callous act considering that Köhler had four or five children from his previous marriage. If the story about Karin was true, and I had no reason to doubt Mrs. Metzger, I wondered if perhaps the motivation for his behavior went beyond a simple "dislike" for small children. It was the second Mrs. Köhler and Karin with whom Köhler moved to the United States in 1935. Köhler's second wife was his widow, the woman who at that moment was vacationing somewhere in the Black Forest. It amused me to consider the possibility that Mrs. Köhler and I might at that very moment be sitting in the same town; Bebenhausen is in the region of the *Schwarzwald*— the Black Forest.

Metzger said it was easier for Köhler to leave Germany and take up residence in the United States than it was for the other German scholars escaping from Nazi Germany. Köhler, he said, had made many trips to the United States prior to 1935, had many friends in the United States, liked the United States, and felt comfortable there. Metzger also mentioned that Köhler's brother, Wilhelm, taught at Harvard.

During his visit to the United States the previous year, Metzger had met with Hans Wallach, the professor of psychology at Swarthmore College who had worked closely with Köhler during his years in the United States. Wallach had studied with Köhler at the University of Berlin, moved to the United States with Köhler in 1935, and taken a post at Swarthmore College along with Köhler. Later in his career, Wallach joined the staff of the Graduate Faculty of the New School, but he moved back to Swarthmore where he became chairman of the Department of Psychology. Wallach was very bitter; he expressed resentment over the fact that he had spent so many years under Köhler's reign, that Köhler's death was to some extent a liberating experience for him. Metzger understood Wallach's feelings. Köhler was sensitive, but almost brutal; he had an aristocratic attitude that made him cold and aloof.

Wertheimer, on the other hand, was exactly the opposite of Köhler; friendly, warm, and gregarious, Wertheimer had great respect for people. Metzger expressed considerable fondness for Wertheimer. He said that there was something holy about Wertheimer, that he had penetrating eyes, that he reminded Metzger of an Old Testament prophet.

Although Wertheimer's research on the phi phenomenon marked the beginning of Gestalt psychology, Wertheimer received almost no acclaim within German academic circles. According to Metzger, Wertheimer did not receive a salaried appointment to a German university until 1929, when Schumann, the director of the Psychology Institute at the University of Frankfurt, resigned, and Wertheimer took his place. The appointment was a brief one, however, because in 1933, Wertheimer, who was Jewish, was forced to flee from Nazi Germany. During Wertheimer's earlier stay at the university, in the years preceding World War I, he did not hold a formal appointment to a salaried post; he was provided with research facilities through the courtesy of Professor Schumann. Later, during World War I, Wertheimer worked in Berlin on a government project on sound detection, an area of research that gained in importance with the development of the submarine.

According to Metzger, Wertheimer's family was wealthy, thus enabling him to pursue his scholarly interests even though he did not hold a formal university appointment. Wertheimer's contribution to psychology was great. He provided the intellectual impetus that led to the growth of Gestalt psychology, a school that has been largely incorporated into contemporary psychology, especially perceptual psychology and cognitive psychology. In light of this, it is both sad and ironic that he was not appointed to a professorial chair until 1929, when he was already forty-nine years old. It is sad because this small recognition was so late in coming, and ironic because even though it was Wertheimer's seminal thinking with which Köhler and Koffka had the good fortune to come in touch, it was probably Köhler's influence, as director of the prestigious Psychological Institute at the University of Berlin, that finally led to Wertheimer's appointment at Frankfurt, a far more modest intellectual setting than Berlin.

The Nazis carried anti-Semitism to its extreme and final limits, but anti-Semitism in Germany did not begin with them. The fact that Wertheimer was Jewish probably contributed to the lack of recognition he received in German academic circles. According to Fritz Ringer, author of the *Decline of the German Mandarins:* "In 1909-10, less than 3 percent of full professors at German universities were of the Jewish religion, and another 4 percent were converts. Protestants and Catholics held over 93 percent of the full professorships, although they supplied less than 81 percent of the instructors. At the biggest and most prestigious of the German universities, in Berlin, there was not a single Jewish professor in 1909-10.'' Köhler, on the other hand, was thirty-three years old when he was appointed acting director of the Psychological Institute at the University of Berlin in 1920, and Metzger was thirty-three when appointed to succeed Wertheimer as director of the Psychology Institute at Frankfurt in 1933.

My conversation with Metzger returned to Tenerife, and I asked him if he knew why, in view of the fact that the apes at the station came from the German Cameroons, the station was not situated in the Cameroons. Metzger said that it was too hot in the Cameroons. If it was too hot in the Cameroons, I asked him, why then was the station not located in Germany? He told me that it was too cold in Germany. Thus, Tenerife was chosen because it wasn't too hot and it wasn't too cold. I wasn't sure whether or not Metzger was kidding, so I decided not to pursue the matter further.

Metzger told me that the person in the United States who knew Köhler best was Hans-Lukas Teuber. I told Metzger that I had written Teuber twice and had not received an answer. Metzger insisted that I get in touch with Teuber, that Teuber could be very helpful.

*   *   *

Late that afternoon, I took a cab to nearby Schloss Weitenburg, a medieval castle recently converted into an inn, and stayed there until early Monday morning, at which time I took a train to Koblenz where I met with Dr. Giessler at the Bundesarchiv.

Giessler had located documents dealing with treaty policies between Germany and Spain relating to the neutrality of Spain during World War I. The formal policy stated that Spain would not permit any German nationals (German citizens residing in Spain at the time of the outbreak of the war) to leave Spain to return to Germany, a policy that supported Köhler's story that he was essentially marooned in Tenerife for the duration of the war. So much for formal policy. Other records indicated that German citizens residing abroad were strongly encouraged to return to Germany. In one case, a naturalized British citizen of German origin (a former German consul named Ahlers) was arrested and tried in Britain for recruiting German citizens to return to Germany and to the German military. His case was considered an act of treason. He was found guilty and sentenced to death. The records made it clear that German men living abroad were requested to return to Germany unless they were on a special assignment or special duty. A careful search of the records of those Germans requested to return to Germany following the outbreak of the war did not show Köhler's name. He was apparently among those persons on a special assignment or special duty for the government.

* * *

Since the time I left Tenerife, I had learned a great deal about what went on there during the years of World War I. Although the information obtained in Germany was less than I expected, I felt optimistic about my chances in Tenerife. During the years of World War I, Tenerife had a relatively small British community and an equally small German community. If there were people still living in Tenerife who had lived there during World War I, they should not be too difficult to locate.

9.

Tenerife in the Summer

On Wednesday, July 23, I flew from Frankfurt to Madrid, where I made connections with a flight to Tenerife. My plane landed at Los Rodeos airport shortly before sunset.

On Friday, I went to the Hotel Martiánez, the site of the old hotel that Manuel González y García had said was the place where the apes were housed when they first arrived in Puerto, the place where they were maintained before they were moved to La Costa. I hoped that there might be someone there who knew something about Köhler and the ape station. The assistant manager who greeted me introduced me to Pedro Fernández, the present owner of the hotel. Fernández told me that the present hotel, which was built in 1970, stands on the site of the old hotel, but that the garden of the old hotel still remains. According to Fernández, the old Hotel Martiánez was opened in 1908 as a sanatorium. Pedro's father, the owner of the old hotel, spent the years of World War I in Germany, where he married a German women (née Marle), the woman who was to become Pedro's mother. Pedro did not know who the tenants of the hotel were at that time, and according to his accountant, there were no records from the old hotel—they were all burned.

After my meeting with Fernández, I left the hotel and walked around the block to the rear of the building to a set of ornate cast-iron gates large enough to allow horse-drawn carts to pass through. The gates opened onto a large garden enclosed by twelve-foot-high brick walls. It was here that the apes were kept before they were transported to the compound at La Costa; this was the place where Manuel said he first encountered the animals after their arrival from the Cameroons.

* * *

The following Monday, at a previously appointed time, I called at the office of Anthony Yeoward, the owner and manager of the Yeoward Company, the British fruit exporters who, according to Manuel, purchased La Costa for the purpose of disrupting Köhler's espionage activities. Yeoward, who appeared to be in his mid-forties, was waiting for me when I arrived at his office. In summarizing the nature of my research, I told him that I had come across correspondence from the Yeoward Company in the World War I files of the British Foreign Office, and that Manuel González y García had told me that the company had purchased La Costa for the purpose of evicting Köhler. Yeoward said that he had heard about the ape station and the rumors that it had been a cover for German espionage, but that he doubted Manuel's story because it was his impression that La Costa had been acquired as a part of the company's general land acquisition policy, which began during the years *after* World War I.

Yeoward's clerk retrieved the records of the purchase, which showed that the property (one two-story house, one stable, four smaller houses for workers, and one warehouse) was acquired from Melchor Luz y Lima on July 18, 1918. Yeoward was surprised to learn that the property had been purchased *before* the end of the war, and added that negotiations for the sale of the property probably began a considerable time before the date of the official transaction.

Yeoward said that there was a man who might be able to shed some light on the problem, that the manager of the Yeoward Company during the years of World War I, William Arthur Clark, was alive and resided in Tenerife. Unfortunately, he was on holiday in Liverpool, England, and was not expected to return to Tenerife until October. Clark, who joined the company in 1911, was quite old (in his nineties), but in good health.

There was another person who Yeoward felt might know something about the circumstances of the purchase of the property: Isidoro Luz-Carpenter, a politically active man who had held a number of important governmental appointments including the post of mayor of Puerto de la Cruz for twenty-six years, the son of the man who sold La Costa to the Yeoward Company, and a resident of La Costa at the time the plantation was leased to Köhler. Yeoward gave me his address.

I asked Yeoward if there was electricity at La Costa when the property was purchased. Yeoward and his assistant, Señor Manuel Abreu-González, assured me that there was not; they said that the entire area of the plantation had remained rural until only about fifteen years ago. If Köhler had operated a radio, he would have needed electrical power.

I told Yeoward that Manuel had mentioned that a Señor "Acobales" was responsible for shipping the apes to Germany after the war; I asked him if he had ever heard of such a person. Yeoward and Señor Abreu laughed as they explained that the mysterious "Acobales" was probably a fractured Spanish pronunciation of "Jacob Ahlers," the German consul in Tenerife at the time of World War I. Ahler's son, also named Jacob, was the present German consul; his office was in Santa Cruz.

As I was leaving, Yeoward suggested that I call him in a few days, in the event that additional information of interest might come his way.

* * *

The next day I called Isidoro Luz-Carpenter and received an invitation to visit him at his home that evening.

The driveway to Don Isidoro's house was partially hidden by the walls and tall shrubs that lined the busy road connecting Las Arenas with Puerto de la Cruz. The large, rambling stucco house could not be seen from the road and appeared at the end of the driveway as something of a surprise. A servant greeted me and led me to an elegant sitting room in which the walls and tables were heavily adorned with objets d'art, symbols of considerable culture and wealth.

Only a few minutes passed before a distinguished looking gentleman, whose appearance befit the room and its furnishings, entered and introduced himself as Don Isidoro. His brisk movements and speech plus his soldier-like bearing gave him a vitality that made his appearance seem younger than his seventy-plus years. Although his comportment indicated that he was a person of authority who was accustomed to giving directions, the warmth of his smile and the tone of his voice made it easy to relax in his presence and speak candidly. He listened attentively as I told him about my interests in Köhler and the ape station. He brightened up when I mentioned that Köhler became director of the Psychological Institute at the University of Berlin after he left Tenerife. It seemed that Don Isidoro had lived in Berlin during the 1920s, during the years he studied medicine there. He was not, however, a practicing physician; he spent most of his career in politics and government service, and was the owner of a large resort hotel in Puerto, the Miramar.

Don Isidoro confirmed the fact that it was his father, Melchor Luz, who in 1912 leased La Costa, the family home, to Köhler, but that it was Jacob Ahlers with whom arrangements for the lease were made. It was at this time that his father bought the house and land at Las Arenas where Don Isidoro now lived. He explained that the house in which we were seated was built as an addition to the old buildings where the family first lived after they left La Costa. The house at Las Arenas is only a few miles from La Costa. As a boy, Don Isidoro and his brother had visited the ape station to see the animals.

When I told the story of my meetings with Manuel, Don Isidoro nodded his head in agreement and said very matter-of-factly that he too believed that Köhler was a spy. He said that the ape station was but one part of the German espionage organization in Tenerife during World War I, that another part included the meteorological observatory and sanatorium in the Cañadas Mountains, and a third part was the Taoro, a large German-managed hotel that was closed to tourists during the years of the war. According to Don Isidoro, the Taoro Hotel was popular among German residents of Tenerife during the years immediately before the outbreak of the war, but that soon after the outbreak, most of the residents left Tenerife to return to Germany. Although the Taoro was officially closed, it was still occupied by a staff of Germans who used the hotel as headquarters for the Tenerife Etappe. The German meteorological station and sanatorium in the Cañadas were used as a base for making observations of ships at sea and as a radio relay communication center. According to Don Isidoro, the ape station was also used for radio communication, especially radio communication with submarines.

Don Isidoro added that he could not believe that the occurrence of the three German establishments (the Taoro Hotel, the meteorological observatory-sanatorium, and the ape station) at approximately the same time (a year or two prior to the outbreak of World War I) was a coincidence.

I told Don Isidoro that Manuel claimed to have been privy to Köhler's activities as a German agent, that he had firsthand knowledge of Köhler's radio. I asked Don Isidoro if he knew Manuel. He said he did. I then asked him if Manuel had a reputation as a storyteller. Was he given to exaggeration? Was he a drinker? Was there any reason to doubt his word? Don Isidoro gave an emphatic ''no'' to each of my questions and added that Manuel was known to be an honest, sober, reliable, and hardworking man. He said that Manuel was a simple man, an uneducated man, but an intelligent man of good moral character. In describing Manuel, Don Isidoro spoke with a bit of pride and affection; he seemed pleased to be able to recommend Manuel's veracity.

I asked Don Isidoro if there was electricity at La Costa when he lived there. He said there was not; it was his impression that a public source of electricity was not available to La Costa at that time, that if Köhler had electricity he must have generated it himself.

* * *

The following morning I drove to Santa Cruz, to the office of Jacob Ahlers, the German consul in Tenerife. I was met by Dr. Schotz, the vice consul, who led me to Ahlers' offices, a large, airy, and bright suite of rooms in another section of the same building, and introduced me to Herr Ahlers, the West German consul for Tenerife.

Mr. Ahlers, who was casually dressed in an open-collar, short-sleeved shirt, appeared relaxed, but a tired look in his eyes made him seem older than sixty-two. His English was excellent, with just a slight trace of a German accent, but his deep-set blue eyes searched my face as he concentrated on my words; he seemed to be searching for meaning beyond that which my words expressed. Perhaps it was my response on meeting him that led to his searching look. As we clasped hands on introduction, the thought flashed through my mind that I was meeting a ghost, that Jacob Ahlers, the West German consul whose hand I held, was the same "Acoboles" of Manuel's recollection of a Tenerife long past. I had no previous idea of what Jacob Ahlers looked like, neither the man whose eyes I looked into nor his father, but the man I saw at that moment elicited a sense of recognition. Since one cannot have a memory of a person never met or an event that never occurred, false recognition is a cognitive phenomenon that psychological theories are hard pressed to explain.

In my explanation of my mission, I told Mr. Ahlers that his father's name appeared a number of times in the files of the British Foreign Office. He interrupted me quickly to point out that it could not have been his father, because his father was in Germany during the years of World War I. According to Ahlers, his father took him and his mother to Germany for a vacation in July of 1914, that the war broke out while they were in Germany, and that they were, therefore, unable to return to Tenerife until one or two years after the end of the war. Ahlers explained that the correspondence which bears his father's name was probably signed by the vice consul on his father's behalf. It may well have been a coincidence that the war broke out when Ahlers' father was in Germany, but I remembered that the event which is generally agreed upon by historians to have precipitated World War I was the assassination of Archduke Francis Ferdinand of Austria-Hungary, an event that took place in June, 1914, a month before Ahlers' father left Tenerife for Germany. This was, I suppose, a matter of small importance, but I wondered if perhaps Ahlers' father had been requested to return to Germany because war was imminent; Germany's declaration of war in August did not come as a surprise.

I told Ahlers that Manuel had told me that it was Ahlers' father who was responsible for sending the apes to Germany after Köhler's departure, and that the sequence of events was not clear. Since the German consulate was passed on to Ahlers from his father, I asked him if he had records of events for the years that Köhler was in Tenerife. Ahlers said that there were no records for the years of World War I. He quickly qualified his statement by saying that he did not know of any such records. But when he said this, he closed his eyes, shook his head, and waved his nicotine-stained cigar-holding hand in front of his chest in a gesture that looked more like a refusal than a denial. There was a finality about this gesture, a pronouncement that communicated the message that he did not want to hear anything more about records.

Ahlers said that he had heard about the ape station, but that he had no personal recollection of it and did not recall anything his father might have said about it. He also said that he did not recall the names "Teuber" or "Rothmann." He said he did not know what agency of the German government sponsored the ape station, but he did know that the Kaiser Wilhelm Gesellschaft made a gift of a meteorological observatory to the Spanish government in 1912, and that the observatory was located in the crater beneath Teide at the base of the Cañadas Mountains, almost directly east of Teide.

Ahlers drew a map on the back of an envelope indicating the site of the observatory. He smiled and laughed softly as he talked about this German "gift." Included among the instruments and equipment of the observatory was an encyclopedia—a German language encyclopedia, which, as Ahlers pointed out, could not be of any value to the Spanish speaking natives. Ahlers chuckled as he pointed to the fact that the site chosen by the Germans for the observatory was not a very good one, since its location on the floor of the crater, sheltered by the steep mountains, did not permit accurate meteorological observations of wind velocity and direction. Furthermore, the mountains surrounding the observatory considerably reduced the amount of sky that could be seen; that is, by putting the observatory in a valley, the advantage to be gained from a reduced horizon line that results from a high elevation was lost—the mountains cut off the view of the sky.

Ahlers said that shortly after the Spanish government took possession of the observatory, they moved it to Izaña, the peak of a ridge of mountains several miles east of the old location, an unobstructed spot where years later a television relay station for the islands was constructed. Ahlers emphasized the fact that it seemed strange that the German scientists had established an observatory in such a spot as they did and had equipped it with a German encyclopedia and other German language documents. He smiled as he conveyed these facts in a somewhat hushed tone of voice, suggesting that he was making me privy to confidential information.

I looked at the map Ahlers had drawn and realized that the spot he had marked as the location of the observatory was the same place Anthony Yeoward had identified as the location of the sanatorium, the same place Don Isidoro had said was the site of the German Etappe establishment in the Cañadas. The information given to me by Ahlers confirmed what I already knew.

Ahlers seemed pleased to draw the map and discuss the observatory, but reluctant to talk about the ape station. Maybe he didn't know anything about it, but I suspected strongly that he did. Surely, his father had talked about it. And if he didn't remember what his father had said, there must have been consulate records to which he had access. As strongly as I felt Ahlers knew a great deal more than he told me, I felt that he was not going to tell me more.

Ahlers was primarily a businessman. His post as German consul, which he inherited from his father, was an honorary one that was scheduled to be terminated within the next several weeks. The office of the German consul was in the process of being moved from Ahlers' building; he would be replaced by a full-time professional consul, while at the same time the British government would close its consular offices in Tenerife and Las Palmas. Germany lost both World War I and World War II, but its domination of business interests in the Canary Islands in 1975 was clear. It is somewhat ironic that the goals of economic expansion that Germany set out to achieve by means of war were finally successfully achieved by peace.

* * *

The following day, I called Anthony Yeoward, who told me that
his agent, Manuel Abreu-González, had talked with Guillermo
Luz-Carpenter, the brother of Isidoro Luz-Carpenter. According
to Yeoward, Don Guillermo had told Abreu that there was no
doubt in his mind that the ape station was a cover for German
espionage. Don Guillermo, who spent the years of World War I
in the region of Puerto de la Cruz, had lived with his brother,
Don Isidoro, at La Costa until the time that it was leased to
Köhler. Yeoward indicated that he trusted in the reliability of
Don Guillermo, and added that Don Guillermo also said that the
observatory in the Cañadas and the Hotel Taoro were part of a
common plan. Yeoward thought that I was "really on to something," and promised to keep his ears open for any other information that might be of interest to me.

* * *

In the early afternoon, I drove to La Costa to look again at the
old plantation and buildings there. When I arrived at the driveway leading from the narrow dirt road to the house, I parked my
car, walked to the cliff overlooking the sea, and paced off the
distance from the edge of the cliff to the house. It was about
three hundred yards. From my vantage point on the cliff, it was
apparent that the house at La Costa was much closer to the sea
than were any of the houses on neighboring plantations. Moreover, La Costa was closer to La Paz, and thus to Puerto de la
Cruz, than any of the other plantations. La Costa's proximity to
La Paz and Puerto would have been an important factor in pin-
pointing the exact location of La Costa from a ship at sea. Furthermore, the water at the coastline at the base of the cliff was
deep enough to allow large ships to come within a very short
distance of the beach.

I stood on a high wall in front of the adjacent building and
found that I could see over the tops of the banana trees and far
out to sea; the elevation of the land and the height of the cliff
provided a broad unobstructed view of the sea and the northern
coastline. Furthermore, the roof of the house was considerably
higher than the point where I stood, which meant that the view

from the house provided an even better vantage point. In the southwest, Teide was in clear view.

I inspected the other buildings on the plantation. They were in good condition and appeared still to be in use. I wondered what Köhler had used them for. I wondered too about the connection between the German installations in the Cañadas (the sanatorium and meteorological observatory) and La Costa. I wasn't sure what to look for, but I decided to drive to the Cañadas the next day to locate the spot that Manuel, Yeoward, Don Isidoro, and Jacob Ahlers had told me about.

* * *

It was mid-morning of the following day when I reached the mountains. A short distance beyond Portillo, a crossroads at the entrance to the basin of the Cañadas, I turned left off the highway onto a dirt road. According to both Ahlers' map and Yeoward's directions, I was on the correct road in the correct area of the floor of the crater—bordered by the Cañadas to the east and south, and by Teide to the west. After a short distance on the dirt road, I came to a fork and took the road to the right, the one that seemed to be headed in the direction that Yeoward and Ahlers indicated. Soon I came to a chain that blocked passage to the road. I backed up and took the fork to the left, a rocky road that took me to the ridge of the Cañadas.

The terrain was fascinating: red-orange volcanic dust and cinders, craggy rocks, sparse tiny vegetation, a cloudless sky as blue as any I have ever seen (the thick clouds that shaded Puerto de la Cruz were several thousand feet below), crystal clear air, and a fresh crisp wind gusting up to about fifteen miles per hour. From time to time, I stopped the car to look for the remains of the old installations on the floor of the volcanic crater below. I was impressed with the silent vastness of the setting. Aside from the sensation of air pressing against my body and ears, there was no sign of the wind; nothing moved, and nothing made a sound. The atmosphere had an otherworldly quality.

I continued along the ridge for several miles. After some complex maneuvering in a very tight space, I managed to turn the car around without getting stuck, and to make my way back to the highway. I then turned left and headed in the direction of the Parador, a government-sponsored hotel situated a few miles past the entrance to the Teide cable car station. A short distance beyond the entrance, I turned left onto a dirt road that led to a complex of small buildings built from indigenous rocks; they resembled the adobe huts I had seen in the Southwestern United States. No one seemed to be living there.

A building I thought to be the sanatorium was located at the end of the dirt road, less than a mile beyond the cluster of adobe-type houses. The building, a two-story stone house that seemed to be in good condition, had all its windows and doors shuttered. Near the house were some stone walls that appeared to be the foundations of other buildings not yet completed. According to Ahlers' map, the site of the meteorological observatory was located nearby, close to the walls of the mountains that formed the sides of the basin. I walked a short distance beyond the end of the road but didn't find the site.

From this area of the basin, Teide and the ridge of the Cañadas were both accessible, but it was clear that the high winds at these altitudes would make them uninhabitable, except for relatively brief periods. It was also clear that the tall walls of the Cañadas would confound meteorological measurements and astronomical observations.

It was quite conceivable, however, that the sanatorium and its surrounding region could serve as a base, a relatively sheltered inhabitable region from which observers could commute to and from Teide. Perhaps the peak of Teide, which is visible from the sea at a distance greater than a hundred miles, was used as an outpost where squads of observers rotated brief tours of duty (three or four days). From this point, they could have used battery-powered radios to report the location of ships at sea to a headquarters in the basin of the Cañadas. If the sanatorium served as relatively permanent living quarters, the meteorological observatory may have been the location of a high-powered radio designed to relay information to and from Germany. In this case, the high cliffs of the Cañadas may have been used to support a radio antenna, and the observatory may have housed an electrical generator that provided power for the long-distance radio. Thus, the peak of Teide may have been used for observation, the sanatorium as living quarters, and the meteorological observatory as a radio station. As I looked out over the terrain, I could see nothing that made the logistics of such a scheme implausible.

My presence at the sanatorium elicited the same feeling I had experienced at La Costa when Manuel showed me the site of the ape station; it changed the nature of the problem from an abstract historical one to a concrete present-day issue. I had another fanciful notion; I felt that if I could open the locked doors and enter the building, I would find things exactly as they were in 1914. I wondered if Köhler had ever visited the sanatorium. If the establishment in the Cañadas was connected with the ape station, Köhler must have known the men stationed there. The setting—the physical reality of events past—was energizing. In spite of the thin air at this high altitude, I felt a surge of energy as I left the sanatorium and headed for Puerto de la Cruz to interview Manuel again.

*   *   *

It was mid-afternoon when I arrived at the little workshop behind the garden of the Hotel Tigaiga. Manuel remembered me well from our meetings in January. He told me that since I saw him last, he had been visited by an American, some German men, and a Spaniard from La Laguna, all of whom were interested in Köhler and the ape station. Manuel did not remember the names, but I felt quite certain that the Spaniard from La Laguna was Dr. Vincente Pelechano, the chairman of the Psychology Department at the University of La Laguna. I had no idea who the Germans were, but since Pelechano had ties with the Max Planck Institute in Munich, I wasn't surprised to hear that they had accompanied him. I had no clue to the identity of the American, except that he was either writing a book about Köhler or completing a book that Köhler had left unfinished at the time of his death. Manuel could not remember the details of the interview with Pelechano and his party. A curious aspect of the decline in memory that accompanies old age is that recall of relatively recent events is often poorer than recall of very old events.

I asked Manuel whether or not Köhler had electricity at La Costa. He stated with great certainty that Köhler did, and added that Köhler had electric lights as well. Manuel was not certain whether Köhler generated his own power, but he thought the power came from Las Arenas.

As for Manuel's consistency, there were no contradictions between the statements made in January and his answers to my questions at this time concerning those statements; he told me exactly what he had told me in January. There were, however, a few bits of information that Manuel added to what he had told me earlier: he recognized "Dr. Teuber" as a friend of Köhler's and said that Teuber and his wife came to Tenerife from Africa. I asked him if the Teubers had children with them. Manuel said that they did not, and added that it was the Köhlers who came to Tenerife with children: a boy and a girl. It was confirmed that "Acobales" was Jacob Ahlers, and that trucks belonging to Ahlers were used to transport the apes from El Ciprés to Santa Cruz, where the animals were loaded on ships and sent to Germany some time *after* Köhler's sudden departure.

* * *

That evening, I read through the notes of my most recent interviews. I was frustrated by the dead end I reached each time I tried to discover if Köhler did in fact have the electric power necessary to operate a radio. Although both Don Isidoro and Manuel insisted that Köhler had operated a radio, Don Isidoro and Yeoward said that he did not have electricity.

When Manuel first told me his story, I had studied *The Mentality of Apes* in hopes that it might contain some clues. Once again I turned to Köhler's book, this time to the German edition, *Intelligenzprüfungen an Menschenaffen*. As I leafed through the pages and studied the photographs, I remembered that unlike the English translation, the German edition had a frontispiece, an illustration placed before the title page. Done by Köhler's first wife, Thekla, the drawing was of the house at La Costa. Although I had looked at it several times before, this time, something new caught my eye—something that I must have seen before but had never really attended to. Mounted on the front wall of the house was a vertical pole that extended above the roof, and attached to the pole were two wires that appeared to be power lines. Thekla Köhler's message may have taken sixty years to reach me, but it arrived right on time.

Subsequently, I learned that there was a public power source at Las Arenas in 1914, but it was not clear if power lines extended as far as La Costa. Whether or not Köhler had generated his own power was a secondary question; the important point was that there had been no electricity at La Costa before Köhler lived there, and that Köhler had been responsible for its installation. Whatever his reasons for installing electricity, it was clear that he had available to him the power necessary to operate a radio.

*   *   *

There were a number of leads that needed to be followed up in Tenerife, but some of those that looked most promising could not be pursued at that time. I would have to return. It was already August; my sabbatical leave would end with the forthcoming fall semester. I returned to Albany the next day.

10.

Swarthmore and Philadelphia

After a year's sabbatical leave, readjusting to the routine of the university wasn't easy. It wasn't so much the nature of the work demanded of me as it was the sense of frustration I experienced from the interruption of my search for Köhler's past.

Early one morning, soon after my return, I awakened from a dream in which I was on the island of Tenerife during the summer of 1914. It was a vivid dream that lingered through that twilight phase between sleep and wakefulness when the distinction between fantasy and reality is vague. It was a Sunday morning, so I indulged myself by lying in bed thinking about the dream, imagining how it might have been in Tenerife in the summer of 1914. As I thought about the places I had seen and the events that I knew to have occurred, a story came to mind, a story in which a young American psychologist, whom I named Kenneth Hull, meets an equally young German psychologist, whom I named Gerhard Müller.

Until my trip to Tenerife, my image of Köhler had always been that of an elderly, gray-haired man close to the end of his career; now I could see him as an energetic young man eager to make his mark in the world. The imminence of World War I and

of the clash between the United States and Germany provided
the background for the clash between Müller, whom I cast as a
classicist who fancies himself a romantic, and Hull, whom I cast
as a romantic who fancies himself a classicist.

A story line that wove fact with fiction evolved almost effort-
lessly. I made notes of my thoughts during the rest of the morning and spent the remainder of the day outlining the story. The
conflict between the two characters was clear, but the denouement was not. It would be three years before I would complete
"The Mountains of Tenerife."

Meanwhile, my work at the university demanded a considerable amount of my immediate attention. As for my research on
Köhler, the best I could do was to set aside some portion of my
unencumbered time for following up leads in the United States
and for making new plans for trips to Tenerife and Germany.

During the first half of the fall semester, I tried to reach
Hans-Lukas Teuber at the Massachusetts Institute of Technology,
but with no success. I was, however, able to reach Hans Wallach
at Swarthmore College and arrange to meet with him at his
home on the morning of October 25.

* * *

Professor Wallach, who took his Ph.D. at the University of Berlin
under Köhler's direction, began his studies there in 1926, and
later served as Köhler's assistant until 1935, when Wallach, who
is Jewish, left Germany for the United States. Wallach was very
open and very frank in his responses to my questions; he had the
directness of a man who appeared a bit weary with the time-
wasting conventions of cordial introductions. He appeared to be
prepared to talk immediately about the essential information I
sought.

He told me that Köhler came to the United States in the fall
of 1934 to give the William James Lectures at Harvard University, where Köhler's brother Wilhelm was already a member of
the faculty. According to Wallach, Köhler was offered a professorship at Harvard at that time, but did not accept it because his
position as director of the Psychological Institute at the University of Berlin was a very lucrative one. A professor's salary con-

sisted of a stipend from the government plus a percentage of the students' tuition payments; the larger the class enrollment, the greater the professor's salary. As director of the Psychological Institute, Köhler was responsible for the assignment of courses to faculty. Although Köhler, whom Wallach described as being half psychologist and half philosopher, would have preferred to teach the history and philosophy of science, a relatively unpopular course with a low enrollment, he assigned himself an introductory course in psychology, a popular one in which enrollment sometimes numbered between five hundred and six hundred students. Köhler's income from tuition exceeded his salary from the government, a salary that, according to Wallach, Köhler gave entirely to his first wife and their children.

During the spring semester of 1935, when Köhler was a visiting professor at the University of Chicago, he received word from Germany that he had been dismissed from his post as director of the institute, although his appointment as a professor at Berlin would be continued. Wallach said that it was for financial reasons as well as personal and professional pride that Köhler resigned from the University of Berlin and sought the post at Harvard offered him a few months earlier.

When Harvard University would not make Köhler a second offer, he turned to his American friends in academic circles and found among them Professor Robert MacLeod, a former student at Berlin who was now a member of the Psychology Department at Swarthmore College. Köhler accepted MacLeod's offer of a research professorship, a position that would not demand a heavy teaching schedule or administrative responsibilities. In the summer of 1935, he returned to Germany to settle business matters, and, after a brief stay, left Germany permanently for the United States. Köhler was accompanied by Wallach, for whom Köhler had arranged a post at Swarthmore.

There is no question that Köhler was opposed to the Nazis and sympathetic to his Jewish colleagues, but Wallach made it clear that this was not the chief reason for Köhler's departure from Germany. Köhler was not Jewish; he was not forced to flee Nazi Germany in fear for his life as Wertheimer was, nor was he a political zealot whose principles would not permit him to tolerate principles contrary to his own. Köhler was uninterested in

politics—provided that a political ideology did not interfere with
his personal life and his work.

I understood Wallach; what he said was consistent with the
pervasive attitude of German intellectuals described by Fritz
Ringer in his book *The Decline of the German Mandarins: The
German Academic Community, 1890-1933.* The intellectual environment of Germany during Köhler's formative years, the years
from the turn of the century to the period preceding the Social
Democratic revolution of 1918, was very different from that of
other European countries, and this difference must be understood if Köhler is to be understood. A fundamental difference of
singular importance is centered on the meaning of humanism.
For French and British scholars, the concept of humanism either
openly proclaimed or strongly implied a positive attitude toward
egalitarianism, an attitude that influenced the development of
democratic institutions and democratic governments. For the
German intellectual class (the government-supported university
professors and their university-educated associates), however,
the concept of humanism neither proclaimed nor implied a positive attitude toward egalitarianism. For the German academic
intelligentsia, the concept of egalitarianism was vulgar, and the
pressure of the masses to exercise their will through a democratic
government or a communist government was a threat to the
lofty status of the academicians.

Other important differences between German scholars and
other western European scholars centered on metaphysical as-
sumptions concerning the basic foundations of civilized soci-
eties. The German academic intelligentsia believed that the state
derives its legitimacy from neither divine right nor the interests
of the people, but rather from its services to the intellectual and
spiritual life of the nation. The German intellectual was not
viewed merely as a contributor to the well-being of the state, but
was, instead, the embodiment of the very reason for the state's
existence. This becomes clear when you consider the German
meaning of "learning" and "culture." Learning implied a "spiritual cultivation," the incorporation of objective cultural values
unencumbered by any suggestion of a responsibility for utilitar-
ian application to the needs of society. It was believed that the
specific cultural values that justify the existence of a society can
be attained only through pure learning, that is, learning for the

sake of learning. Since there were in fact some very practical by-products of German intellectual activity (the training of physicians, lawyers, and technicians, for instance), the monarchy willingly provided the funds for support of the bureaucracy that controlled the intellectual establishment. (A Ministry of Culture was responsible for the appointment of professors to posts at German universities. If an academician were looking for a high-paying position at a first-rate university, it helped to have friends in high political office.)

In spite of government subsidy, the German intelligentsia comprised strong adherents to a doctrine of individualism. Culture was a state of personal attainment achieved by means of pure learning, not a condition of society. The values reflected by society were thought to be the result of individual achievements rather than group achievements. Furthermore, there existed a quasi-mystical attitude that the contemplation of the proper areas of study led to wisdom, virtue, and the elevation of the learner to something resembling a state of grace. The importance of the concept of this state cannot be overemphasized, because it provided members of the German intelligentsia with a unique status that made them the social equals of the aristocracy. Most important, the aristocracy accepted the concept, as evidenced by the fact that aristocrats intermarried with common-born citizens who attained high status in the German academic establishment. Köhler was a case in point; although he was common born, his second wife was of noble birth—a Swedish aristocrat, but an aristocrat.

Köhler was deeply steeped in the German intellectual tradition of his time. His father, Dr. Franz Koehler, was the principal of a school; his brother, Wilhelm, held a Ph.D., and was a university professor and director of a museum. Köhler took his Ph.D. at the University of Berlin under the direction of Carl Stumpf, holder of one of the most distinguished university appointments in Germany, and then had the good fortune to meet Max Wertheimer and Kurt Koffka at the Frankfurt Academy at the time of his first academic assignment following graduation from Berlin. He was appointed professor and director of the Psychological Institute at the University of Berlin at age thirty-five at a time (1923) when the average age of a professor there was about sixty. Köhler did well within the German intellectual establishment. He wasn't opposed to war. He was opposed to social forces that threatened his special position in German society. Throughout World War I, the German intellectual establishment had strongly supported Kaiser Wilhelm and the monarchy. Their interests were best served by maintaining the status quo.

Although there were no dramatic changes in the status of the intellectual establishment immediately following the fall of the monarchy in 1918, the stage was set for the denouement that was to occur between 1929 and 1931, when the Nazis took control of the German National Student Union. Köhler did not leave Germany purely out of sympathy for his Jewish colleagues. Anti-Semitism did not begin with Hitler. The evidence is plentiful that Jewish citizens had been discriminated against long before the Nazis took power. It seems clear that at least one of the reasons for Köhler's decision to leave Germany in 1935 was the fact that the Nazis had taken control of the Ministry of Culture and fired Köhler from his position as director of the Psychological Institute, although he retained his tenure as a professor. Aside from this personal insult, Köhler must have realized that the days of intellectual domination of German society were over. The values of German society made a complete turn in the opposite direction: under the Nazi Party, the German intellectual establishment was required to dedicate itself to the welfare of the state, a condition that Köhler could not tolerate.

Wallach told me again that he could not recall anything Köhler ever said about the ape station or his days in Tenerife, but added parenthetically that this was typical of Köhler, that Köhler was one of the most secretive persons he had ever known. Although Wallach did not express affection for Köhler and did appear to be embittered, just as Wolfgang Metzger had said, Wallach's outspoken remarks were not derisive. As for Köhler's first family, Wallach said that Köhler never talked about them, but that he had heard from others that Köhler had four children by his first wife, who was the granddaughter of a famous and popular German neo-romantic painter named Achenbach. Wallach said that those who knew Köhler best were Hans-Lukas Teuber and Richard Held, both at MIT, and Mary Henle.

I told Wallach that I had been unable to reach Teuber, and that Mary Henle had not been helpful. Wallach seemed surprised when I told him that Henle had discouraged me from trying to reach Mrs. Köhler because Mrs. Köhler was seriously ill. After a pause, during which Wallach appeared to be searching his memory, he said that he had not heard about Mrs. Köhler's illness. He was puzzled; he said he had seen Mrs. Köhler at the college (Swarthmore) a short time ago, and that she had appeared to be in good health and had said nothing about an illness. Wallach remembered that Mrs. Köhler had not been well some time ago as a result of an automobile accident, but that she was now fully recovered.

In an effort to satisfy his own curiosity as well as help me, Wallach telephoned Mrs. Köhler's residence but was unable to reach her—she was visiting a friend in Hanover, New Hampshire, and was not expected to return until November 2. Wallach assured me that Mrs. Köhler was not incapable of withstanding an interview with me and suggested I get in touch with her after her return.

* * *

About one month after my meeting with Wallach, I received a letter from Richard Solomon, a professor of psychology at the University of Pennsylvania who had earlier suggested I get in touch with Wallach, and who had recently written a letter in support of my application for a research fellowship. I had chatted with Dick a few weeks earlier in Denver, Colorado, where I presented a paper at the annual meeting of the Psychonomic Society. In his letter, Solomon said that he had talked recently with Henry Gleitman, a friend and fellow professor of psychology at the University of Pennsylvania who had known Köhler from earlier days when Gleitman was a member of the psychology department at Swarthmore. Solomon told me that Gleitman would be happy to talk about his association with Köhler.

I had met Professor Gleitman once in the fall of 1964 at the Graduate Faculty of the New School on the occasion of an oral defense of a doctoral dissertation. Gleitman had chaired, and I had served as a reader. I called Gleitman a week or two after I received the letter from Solomon, and made an appointment to meet with him in Philadelphia.

On December 18, I went to Philadelphia and met Gleitman at his office. Since Solomon was acquainted with my research and had already talked to Gleitman concerning my interest in Köhler, Gleitman was well prepared to answer my questions and give me additional information.

Gleitman was born in Germany and came to the United States as a European refugee in 1939, at age fifteen. He first met Köhler in 1949, the year Gleitman completed his Ph.D. at the University of California at Berkeley (he studied under Edward C. Tolman) and joined the staff of the department of psychology at Swarthmore, a high-powered department for a small college. During Köhler's years at Swarthmore—and partly because of his presence there—the faculty of the department of psychology included, in addition to its chairman, Robert MacLeod: Solomon Asch, David Crutchfield, William Prentice, Hans Wallach, Edwin Newman, and Gleitman. Its master-degree graduates included Richard Held and Ulric Neisser.

Although Gleitman met socially with Köhler on a number of occasions, his primary association was academic. Aside from the large differences in their ages and academic status, it was clear that Köhler maintained a social distance which exceeded the ordinary boundaries of collegial relationships. I was not surprised to learn that Gleitman was in awe of Köhler; Köhler's reputation for brilliance was well established and, as Gleitman learned soon after their early meetings, well deserved.

According to Gleitman, Köhler was a cultured gentleman; he was at home discussing art, music (he played the piano well), philosophy, literature, science, and many other subjects. His depth of knowledge in so many subjects was so extensive that someone who had met him for the first time might spend an evening of conversation with him without ever knowing what his field was. In addition to his profound intellect, Köhler had a great deal of charm; he knew how to compliment a woman in a manner that a feminist would not find objectionable. He could comment favorably on a feminine aspect of a woman so as to flatter, and at the same time enhance the woman's feelings of esteem as a person, not a sex object.

Part of Köhler's charm was his sense of humor, an impish quality that was expressed in a smile rather than a laugh, amusement rather than hilarity. Köhler told little jokes; Gleitman recalled that in his criticism of someone's work, Köhler had said: "So much philosophy of science, so little science." Another part of his charm was his detachment from commonplace things. Gleitman said there was something Olympian about Köhler; his presence and superior achievements gave him an air of lofty detachment. Although some thought Köhler arrogant, Gleitman did not. Gleitman said that Köhler was "a magnificent figure of a man with grace and charm. . . . Köhler was the perfect German gentleman; he possessed genuine elegance." Gleitman asked me whether Köhler was highborn.

I asked Gleitman to describe Köhler's physical stature. He said that Köhler was not a big man, that he was about 5 feet 8 inches or 5 feet 9 inches tall and weighed 145 to 150 pounds. Gleitman, who has an active interest in theater both as an actor and a director, emphasized that it was not Köhler's physical size that made him impressive, but rather his presence, that special quality of poise and distinguished bearing that certain actors have which enables them to arrest the attention of their audience. Gleitman could not remember anyone with as much presence as Köhler. In addition to his stately air and exceptional presence, Gleitman saw Köhler as a strikingly handsome man, a dashing personality in the dramatic sense, a leading man.

I asked Gleitman whom he would cast as Köhler if he were directing a play or a movie about him. His first response was Claude Rains, the Claude Rains of *Antony and Cleopatra*. His second response was Laurence Olivier during his best years—a strong, powerful, middle-aged man. He said that Köhler was like the Olivier of *Sleuth*, but without the homosexual overtones. Gleitman felt that Köhler possessed what the Freudians refer to as an appropriate amount of narcissism, that he showed proper concern for his appearance and proper respect for his physical well-being. Köhler dressed well; he was always properly attired for the occasion, but not flashy or conspicuous. No one article of clothing stood out, but one was conscious of the fact that he was well dressed. Gleitman had selected two actors who for him epitomized beauty, power, intelligence, stage presence, sophistication, charm, wit, and noble bearing.

From Gleitman's description of Lili Köhler, Köhler's second wife, she was ideally cast for her role. Gleitman said that she and

Köhler were well suited for each other, that their marriage was a good one, that they were dedicated to each other, that she was the perfect complement to his character, personality, and appearance. Gleitman first said that Mrs. Köhler was beautiful, but then changed his mind and said she might better be described as handsome, that "she matched the part." Although Gleitman couldn't think of an actress whom he would cast as Mrs. Köhler, he felt it would not be a leading lady such as Katharine Hepburn, because Hepburn would upstage her own role. He felt Mrs. Köhler was a lady-of-the-manor type, but definitely someone who would be cast in a backstage role.

Although Wolfgang and Lili Köhler may have approached perfection as a couple, their daughter, Karin, who attended Swarthmore as an undergraduate, may have fallen short of the high standards set by her parents. Gleitman was vague in his description of her. The Köhlers were, it appeared, a tough act to follow. Earlier in the interview, Gleitman had said that he felt that Köhler could have used "a little unbending as a human being," that Köhler was not close to anyone, except possibly his wife.

I asked Gleitman if he ever noticed a tremor in Köhler's hands. He said he did, and demonstrated the tremor by extending his arm, which showed a displacement at the finger tips of about one inch. Gleitman thought the tremor was neurological in origin. He was surprised to learn that it had begun as early as 1925.

Köhler was brilliant but not flawless. Gleitman, who was the resident behaviorist at Swarthmore, felt that Köhler knew little about American behaviorism and didn't really care to learn more. In the 1950s, Köhler spent a great deal of effort trying to develop a direct-current model of cerebral activity. Gleitman felt that Köhler was never as interested in psychology as he was in physics. Unfortunately, in his efforts to support the idea that psychological events can be reduced to the level of the physics of electricity, he ignored a considerable amount of information on neurophysiology. Köhler felt that it was necessary that a physiological basis for Gestalt theory be established, that his work in science would not be remembered if he did not adequately establish a physical model to accommodate the psychological principles of Gestalt theory. In view of current developments in neu-

Manuel González y García, circa 1916, sitting with a chimpanzee on his lap and an orangutan at his side.

Tschego using sticks to obtain food placed beyond her reach.

Grande standing on three boxes piled together to provide a platform from which a bunch of bananas can be reached. Sultan looks on.

The lawn tennis court of the Hotel Martiánez, circa 1917. At left, an unidentified couple; at center, Mr. and Mrs. Ernst Groth; at right, Thekla and Wolfgang Köhler. The first three children from right to left, Peter Koehler, Marianne Koehler, and Claus Köhler-Achenbach.

The staff of the German council for Tenerife during the years of World War I.
From left to right: G. Peiplemann, Witt, Ernst Groth, von Sternfels, and
Alfred Bäger.

Left to right: Claus Köhler-Achenbach, A. Gelb, Max Wertheimer, Wolfgang Köhler, Marianne Koehler, and Peter Koehler, in Harz, 1922.

Thekla Achenbach Köhler in Niehagen, Germany, circa 1937.

Wolfgang Köhler in his classroom at the University of Berlin, circa 1929.

Manuel González y García on January 23, 1975.

The postcard sent by Wolfgang Köhler in Berlin to Manuel González y García in Puerto de la Cruz, dated February 18, 1921.

A portion of the courtyard at El Ciprés.

La Costa as seen from the road from the sea.

La Costa as seen from the south.

The diesel-powered generator used to produce electricity at the German meteorological observatory at La Grieta.

A view of the lava basin of the Cañadas Mountains taken from the cable car to Mount Teide. The German meteorological observatory was located at the base of La Grieta, the tallest mountain in the background.

The author views the steel I-beams used as the foundation for the German observatory located at the peak of Mount Teide during the early years of World War I.

Mount Teide in the background, overlooking the site of the German meteorological observatory.

Kaiser Wilhelm II's hunting lodge, donated to the German meteorological team at La Grieta.

The staff residence for the sanatorium in the Cañadas Mountains.

Wolfgang Köhler, circa 1947.

rophysiology, it would seem that his efforts in this direction failed.

Gleitman said that when questioned concerning matters relating to the neurophysiological model he was trying to establish, Köhler became extremely defensive. According to Gleitman, who on at least one occasion asked Köhler a relatively simple question, Köhler went into a lengthy explanation far beyond Gleitman's comprehension. Köhler had attributed far more knowledge to Gleitman than Gleitman possessed, and then attributed underlying motives to Gleitman's question, motives that were not intended. In his answer, Köhler became hostile and "paranoid." It seemed more than likely that Köhler realized some of the shortcomings of his work; he must have known that he couldn't adequately construct a neurophysiological theory that would be compatible with existing neurophysiological data and still support the principles of Gestalt psychology.

I was fascinated with Gleitman's vivid description of Köhler, and pleased to get impressions that went beyond photographs and census data, but I was also interested in more substantive information concerning Köhler's years in Tenerife. Except for an amusing movie of the apes that Köhler showed at a party in his home, Gleitman's only recollection of Köhler's talking about Tenerife was an anecdote concerning an incident during the war. Köhler had sent his helper (Gleitman recognized the name "Manuel González y García" as that of the helper) in a boat to pick up some apes, and the helper was intercepted by a British ship whose crew interrogated Manuel and inspected the crates containing the animals. The joke was that the British were so suspicious of Köhler that they went to the trouble of following Manuel and inspecting the crates. The joke wasn't a big one, but it did confirm one of the stories Manuel had told me.

* * *

After our meeting, Gleitman called Professor Solomon Asch, another member of the psychology department at the University of Pennsylvania who had served with Köhler at Swarthmore, to apprise him of my wish to talk to him. In the late afternoon, I called Asch from the psychology laboratories. Asch felt that it was not necessary to meet because he remembered little about what Köhler said concerning his days in Tenerife, and that what he did remember, he could tell me over the phone.

Asch recalled that Köhler had some difficulties obtaining certain books in physics (one of the few facts that Mary Henle recalled for me in her first letter). He said that Köhler was very busy writing during this period, that it was Köhler's good luck to be stranded in Tenerife during World War I, since his isolation provided him with an ideal place and ideal conditions in which to work. Asch remembered that Köhler did not talk a great deal about his days in Tenerife, but allowed that it was likely that there was not a great deal to be said. He claimed that Köhler could not leave the island because British ships surrounded it, and added that he did not think it unusual that Köhler said little about Tenerife, because this was in keeping with Köhler's German style. Köhler volunteered little information concerning his private life and never complained.

There was very little that Asch added to what I already knew; he suggested that I get in touch with Hans-Lukas Teuber, who he felt would know more about Köhler and his days in Tenerife. As our talk came to a close, Asch volunteered that Köhler was completely apolitical—that Köhler had no personal interest in or involvement with any political factions.

* * *

The fall semester ended in mid-December, and the spring semester was not scheduled to begin until the end of January. As the days passed, I grew more and more impatient with the constraints that my work at the university imposed on my time. Although my experimental research was going smoothly— which means that the data from my laboratory were supporting my hypotheses—I found that I was more excited by the prospect of spending the spring break in Tenerife. There, I hoped to interview some of the people who had not been available the previous summer. There, I would once again pick up the trail.

11.

More Information From Tenerife

The winter months of Albany have an accumulative effect on one's mood. The barren trees of November and the early snowfalls of December have a pleasant freshness to them. But by the end of February, the trees take on the lifeless qualities of monstrous skeletons, and the interminable snow is a constant reminder of the inhospitable coldness of the outdoors.

When March finally arrived, I was delighted to leave the cold, gray landscape of the university for the warm air and clear skies of Tenerife. But I had no desire to spend my precious hours lazing in the sun. And so, on the first day of my arrival in Puerto de la Cruz, I called Anthony Yeoward to arrange a meeting for the following day. The appointment made, I set off to find the Taoro, the hotel that Isidoro Luz-Carpenter had said served as headquarters for a German espionage ring during the years of World War I.

The Taoro, which is located above Puerto de la Cruz, on the highest hill in the Orotava Valley, belongs now to the Spanish government, and the grounds that surround the hotel are a public park visited primarily by tourists. I went to the front entrance of the hotel, which had been closed to guests for the past two years, and was met by a caretaker who explained that no one was permitted in the rooms of the hotel without written permission of the government, but that he would be willing to take me to the roof of the hotel where I could take photographs. I followed Domingo through the empty foyer of the old hotel—the largest in Tenerife—to the elevator, which took us to the top floor of the ten-story structure and then to the staircase leading to the roof.

The roof provided an expansive, uncluttered view of the sea and the northern coastline of Tenerife; I could clearly see the banana plantations east of La Paz. In spite of the fact that La Paz is located on a cliff overlooking Puerto, the hill on which the Taoro stands plus the elevation offered by the original eight-story hotel built in 1914 (two more stories were added shortly before the hotel was recently closed) would have lifted the observer to a considerably greater height than the banana plantation at La Costa. In 1914, before the large hotels were erected in La Paz, it would have been possible to see Köhler's house with ease—the two-story construction of the house puts it well above the tops of the surrounding trees. As the crow flies, the distance between the hotel and La Costa is only about one and a half miles.

The Taoro provides an excellent view of many sights: the Martiánez Hotel, which is located in the northeast, just at the bottom of the hill from the Taoro; the old port and customhouse (the port where Köhler's apes arrived in 1912); all aspects of the Orotava Valley; other hills within the valley; and Teide. It was a particularly clear day, and Teide was free of clouds. Although the narrow, twisting road from Puerto to the Cañadas and Teide is twenty to twenty-five miles long, the direct distance from the hotel appeared to be about ten miles. Wireless communication between the meteorological station in the Cañadas and the hotel or La Costa would be relatively simple even with a small radio transmitter. If either the meteorological observatory or the hotel had a powerful transmitter, messages from La Costa could be monitored, amplified, and transmitted to distant places by one of the other sets.

I asked Domingo if the Taoro had its own source of electricity. He said it did, but that he was not certain whether the diesel-powered generators were installed before or after World War I. When I asked him if I could see the generators, he reminded me politely that I could not visit any rooms in the hotel without official permission.

* * *

I met with Anthony Yeoward at his office on the morning of the following day. Yeoward told me that William Clark, the agent for the Yeoward Company in Tenerife at the time of the purchase of La Costa, had returned to Tenerife, and that he would arrange for me to meet him. Yeoward also agreed to let me see the interior of the house at La Costa, and said that he would call the residents to inform them of my forthcoming visit. Lastly, Yeoward wrote a note of introduction to Lady Abercromby, a British resident of Tenerife, whom Mr. Yeoward identified as a person well acquainted with other residents of Tenerife who might be of help to me.

* * *

I called Lady Abercromby, who preferred to be called Molly, and made an appointment to meet with her at her house that evening. When we met, I told her about my research.

Molly thought she knew nothing of importance for my purposes; she didn't remember hearing anything about Köhler or the ape station, and stated emphatically that she had no first-hand knowledge of events in Tenerife during World War I! She mentioned, however, that she might know people who did know something about it, and asked me if I would like to talk with them. I told her I would.

Molly did contribute one bit of interesting information; she said she had been to the peak of Teide several years ago and remembered seeing the remains of some kind of apparatus installed by Germans when they maintained the meteorological observatory in the Cañadas. She couldn't describe it precisely, but she did remember that it was some kind of steel framework embedded in a concrete foundation. She didn't know what it was for, but she recalled hearing that it had something to do with the observatory.

* * *

The next morning I received word from Tony Yeoward that William Clark would be available to meet with me at his house that morning at eleven o'clock. Clark's house was in Las Arenas, just a short distance from Isidoro Luz-Carpenter's. I pulled into the driveway through the open gates hinged to the tall stone wall that ran along the road front; drove through a garden filled with an assortment of well-kept tropical plants, including an orange tree covered with ripe fruit; and parked my car on the circular path in front of the main entrance of the house—an elegant building constructed in a Spanish mode of recent times. Two gardeners greeted me as I walked to the front door where a maid met me and led me to the large center entrance hall. The interior of the house showed the same signs of care as the exterior. The proportions of the house were unusually large, which added to the clean, uncluttered impression that it gave.

After a short wait, Mr. Clark entered the foyer. He was obviously pleased by my visit, not so much because he felt flattered by my interest in information he might have, but rather because I was someone with whom he could spend a pleasant morning chatting. An old man (he would turn ninety-one on October 9), he was nevertheless in good physical condition. He took me to a veranda overlooking the garden at the rear of the house. As he directed me to a chair to his left, he explained that the hearing in his right ear was poor. From the veranda, I could see Isidoro Luz-Carpenter's house; it appeared to be about a quarter of a mile away. The property on which Mr. Clark's house is located is quite large; the land had been part of a banana plantation prior to its purchase from the Yeoward Company.

Mr. Clark told me that he came to Tenerife in 1912 to cultivate bananas for the Yeoward Company; in 1918 he became manager of the Tenerife office. As we talked about his early years in Tenerife, he smiled and laughed a great deal; and when he spoke of hardships, frustration, and grief, he expressed no bitterness. Mr. Clark told me that before coming to Tenerife, Tony Yeoward was in the London office of the company, and that it was Clark who had met Tony in Barcelona, introduced him to the British community and to Spanish business associates, and made arrangements for him to live with a Spanish family for the purpose of learning their language. From Barcelona, Tony came to the island and took charge of the Tenerife office.

When coffee was served, I began questioning Mr. Clark about World War I and Köhler. He said he remembered nothing about the ape station or Köhler, that when the Yeoward Company took possession of La Costa, everything had been cleared out. He then indicated that he did have some recollection of someone having a few monkeys there, but he thought it was as a hobby. Mr. Clark's memory for events was obviously poor—he could not remember the name of the German leader during World War I, Kaiser Wilhelm. He did remember, however, that throughout the years of the war, the Spanish government was much friendlier with the Germans than with the English. He remembered the German consul, Jacob Ahlers, as a very nice man: "He wasn't aggressive like so many other Germans."

In our discussion about activities in Tenerife during the years of the war, Mr. Clark mentioned that it was not until a few years ago that he visited the south side of the island, that his work was in Puerto and Santa Cruz, and that he had no interest in other parts of the island.

The most important bit of information that he provided concerned the purchase of La Costa in 1918. Mr. Clark indicated that before World War I, the company leased farms on which they cultivated bananas. He thought that only one farm, Lagar, was purchased prior to the war, and that only one farm, La Costa, was purchased during the war. At the time of La Costa's purchase, Mr. Clark was assistant to the manager, Mr. Artus. In response to my question concerning who was responsible for the purchase of La Costa, Clark said that instructions were sent from Liverpool by Mr. Richard Yeoward, Anthony Yeoward's grandfather. In view of the fact that the Yeoward Company was leasing many farms at that time, I asked him why La Costa was singled out for purchase. Mr. Clark said he did not know why, but thought it unusual that the company should buy a farm they weren't leasing, rather than one they were.

According to Mr. Clark, the company policy following the war was to purchase the farms the company had been leasing, farms on which bananas had already been carefully cultivated. It is important to note that the cultivation of bananas in the Orotava Valley did not begin until about the turn of the century.

Before this time, the land was used for the cultivation of grapes and vegetables. I remembered Señor Abreu, Anthony Yeoward's assistant, telling me that banana trees on La Costa were rather sparse at the time the property was acquired, that a great deal of work went into the development of the plantation after its acquisition. According to Mr. Clark, the company's policy of expansion did not begin until after the war, when a number of farms were purchased within a relatively brief period of time.

Why was La Costa the only farm singled out for purchase from Liverpool by Mr. Richard Yeoward during the years of World War I? As Mr. Clark thought about it, he mentioned that the company suffered some severe financial setbacks about the same time as or shortly before the purchase of La Costa. Five steamships owned by the company had been sunk by German submarines. The loss of the company's fleet may have created strong anti-German feelings in Mr. Richard Yeoward, feelings that may have been stronger than those typically engendered by patriotism and the desire to serve one's country in time of war.

All of this tied in with Manuel's story that La Costa was purchased for the purpose of uprooting Köhler, of forcing him to move his operation. Furthermore, it was consistent with the information from the British Foreign Office files, which indicated that the British were unsuccessful in their attempts to compel the Spanish government to stop German agents from engaging in espionage activities. Short of direct aggressive intervention, which the British threatened, there was little they could do. Pressuring Köhler by means of forcing him to move may have been one of the alternative actions available as a counterespionage activity.

Mr. Clark couldn't recall details about German espionage in Tenerife during the war, but it was his impression that German activities were centered in Santa Cruz. He laughed when he mentioned that the Spanish referred to the Germans during the war as "niños bandidos"—naughty children. According to Mr. Clark, the Germans got on well with the Spaniards: "There is no doubt that the Spanish liked them. . . . The Germans behaved as if they were people who were going to rule the world. The Spanish admired them for their aggressiveness and strength."

* * *

After the meeting with Clark, I drove directly to La Costa, where the middle-aged woman I had met on my first visit there greeted me. She showed me each room of the two-story, square (about forty feet by forty feet), stucco building. There were no surprises—the interior looked pretty much as I had imagined it would: high-ceilinged rooms that included a kitchen, dining room, sitting room, and one or two other small rooms downstairs. A narrow staircase close to the entrance led to a second floor hallway that connected several upstairs bedrooms. The bedroom in the northeast corner of the second floor, the largest bedroom (the one Köhler and his wife probably occupied), had two large windows. The one on the east side, through which I could see the area that had been the animal compound, overlooked the northeast coastline of the island; the one on the north side looked directly out over the sea, past the single tall palm tree that marked the house and the plantation. In the corner between the windows there was a very large cabinet with two locked doors hinged to open in the center. As I studied the cabinet, I was reminded of Manuel's claim that Köhler concealed a radio in the house; I wondered where he had kept it.

The view from the north window of the bedroom on the northwest corner also overlooked the sea, and the view from the west window overlooked La Paz, Puerto de la Cruz, the Taoro Hotel, and the western section of the Orotava Valley. There appeared to be no structural changes of any kind, so it seemed likely that, except for the permanent installation of electricity and a public water supply system, the house was the same as it had been when Köhler lived there.

There was a small porch located just off the hallway that connected the bedrooms and the staircase to the ground floor. The porch, which the present residents used as a laundry and play area for the children, provided an excellent uninterrupted view of Teide and the Cañadas. Because the terrain surrounding the house was relatively flat, I could see in all directions for a considerable distance. If someone were watching, it would be very difficult to approach the house without being noticed.

* * *

The next morning I drove to the Cañadas. My plan was to hike to the peak of Teide and photograph the view from there, and to look for the remains of the apparatus Lady Abercromby had said were left by the German meteorologists during World War I.

When I got to the base of the mountain, large clouds had moved in and completely enshrouded the peak. Weather conditions didn't improve after an hour, so I decided to visit Izaña, the third highest mountain in Tenerife, and the present site of the Spanish meteorological observatory. Izaña is also the location of an astronomical observatory and the central television and radio relay and transmission station for the Canary Islands. I hoped that someone at the observatory might be able to give me information concerning the location of the old observatory.

I had no trouble finding the new observatory, a very large two-story stone fortress-like building with several smaller buildings attached. I pulled in next to the sole car parked there, but before I stopped, several large dogs were pacing at the car door waiting for me to get out. Among them was a very large German shepherd. As I surveyed the dogs, trying to decide whether or not they were hostile, a man of about thirty years of age came to my car and greeted me. His name was Ramón Juega Buide, and he was a meteorologist from the Spanish mainland employed by the Spanish government for a ten-year tour of duty on Tenerife. His primary responsibility was to monitor and maintain the weather instruments at the observatory and to relay information periodically to a central station that collated the data together with information from other similar stations. Ramón and one other person shared the responsibilities for maintaining the station; they alternated on a three-day interval.

After I introduced myself and explained the reason for my visit, Ramón said that he knew the location of the old observatory and would be happy to escort me personally. He added quickly that the old site was not good for meteorological observation because the wind velocity and direction were distorted by the walls of the Cañadas, and because the surrounding mountains curtailed the observer's view of the sky. Ramón pointed out that the second highest peak in Tenerife was located just above the site of the old observatory.

Before we drove to the site, Ramón took me to a nearby building, a one-story prefabricated aluminum structure that resembled a military barracks in both appearance and size. We entered through the front door, which led to a narrow enclosed porch and to a second door that opened into a parlor complete with furnishings that dated back many years. The building, which had been moved to Izaña in 1919, was the same building that had served as Kaiser Wilhelm's hunting lodge in equatorial Africa before he donated it to the German government for use as a meteorological observatory in 1912. This was the building alleged to have been the location of a radio used to communicate German military intelligence during the early months of World War I.

A doorway from the center of the parlor led to a hallway that ran the length of the building, dividing it in two. About a dozen rooms, most of which appeared to have been sleeping quarters, opened onto the hallway, and at one end of the hall there was a large kitchen and large bath with several toilets and showers. The building, which was obviously designed to house a sizeable staff, was in surprisingly good condition, and many of the rooms contained items of furniture left over from years past—heavy well-constructed pieces made from oak. One room had two desk-type cabinets with drawers. Ramón pulled two drawers out of one of the cabinets and showed me that they were empty. He then reached into the empty space from which the drawers were taken and produced a cleverly concealed inner drawer; the concealed inner drawer was the lining of the obvious exterior drawer.

After I photographed several rooms of the old observatory, we drove to Portillo and took the road into the floor of the crater, the dirt road that winds along the base of the Cañadas. We drove for about five miles before reaching the site of the old observatory, the place where the building we had just left was originally erected in 1912, the place where the building stood during the years of World War I. If you didn't know what to look for, it would have been easy to miss. The site was in a flat region relatively uncluttered by rocks, close to the base of the Cañadas, about 150 yards on the north side of the road beneath La Grieta. It consisted of nothing more than two concrete platforms, which served as the foundations of two buildings, one of which was the building we had just left.

I photographed the site and the view from the site. We didn't spend much time there, because the weather had become cold and windy. Ramón mentioned again that this was a very poor site for an observatory because the direction and velocity of the wind could not be measured accurately; he said that he could not understand why the Germans built the observatory here.

We left the site of the German observatory and drove about two miles to the old sanatorium. The direct distance was probably half this, since the road connecting the two places had a large bend. The important point is that the two places could easily have been in communication with each other and most likely were—there were no other places inhabited by people for many miles.

I discovered that the building I had visited the previous summer was not the sanatorium; it was the residential building for the staff. According to Ramón, the sanatorium never had any patients, a fact consistent with information from the Foreign Office files and with Isidoro Luz-Carpenter's story.

*   *   *

Several days later, Molly Abercromby invited me to meet Austin Baillon, a friend of hers who had a keen interest in the history of Tenerife. I met Molly at her house early that evening, and after a short drive through Puerto de la Cruz to the ocean front at the old harbor, we arrived at Austin and Julia Baillon's residence, Casa de la Cruz. The oldest house in Puerto, Casa de la Cruz had served as the customhouse when Puerto de la Cruz was still an active seaport and port of entrance for ships sailing from foreign countries. The building was a very large three-story stone structure with an open courtyard in the center. The first floor of the building served as a shop where the Baillons sold folk art, curios, jewelry, and other items of interest to tourists; the second and third floors were the Baillons' living quarters, rooms with dimensions that reminded me of the spacious artists' lofts in Manhattan's Soho section.

From the balcony off the parlor, situated in the northwest corner of the building, I had a broad view of the ocean, with nothing but a breakwater and concrete pier below. According to Manuel González y García, this was the place where Köhler's animals were put ashore when they arrived from the Cameroons; it was here that the animals cleared customs, so to speak, before they were taken to the courtyard of the old Martiánez Hotel, to the place where Manuel first encountered them.

Austin Baillon, an energetic and zestful man in his early sixties who had recently retired from a post in South America with the Shell Oil Company, was eager to hear my story about Köhler and the ape station. He listened attentively and indicated several times his enthusiasm for my research. Although Austin's family had lived in Tenerife throughout his life, Austin had been educated in England, served as an officer in the British Army during World War II, and worked in other parts of the world before returning to Tenerife. There, he and his wife purchased Casa de la Cruz, and opened their shop, La Antigua Casa de la Real Aduana.

Although Austin, who had an interest in World War I, did not recognize Köhler's name, he did recall hearing something about a man who had some monkeys. He then described the box-stacking experiment in which the apes were required to construct from boxes a platform that would give them access to a suspended bunch of bananas that was otherwise out of reach. Austin also recalled that his father, the late Alexander Baillon—past plantation manager for Elder and Fyffes Company, fruit exporters—had written something about German scientists on the peak of Teide about the time of World War I. He consulted his father's *Memoirs* and found a brief reference to evidence of the presence of German meteorologists on the peak, but no details of events directly associated with Köhler.

* * *

Although my search in Tenerife did not produce dramatic findings that added a great deal to what I already knew about Köhler and the circumstances surrounding his stay in Tenerife, I did make a serendipitous discovery. While reading Alexander Bail-

lon's *Memoirs* looking for clues pertaining to Köhler, I learned
that Baillon was closely associated with the late Ernest Hooton,
the founding father and leading figure of American physical
anthropology.

According to Baillon's account, during the summer of 1914,
Hooton came to Tenerife, where he unearthed a number of bur-
ial sites in caves used by the Guanches, the aboriginal inhabitants of the Canary Islands. Measurements of the relics he unearthed provided the data for his classic *The Ancient Inhabitants
of the Canary Islands*, the book that established Hooton's international reputation. While these facts were stated clearly by
Hooton in the preface of his book, the story of how Hooton got
the skeletal remains of his subjects from Tenerife to the Peabody
Museum of Harvard University had never been told, at least not
in print.

In his *Memoirs*, Baillon revealed that the Spanish government
forbade Hooton from removing the bones and related artifacts
from Tenerife, thus frustrating Hooton's efforts. Shortly after
Hooton's departure, Baillon managed cleverly to use the facilities of the fruit exporting company that he managed to smuggle
Hooton's collection from the caves of Tenerife to the stores of
the Peabody Museum via Liverpool, England, a port of debarka-
tion used commonly by the Elder and Fyffes Company. The
details of Baillon's coup would be told in a 1979 issue of the
Anthropological Quarterly.

Although the inside story of how Hooton obtained skeletal
remains of Guanches was not related directly to the specific
goals of my research, it did provide me with a closer feeling for
the *Zeitgeist*—the spirit of the time—during which Köhler lived in
Tenerife. Attitudes have changed since then. Today, it is very
likely that concern would center on the legal issues of Baillon's
behavior and Hooton's complicity. Whatever Baillon's motivation, it is clear that it was neither fame nor fortune. On the
island of Tenerife during the summer of 1914, the story told by
Baillon was one of bold men performing bold acts. Were there
parallel events taking place in Köhler's life?

12.

The German Military Records

During the spring semester, there were three events that contributed to the progress of my research on Köhler: a letter from Austin Baillon, a telephone conversation with Hans-Lukas Teuber, and a transcription of the German military records from Freiburg.

The letter from Baillon contained a statement by Señor Tomas Hernández, an old native of Tenerife who had *personal recollections* of the ape station during the years of World War I. The following is an excerpt from Don Tomas's statement to Austin Baillon in April 1976:

In the year of your birth 1912, there came to Puerto de la Cruz some people of German nationality who brought with them eight animals, of which five were chimpanzees, one a gorilla, and two orangutans. These animals were maintained under the observation of a physician, and had been brought to this location in order to be part of scientific experiments.

The animals, which soon came to be known as "Machangos," were housed in well-constructed individual cells supported by iron braces. The compound where the animals were maintained was located in the place known as "La Costa," land belonging to the Yeoward Company which at that time belonged to Melchor Luz y Lima, who pointed out to the local authorities that this location was used for various etapas [espionage centers]. This farm is situated along a cliff to the east of Playa de Martiánez at about 70 meters above sea level; and there they remained for several years. It was at this place, I think, that the two orangutans died. . . .

Two years later, in 1914, the First World War began. It was then said that the owners of the animals were spies. That at night in front of the cliffs at La Costa, lights from German submarines sailing close to the coast were frequently seen, but the exact nature of the submarines' activities there was not known. The certain thing was the "Machangos," the apes. They were transferred to a farm known as "El Ciprés" located on the municipal boundary of the Valle de Orotava. And that at the end of the war the animals and owners left the valley. The only remaining person was the custodian, guard, and maintenance man, Manuel González y García, a local resident of this region who presently lives among us.

If there were a connection between offshore submarines and the inhabitants of La Costa, and if Köhler were operating a radio, the strong inference would be that he was communicating information to the submarines. The reason for the submarines coming close to the coastline to receive radio messages may have been a strategy designed to protect against the interception of the communication by the British Navy. Other things being equal, the reception of a radio signal depends upon the strength of the signal and the distance from the source of transmission. This is the basic principle underlying the modern navigational systems that guide airplanes, keeping them on the beam. By cruising close to the coastline just offshore of La Costa, a very low intensity signal would be strong enough to allow communication with a nearby submarine, but weak enough not to be detected a short distance beyond the offshore location by British ships. The presence of German submarines off the coastline of Tenerife was certain; the possession of a radio by Köhler rested on Manuel's statement.

* * *

The second event that contributed to my research was a telephone conversation with Hans-Lukas Teuber, the man thought to be best informed on Wolfgang Köhler. I called Professor Teuber at his office at the Massachusetts Institute of Technology on the morning of May 19, and asked for an appointment to meet with him.

Teuber told me that he would be very busy the following week, that he was very pressed for time and would be leaving the country on June 17. I told him that it was important to talk to him because he knew Köhler well. He agreed that he did know Köhler well, that Köhler had been a surrogate father to him and to Richard Held, a professor of psychology and a member of Teuber's department. Teuber suggested that we discuss what was on my mind on the phone.

In answer to my question concerning the origins of the ape station, Teuber said that Max Rothmann and Carl Stumpf were directors of the Prussian Academy of Science and were responsible for the selection of Köhler as director of the station. Teuber said that his father and mother were the actual founders of the station in that they preceded Köhler, but that Teuber's father was called back to Germany to serve in the military, while Köhler stayed on and was stranded there by the war.

I asked Teuber why his father was called back to Germany to serve in the military and Köhler wasn't. He said that he was not altogether sure what the reason was, and quickly added that Köhler was from one of the Baltic countries, that perhaps he wasn't a German citizen "or something like that." He said: "It may have all happened too suddenly," that perhaps his father was called back to Germany earlier because he had a reserve commission, and concluded with: "I never actually asked him why he wasn't called back. He was stranded."

According to Teuber, Robert Yerkes, an American who pioneered research on the great apes, visited Tenerife prior to the establishment of his own ape station in Orange Park, Florida, and used the station at Tenerife as a model for his own station. Teuber mentioned again that it was his father and mother who were responsible for the establishment of the station, that prior to Tenerife, they had been in continental Africa, where they recorded folk music on some sort of primitive wire recording device. When Teuber's father returned to Germany from Tenerife, he entered the military and served until the end of the war, after which he turned to the study of information processing; engineering; and applied, industrial, and mathematical psychology.

Teuber said that Rothmann, who visited Tenerife but once, and Stumpf were responsible for obtaining the funds for the station, and that they did this by dint of their status in the Prussian Academy of Science. Teuber added that Rothmann achieved fame through his work on the decortication of dogs, and that he was planning to extend his research to apes at the station in Tenerife following the war. Rothmann died before he could realize this ambition; after his son's death in the war, he grew despondent and killed himself.

I asked Teuber if he knew why Köhler took the post as director of the ape station, that it seemed odd that he should leave the company of Wertheimer and Koffka in Frankfurt at the very time that the three of them were formulating the basic principles of Gestalt psychology. I told him that I thought it was especially odd in view of the fact that Köhler had no experience working with animals prior to his stay in Tenerife, and showed little or no interest in animals following his stay. Teuber said that Köhler saw the post in Tenerife as a ''good opportunity, a special opportunity,'' that it was Stumpf who selected him. Teuber also mentioned that the post in Tenerife gave Köhler the opportunity to test his ideas against those of Edward Thorndike, the American psychologist who favored a mechanistic trial-and-error theory of animal learning.

I asked Teuber what he knew about Köhler's first family. He said he knew nothing except that Köhler's son was a physician who lived in Heidelberg or an area close to Heidelberg. He said he didn't know the son's name or anything more about the children or about the first Mrs. Köhler, that perhaps the second Mrs. Köhler might know something.

Teuber told me that he had written a necrology on Köhler that was published in a German journal, and that he would send me a reprint. I told him I would be in touch with him after his return to the United States.

* * *

The third event important to my research was the arrival of the transcription of the German military records pertaining to activities in the Canary Islands during World War I, the documents I had obtained a year earlier from the military archives in Freiburg. The records provided prima-facie evidence of German espionage in the islands and other parts of Spain. They were not, however, as complete as I had hoped. Although the records contained some of the correspondence received from the Etappes in the Canaries, they did not contain the actual files of the Etappes in the islands. The reason for this was explained in part by a "Top Secret" memorandum from Berlin to the German naval attaché in Madrid, dated March 15, 1920. The memo, which gave notice to the military attachés that their offices were to be closed by March 31, instructed the attachés on the Spanish mainland to "destroy codes" and submit their files to the German Embassy in Madrid. However, documents of the Canary Island Etappes were "to be sent home if safe," with an added caution to "destroy compromising material if safe forwarding cannot be guaranteed."

Although the war ended in November 1918, and the Treaty of Versailles, signed in June of 1919, became effective in January of 1920, the German government was still concerned that German military documents should not be intercepted and confiscated by the Allies.

Whatever the final disposition of records from the Canary Island Etappes—whether safely transported, intercepted, or destroyed—documents from these files were not among those I received from Freiburg. Furthermore, the records received did not contain a single document dated for the years of 1917 and 1918, the years during which Germany intensified her submarine warfare in the Atlantic and expanded her network of operations beyond the Canary Islands. Perhaps the task of keeping records became less essential as the intensity and duration of the war increased.

* * *

One of the earliest documents from the files was a memorandum from Las Palmas. Dated August 26, 1914, the memorandum was addressed to the offices of the Woermann steamship line in Hamburg and was from F.W. Behrens, the German vice consul in Las Palmas. Behrens' statement made it clear that it was possible to travel between Germany and the Canary Islands during the early days of the war. The fact that his ship sailed via England suggests that he either possessed a bogus passport or was hidden aboard the ship and not detected by British customs inspectors. Whatever the means, Behrens' memorandum supported Isidoro Luz-Carpenter's impression that Germans were able to travel between Germany and Tenerife.

The first substantive document was a ''Top Secret'' memorandum. Also dated August 26, 1914, the memorandum was from the chief of the Etappe in Las Palmas—a German naval officer named Korvettenkapitän Leonhardt, who signed this document and all subsequent documents written by him, ''Leonardi.'' The reason for the subtle change in his name (the dropping of the ''h'' and substitution of ''i'' for ''t'') was not explained, but it seemed reasonable to assume that he intended to disguise his personal and ethnic identity.

The memorandum, a summary of the activities of the Etappe since August 1, 1914, provided information that dovetailed nicely with the events of the early days of the war as described by Corbett in his account of the British naval activities in the area of the Canary Islands. The Etappe in Las Palmas was responsible for maintaining ''encountering lines'' for the service of German ships in the Atlantic off the northwestern coast of Africa. The memorandum mentioned seven ships used by the Etappe as colliers, the number of tons of coal each carried, the dates of their departures from Las Palmas or Tenerife, and the direction in which each of the ships was sailing. Since wireless sets were not standard equipment on all ships at that time (only one collier had a radio), the encountering lines were established so that a German warship in need of fuel or supplies would know the specified route of a collier (the encountering line), and thus be able to intercept it and refuel or exchange passengers at sea if necessary. In this way, the ship could avoid the risk of being trapped in a harbor by the British Navy. However, moving several hundred tons of coal from one pitching ship to another in a rough sea was not a simple matter. Thus, a warship and an encountered collier would more often seek a safe harbor where the transfer could take place. The memorandum mentioned that the *Duala*, a collier that left Las Palmas on August 2 with twelve hundred tons of coal, was met at its position at Terro by the *Kaiser Wilhelm der Grosse* (a German ship subsequently sunk by the British warship *Highflyer* in the late afternoon of August 26, 1914). The *Duala* was then escorted to Rio de Oro where it transferred its coal before returning to Las Palmas for another load.

Since many hours, and sometimes days, were required to transport coal from one ship to another, it was extremely important that British warships be sufficiently distant to be unable to reach the harbor before the German ship had refueled and was safely out to sea. One of the jobs of the Etappes was to keep track of the location of British ships and to communicate this information to German ships that might be in jeopardy. Another job of the Etappes was to relay information obtained from the colliers to Nauen, a small town west of Berlin, which served as the center for German military intelligence during World War I.

Leonardi's memorandum included a report stating that a German ship (the *Kaiser Wilhelm der Grosse*) earlier "shot the *Kaipara* and the *Nyanga* in the ribs," that is, she had sunk the two ships. However, before sinking the ships, the captain of the German ship took their crews aboard his ship and held them captive. When he intercepted the *Arlanza* (a British ship), he already had on board 125 captured crew members, and was reluctant to add the crew of the *Arlanza* because the already large number of prisoners posed the threat of mutiny. Since he was unwilling to risk accommodating the crew of the *Arlanza*, he couldn't sink her. In August of 1914, German naval officers did not kill innocent seamen in cold blood. The sinking of ships at this time was a relatively civilized business. The German cruiser would intercept an Allied merchant ship, order her to position herself for boarding, board the ship and request her captain and crew to pack their personal belongings, and transport the captain and his crew to the cruiser while German sailors prepared to scuttle the ship by opening petcocks and/or planting explosives in her hull. If the cruiser were in a hurry, it might fire a few shells into the hull of the merchant ship and thus speed its demise. The surprise attack—the attack without warning or concern for the lives of the personnel of the merchant ships—did not begin until

1915, after Winston Churchill, then first lord of the British Admiralty, ordered the British merchant ships to arm themselves
and to attempt to defend themselves against German warships.
After the first German warship was fired upon, the gentleman's
naval war ended.

The report also explained that the captain of the *Kaiser
Wilhelm der Grosse* would transmit wireless messages only under
the most urgent situations, that messages transmitted from his
ship might be detected by British warships searching for him and
thus make his position known. The *Kaiser Wilhelm der Grosse*
could, of course, receive radio messages without being detected,
but this required that the messages be sent in code. Thus, another important function of the Etappes was to gather information concerning the location of Allied merchant ships and British
warships, and encode the information before broadcasting it to
German ships at sea.

Another way in which the Etappes provided land-based support for German ships was revealed in the part of the report in
which Leonardi explained that the close surveillance of ships by
the British led to an investigation by the Spanish port authorities
in Las Palmas when the *Duala*, a collier, returned. The question
was: what happened to all the coal the *Duala* carried when she
last left Las Palmas?

The issue was settled in favor of the commanding officer of
the *Duala* through the skillful defense presented by the German
vice consul for Las Palmas, F. W. Behrens, a member of the Las
Palmas Etappe, who argued that the *Duala* was driven off its
course to New York by fear of interception by British warships,
that it met the *Kaiser Wilhelm der Grosse* by coincidence and was
forced to give up its cargo. This event may have marked the first
in a long series of frustrations suffered by the British in their
never-ceasing attempt to force the Spanish authorities to inter-
vene on their behalf and stop Germany from using bases in
Spain for the purpose of maintaining German ships and submarines. Other information contained in the memorandum suggested that the Etappes had infiltrated facilities vital to their
work early in the war, and that they began counterintelligence
work in the first days of the war or possibly before the war
began. One item in the August memorandum described a ci-
phered telegram sent to Gibraltar and Cape Verde by the British

consul. Not only was the German Etappe able to decipher the British code (the telegram alerted the British Navy to be on the lookout for a German steamer), but it was also able to hold up transmission of the telegram by the public telegraph office for six hours, "so that the English cruisers would be unable to detect any trace of the steamer." Knowledge of the British code not only apprised German agents of British intelligence, but also provided the means by which they could manipulate the British through the transmission of false information. A message from the German Embassy in Madrid to the German naval staff in Berlin, dated September 27, 1914, gives an example:

> There is the possibility of leaking false news to the press. It would be advantageous to Spielmann to advise of false ship traffic from some coast, for example, "three German cruisers passed Ferrol on a course headed south." At the same time, a coded telegram could be sent to the cover address of the Naval Staff in London according to the English Consulate code, which would give the same false information.

The Germans were quick to explore the ways in which the new technology of wireless communication could be exploited as a weapon of war. The new technology bred new strategies of deception as well as new tools of logistics.

Information concerning the arrivals and departures of British warships in and from both Tenerife and Las Palmas was stated in the memorandum. Leonardi listed seven colliers in Tenerife, each carrying quantities of coal ranging from 180 to 2,500 tons, and six ships in Las Palmas with loads of coal ranging from 250 to 1,250 tons. He explained, however, that the presence of the British warships, plus a message from the German Admiralty in Rome warning of the presence of the British ships in the area of the Canaries, made it very difficult for him to dispatch colliers to the encountering lines. (The fact that Germany was sending naval intelligence from Rome to the Canary Islands is an interesting bit of information in itself, and illustrates the expansiveness of Germany's intelligence network. It should be noted, however, that Italy was neutral at this time, that she did not join the Allies until May of 1915).

Leonardi also mentioned that the German ships in the harbors of both Tenerife and Las Palmas were being watched closely by the British, but added that if it were not possible to safely send the German colliers to sea, he would spread rumors that the ships were preparing to go to sea, which would force the British Navy to send cruisers to the ports in question, and thus distract them from German ships already at sea. This cat-and-mouse game was a consequence of Spain's neutrality; as long as the German ships were anchored in a Spanish harbor, or anywhere within Spain's territorial waters, British warships could not legitimately attack them. This rule was violated from time to time as in the case of the *Kaiser Wilhelm der Grosse*, which was finally trapped by the *Highflyer* in a Spanish port while refueling, and sunk after she refused to surrender.

In his memorandum, Leonardi revealed the somewhat complex nature of the German secret code: "The ship [*Professor Woerman*] cannot be reached by wireless anymore, since wireless messages are now only allowed in *open language*, and the steamer does not possess the *devices* necessary to decipher *sentences* [italics mine]." Relatively primitive forms of code involved the simple replacement of letters or digits in a message with corresponding letters or digits of the code; cryptographers refer to this process as "enciphering." An enciphered message, if intercepted, can be recognized immediately as a secret message because such a message does not conform to the rules of spelling, grammar, or syntax of any known language. Sophisticated codes, on the other hand, treat syllables, words, or whole sentences according to set rules; this process is now referred to by cryptographers as "encoding," and the process of translating the encoded message is "decoding" (the process referred to by Leonardi as "deciphering"). The encoded message appears as a meaningful group of words that do conform to the standard rules of spelling, grammar, and syntax in the appropriate language of the sender, the "open" language to which Leonardi refers. The greater complexity of encoding over enciphering is obvious, and the fact that an encoding and decoding machine was required is not too surprising, especially in view of the famous German "Enigma" encoding and decoding machine. The device, a copy of which British intelligence obtained in the early years of World War II, was used by the German military in

World War II to send wireless messages. Perhaps the device referred to by Leonardi was an early version of the "Enigma"
machine.

Many of the complications and risks of using public wireless
radio stations were obviated by establishing covert radio stations
under the direct command of the organized Etappes. This solution seems a simple one by current standards, but one must bear
in mind that in the Canary Islands of 1914, the simplest of
wireless radios could not be obtained at local commercial out-
lets, and sources of electricity necessary to transmit radio signals
were not readily available. Even if radio sets, or the components
required for their construction, could be obtained, highly
trusted individuals with technical skills and knowledge of the
physics of electricity were essential to construct and maintain a
reliable radio transmitter and receiver.

The necessity for Germany's establishment of secret wireless
radio stations in Spain is clear. However, the viability of such
stations depended on the cooperation of officials within the
Spanish government. This was not necessarily active cooperation
that would be a blatant violation of Spain's neutrality, but rather
passive cooperation—for instance, public condemnation of German espionage activities in Spain, and private instructions to the
police and military to soft-pedal their investigations of alleged
espionage. This duplicity was not a policy of the Spanish government, which was teetering on the brink of revolution, nor was it
true of all government officials. It was perhaps the instability of
the factional government and the poverty of the times that contributed to the illegal and unethical behavior or indifferent attitudes of some officials.

In spite of the unstable conditions of the times, Germany did
experience some problems in using Spain to support its naval
warfare. The German military files contained a translation of an
article from a Spanish newspaper, *La Region*, published in Santa
Cruz, Tenerife, on November 26, 1914. Entitled "The Germans
on the Peak," the article tells of the alleged installation of a radio
in the Cañadas Mountains by a group of German scientists:

> From the time of the arrival in Santa Cruz of the German
> steamship *Walhalla*, people have been saying that some
> German residents of Tenerife as well as the scientific

commission which studies the atmosphere and the sunlight on the peak [Teide] are in possession of some kind
of a secret wireless station. There has been much talk
about this, and it was noted by a person who had worked
there. The German steamer *Krefeld* arrived here some
time ago after having sailed throughout the islands managing always to avoid the English cruisers. The prisoners
of the *Krefeld* who were released here reported that the
steamer had been in constant communication with land
for two days before arriving, thus lending credibility to
the rumor of the secret radio station.

A Swiss mechanic from Orotava, who by coincidence
helped install the German's cottage in the Cañadas,
talked later to his friends of his strong belief that there is
on the peak a device designed to send radio signals:
"This is altogether possible," said the mechanic. "I have
reason to believe that there is a wooden antenna on the
top of the peak, one-meter wide, its point equipped with
a piece of insulated tin, from which radio waves are sent
at night. You probably think," the Swiss continued,
"that this would require electricity. They have a liquid
source of electrical energy, storage batteries which they
keep well hidden in several trunks. These batteries provide the necessary electricity without any difficulty. The
height of the peak on which the antenna was placed, plus
the huge telescope which is also mounted there, explain
everything. The telescope is turned more often to the
seven islands than to the sky. They see, send, and receive."

The explanation of the mechanic had already convinced the listeners, when it was heard that the local
telegraphist of the wireless station was detecting strange
oscillations when receiving telegrams from London, oscillations which caused strange undecipherable words.
The chief of the station reported this to the Governor
and a telegram was sent to the government indicating
the definite presence of a secret wireless station, and that
it was suspected that the secret station had been put on
the peak by the German commission.

The essential ingredients of the document agreed with the
information from the British Foreign Office files found earlier,
especially the earlier report from Mr. Cooper, the British engi-

neer who supervised the construction of the waterworks at Gran Canaria. Both sources stated that among the materials requested by the observatory were "a three-phase dynamo, transformers and a battery of cells." Mr. Cooper's report corroborated the Swiss mechanic's statement concerning the possible use of liquid storage batteries to power a radio at the peak, and provided the additional explanation of how the batteries were charged. If the dynamo, transformers, batteries, and other electrical equipment were necessary for research purposes, one wonders what it was the Spanish soldiers looked for when they conducted their investigations of the peak and the observatory. What was it they didn't find?

Manuel González y García had said that the Spanish military confiscated the radio of two Germans who had been living in the mountains; he inferred that the men had been using the radio to communicate military intelligence. Perhaps events subsequent to the newspaper article did lead to the uncovering of espionage activities on the parts of the German scientists in the Cañadas. In addition to Manuel, the Swiss mechanic, and British engineer V.B.D. Cooper, Isidoro Luz-Carpenter, his brother Don Guillermo, and German consul Jacob Ahlers all expressed suspicion that German scientists in the Cañadas were involved in espionage.

*   *   *

The files contained only three documents for the year of 1915. Each document provided interesting insights into the variety of everyday activities of the espionage center in Las Palmas, and the means by which the Etappe conducted some of its business.

The first document, an anonymous report dated October 4 and sent to the German Naval Staff via The Hague, the Netherlands, contained three items. The first item discussed how the funds deposited in German bank accounts of companies with affiliates in Tenerife could be used by the German government for the purpose of forwarding funds to the Etappe. The second explained how a German spy whose identity had been uncovered lived in jeopardy of being captured by the British, a fact that supported Manuel González y García's statements that

Köhler lived in fear of the British. The third concerned money used to supplement the salaries of the crews confined to German ships anchored in Spanish harbors, and the conveyance of intelligence concerning the armament of an enemy ship.

The second document for the year of 1915, a decoded telegram from Madrid to the Naval Staff in Berlin dated November 1, reported the death of Vice Consul Behrens in Las Palmas on October 31. The telegram also contained information regarding Allied troop movements in connection with the Salonica campaigns, the long-thwarted Allied efforts to move through the Balkans in an attempt to establish a supply route to southwestern Russia and to aid Serbia. The departure of ships for Saloniki, the seaport in central Grecian Macedonia now known as Thessaloniki, occurred just days after Bulgaria joined the Central Powers (Germany, Austria-Hungary, and Turkey) and overran Serbian Macedonia. This was a time when thousands of Allied troops were still marooned on the nearby Gallipoli Peninsula in Winston Churchill's ill-conceived and tragic campaign designed to open a sea route from the Dardanelles and Bosporus straits of Turkey to Russian ports on the Black Sea.

The third document for the year of 1915 was a letter from the Las Palmas Etappe received in Kiel on October 29, 1915. In the letter, Leonardi provided additional information about the operation of the Etappe and requested that the German Admiralty Office provide additional funds with which to pay a Mr. Bäger, a German spy working out of the Las Palmas Etappe. ''We needed Mr. Bäger to cipher and decipher, a function which at times was so time consuming that extra help was needed to keep the activities of the Etappe going. . . . Furthermore, Mr. Bäger made a trip to Tenerife in the service of the Etappe for the purpose of important discussions with the contact man in Tenerife.''

A subsequent letter, dated March 24, 1916, was sent from the German consul in Tenerife to Berlin via Madrid. It added a few more details concerning Bäger's work in Tenerife, namely, that he acted as a representative of the German consul in Tenerife while assisting the contact man (Vertrauensmann) of the Tenerife Etappe.

This letter and the earlier document received in Kiel on October 29, 1915, made it clear that the German consulates in Las Palmas and Tenerife worked hand in glove with the Etappes of their respective domains. This fact was not a surprising one; the data merely confirmed its validity beyond a doubt, and established the additional fact that Bäger worked closely with the German consul in Tenerife.

There were three other documents for 1916. The first, a "Secret" message from the Canaries received in Wilhelmshaven on April 4, 1916, requested advice on the disposition of some undefined "secret equipment" being stored on a German steamer, and some confidential documents.

The second document, a "Top Secret" letter from the Naval Office of the Reich in Berlin dated May 18, 1916, informed the Hamburg-Bremen-Africa Steamship Line that "the second officer of the steamer 'Ingo,' currently in Las Palmas, succeeded in returning to Germany despite the ship on which he sailed, a Netherlands steamer, was kept in England for two days during which time the English searched the ship thoroughly. The British offered the crew five pounds for each German on board whose presence they can prove."

The last document for 1916 was a communiqué to the Naval Staff dated October 19. Sent from Santa Cruz de Tenerife by a person named R. Badenritz, it related observations on steamer traffic in the islands. Among the ships mentioned was the *Alondra*, an armed British steamer of the Yeoward Company that was sunk in December of 1916.

* * *

In an undated letter, Leonardi complained about his life in the Canary Islands and stated that "W.K." shared his feelings: "Also very sad aside from W.K. and myself, is Regman...."

The final document in the files, also undated but almost certainly written after the war, was a summary statement by Leonardi in which he listed the names of a few people who had been of service to the Etappe; each name was followed by a statement of commendation. Chief among these names was Ernst Groth, B.E.-V.M.II, "Head deputy of Jacob Ahlers of Teneriffe [sic], German deputy consul, and Austrian Vice-Consul." The initials following Groth's name are abbreviations that designate occupational classification within the espionage ring.

B.E. is an abbreviation for "Berichterstatter," a German word that means "reporter." This term was used to describe an espionage agent whose duty was to collect intelligence and convey it to the H.B.E—the "Haupt Berichterstatter," or the "head" or "chief" espionage agent. The duties of the B.E. were distinguished from those of the V.M. or "Vertrauensmann," the German term for a secret intermediary. The V.M. was an espionage agent who acted as an administrator and liaison officer for the Etappe in confidential and sometimes delicate activities, such as the bribing of foreign officials, the instigation of rumors, the spreading of propaganda, etc. The B.E. and V.M. designations represent the two basic functions of the spy rings. They were not, however, mutually exclusive categories.

Leonardi wrote the following words concerning Groth's work for the Etappe:

> At the outbreak of the war and for the entire duration of the war, the German Consul, Mr. Ahlers and also Mr. Schacht, B.E.V.M. I 403, both were in Germany. Therefore, Mr. Groth was charged with the duties of both V.M. as well as those of the German and Austrian Consuls, and the director of Jacob Ahler's company. Despite the difficulty and heavy work in each of his jobs, he performed his services with utmost devotion, energy, and discretion. . . .
>
> He negotiated skillfully and successfully with the protesting Spanish Government—the Provincial Government of the Canary Islands is located in Tenerife.
>
> He always kept the Etappe well informed . . . as a V.M. he risked his life as well as the existence of the company.

Aside from information concerning espionage activities in the islands, the German military records made it clear that Ernst Groth, the acting German consul and the manager of Jacob Ahler's business, was a high-ranking espionage agent (Berichterstatter and Vertrauensmann) of the Tenerife Etappe. This in itself did not seem important when I first read the files, but it proved to be a pivotal fact as subsequent information was uncovered.

13.

Berlin in the Summer

I n Albany, May is the kindest month; it breeds lilacs over kill water, the Dutch name for streams, marks the end of the academic year, and heralds the coming of summer. May is a time for celebration on the part of students and faculty alike.

I was especially eager for the semester to end. A few months earlier, I had received word that the Research Foundation of the State University of New York had approved my application for a faculty research fellowship. The stipend was a modest sum, but sufficiently large to allow me to continue research in Germany during the summer.

My primary objective was to search the archives in Berlin, but since it was necessary to land in Frankfurt to make the connecting flight, I decided to visit the Bundesarchiv of nearby Koblenz and Bonn, and then the archives of the Kaiser Wilhelm Gesellschaft in Munich. From there, I would travel by train to Berlin.

* * *

My flight from New York arrived in Frankfurt on July 5. On the following day, I went to the Bundesarchiv in Koblenz. Dr.

Kahlenberg, the archivist who had helped me the year before, was on vacation; in his stead, I met with Dr. Bobarach. My purpose was to double-check the files in search of references to Wolfgang Köhler, and to determine whether E.L. Teuber's name was among those of Germans living abroad during the outbreak of World War I who were requested to return to Germany for military duty. In my conversation with Hans-Lukas Teuber, Teuber had hedged when I asked him why his father was requested to return to Germany in 1914 to serve in the army, while Köhler wasn't.

The files I had reviewed the previous year were retrieved, and none revealed the name of either Köhler or Teuber. Bobarach assured me that he and his assistant, Dr. Verlande, had done a thorough search.

*   *   *

The next day I went to the Bundesarchiv in Bonn, the location of the German Foreign Office files for the years of World War I, and called on Frau Dr. Keipert, with whom I had made an appointment the previous day. Although Dr. Keipert produced several volumes of correspondence between the German Foreign Office and diplomatic representatives in Spain, she cautioned me that the files were not complete. There was among them, however, one document of immediate interest to me, a copy of a letter from the German Foreign Office that apprised the Spanish Foreign Office that Wolfgang Köhler had been appointed director of the anthropoid ape station in Tenerife to replace E.L. Teuber, who had requested to return to Germany in March 1914 for the purpose of continuing his studies at the University of Berlin. Apparently, Teuber had not completed the requirements for his Ph.D., and this was the reason for his return to Germany, not a call to serve in the military.

There was nothing else in the files that was of importance to me. I decided to leave for Munich, where I hoped to find information that might link the Kaiser Wilhelm Gesellschaft with the ape station.

* * *

It was early Saturday evening when I arrived and took a room in a hotel in Schwabing, an old section of Munich. I decided to walk south on Leopoldstrasse in the direction of Ludwigstrasse and the center of the city. It was a warm night, much like the one I remembered from my first visit to Munich during the early postwar years, when Munich was still partly in ruins. As I looked at the new construction that blended in so well with the buildings that remained from prewar years, I was reminded of my first view of Munich, when laborers worked in the warm summer night under the light of crudely suspended strings of small electric lamps, cleaning the rubble of bombed-out buildings. My memory of the scene was still fresh; it contrasted sharply with my sight of present-day Munich. Most of the people I passed in the street were too young to have experienced Munich at the end of the war, but there were those who obviously were not, those whose mutilated bodies bore stark evidence of their experience of Munich during its destruction as well as its aftermath. It would still be a few more years before the last rubble of the war would be gone from sight.

* * *

On Monday morning I called Dr. Horn, head archivist at the Max Planck Institute (the place I had been told was the location of the records of the early years of the Kaiser Wilhelm Gesellschaft). After I explained my interest in determining whether the Kaiser Wilhelm Gesellschaft had any part in the financing of the ape station or any other scientific expedition in the Canary Islands prior to World War I, Horn told me that there were no documents of interest to me in Munich, that central archives located in West Berlin had been established, and that documents from all the Max Planck Institutes of West Germany were to be kept there.

I was disappointed that my trip to Munich had been a waste of time, but heartened by the fact that the newly established archives were located in West Berlin, the city I planned to visit next. Besides, it was still early in the day, and there was plenty of time to catch a train for Berlin that would make the three hundred-mile trip before dark.

* * *

The prospect of seeing Berlin excited me. I found it difficult to concentrate on the book I planned to read during the trip. At first, the customary sounds and sights of travel by train distracted me, and I found myself checking my watch as we passed through towns, and calculating the progress of the train to make certain we were not behind schedule—an event that rarely occurs on a German train. But the primary thoughts that disturbed my reading were those about Berlin, disconnected thoughts based on the fragmentary information I had gathered through the years, the bits and pieces of loosely connected data that seem to defy logical organization. I had the irrational thought that I would have a feeling of familiarity when I saw Berlin, a place I had never been; I was experiencing what might be called an anticipatory déjà vu.

My most vivid impressions of Berlin were probably based on newsreels, newspapers, and magazine photos of its fall at the end of World War II, pictures of Berlin during Hitler's last days, the final scene of the Hitlerian *Götterdämmerung*. But less vivid impressions—impressions of Berlin during the years of the Weimar Republic and Köhler's tenure at the University of Berlin—came to mind more frequently. My thoughts centered mostly on what I considered, in a narrow sense, to be the halcyon days of Berlin, the years of the late 1920s and the early 1930s before the takeover by the Nazis, the years during which Berlin was the heart of a Germany that exerted a powerful influence on the direction and advancement of the arts and sciences throughout the world. I remembered some of the paintings of Max Beckman, Lyonel Feininger, Paul Klee, and Vassily Kandinsky; the satirical drawings of George Grosz; Walter Gropius's Bauhaus school of arts and crafts; the silent film classic *The Cabinet of Dr. Caligari*, Fritz Lang's *Metropolis* and *M*, and the historic talking film *The Blue Angel*; Nobel laureate Thomas Mann's *Magic Mountain*, and Erich Maria Remarque's *All Quiet on the Western Front*; the music of Kurt Weill and the plays of

Bertolt Brecht; the Nobel laureates Max Planck and Albert Einstein; and of course the Gestalt school of psychology, promoted energetically by Wolfgang Köhler through his post as head of the psychology laboratory at the University of Berlin.

I remembered too that in a broader sense, this brief period in German history was far from a golden one: inflation produced billion-mark notes worth little more than the paper on which they were printed; armies of unemployed workers aimlessly roamed the sidewalks and parks; crowded slums were inhabited by rag-clad lumpenproletariat; forces of the extreme left and extreme right clashed in the streets; a frustrated populace with a sad past and an impoverished present saw no signs of hope for the future. Life was not a cabaret. But what a strange city Berlin must have been. Historic contributions to the culture of the world sprang from the ruins of a decaying social system like so many ripe melons blooming from a heap of dung. I knew that present-day Berlin was much different, but on the basis of my most current knowledge, it was still an unusual city, as different from the rest of Germany as New York is from the rest of the United States.

My train made several stops before it reached the border between West and East Germany, and the six seats of my compartment were occupied by the time several East German customs officers and a number of armed soldiers boarded the train. By early afternoon, the weather had grown hot. Not only was it difficult to read, but my reveries of a bygone Berlin were made less enjoyable by the cramped and stuffy compartment. I left my seat to join the many travelers who stood in the breezy passageways looking at the countryside through lowered windows. The breeze created by the fast-moving train felt refreshing, but the countryside became a little stale as the train moved out of the rolling hills of southern Germany into the flat plains of the north. The surrounding fields for as far as the eye could see were in full bloom; they reminded me of the Midwest, the flat, endless corn fields of Illinois and Iowa, and the wheat fields of Kansas.

The train kept a steady pace except for the brief periods when it slowed down as it passed through a town. On these occasions, I noticed that armed guards stood next to the tracks at close intervals along the length of the train, an added precaution against the defection of East Germans. In spite of what I had heard about the tightness of East German security, the guards came as something of a surprise. I retrieved my camera from my compartment in preparation for a long-angle picture when we came to the next town. As I leaned out the window to look through the view finder of my camera to plan the shot, an old woman who had been watching me stepped from her compartment to warn me that the East German guards aboard the train looked unfavorably on photographers. She made it clear that I might be courting trouble. Several other passengers slowly nodded their heads in agreement. I took my camera back to my compartment.

When the train reached Potsdam, the southwestern border crossing point to West Berlin where the East German customs guards would get off, it stopped in an alley formed by tall concrete walls topped with barbed wire. Although I was cautioned not to stick my neck out the open window, I was able to get close enough to the outside to see East German soldiers—some with drawn rifles and others with German shepherd dogs on leashes—kneeling and closely inspecting the undersides of the train. The stories I had heard and read about the desperate means by which East Germans tried to escape apparently were not exaggerated as I had thought; they were beginning to take on a reality I could not have otherwise known.

Berlin is a very large city. Although Potsdam lies on the border of West Berlin, the trip from there through the Grünwald (the Green Forest of Berlin) to the Zoo railway station was a long one. I had no trouble locating my *pension* on nearby Uhland Strasse, and no trouble locating a charming and modest little restaurant a few blocks farther on. After dinner I returned to my quarters by way of the famed Kurfürstendamm, a gaudy, noisy, and crowded commercial street brightly illuminated by advertisements and the spotlights of shop display windows. This part of West Berlin certainly was unlike the other parts of Germany I had seen.

*   *   *

I awoke early the next day. In early July, the light of the rising sun is surprisingly bright by 4:00 a.m. (Berlin is situated at about

the same northern latitude as the Aleutian Islands of Alaska.)
With such an early start on the day, I decided to walk to East
Berlin. My *pension* was only a few blocks from the Berlin Zoo,
which is situated in the southwestern corner of the Tiergarten, a
large park bordered on the east by the Berlin Wall. It was still
early when I reached the Brandenburg Gate, a triumphal arch
through which traffic can no longer pass. The park stops
abruptly at this point, but the tall chain-link barbed-wire-topped
fence does allow a glimpse of East Berlin and the armed East
German soldiers who stand guard on the other side. Behind the
drab concrete wall that stretches north behind the Reichstag and
south to the new Philharmonic Music Hall, large telescopes
trained on the west side of the wall loom from observation towers spaced at close intervals. The concept of West Berlin as an
island in the midst of a hostile sea is an apt metaphor.

I strolled south along the wall and followed it when it turned
east until I came to Checkpoint Charlie, a main crossing point
between West and East Berlin, located on Friedrich Strasse between Koch Strasse in West Berlin and Leipziger Strasse in East
Berlin. The American, British, and French soldiers who occupy
the post on the south side of Checkpoint Charlie do not exercise
any control over people going to or coming from East Berlin; the
crudely constructed reinforced-concrete wall, the barbed wire,
and the steel I-beam antitank devices that resemble iron garden
sculpture were put there by the East Germans. The border-cross-
ing ritual established by the East Germans is a tedious system,
the complexity of which is somehow amplified by the fact that
although you are passing from the Bundesrepublik Deutschland
(Federal Republic of Germany, or West Germany) to the
Deutsche Demokratische Republik (German Democratic Republic, or East Germany), you remain within the city of Berlin—and
within the country that once was Germany.

The crossing ritual begins when you pass the small building
that houses the allied military guard. As you walk the short
distance of the no man's land between East and West Berlin
(about one hundred feet), your eye is almost immediately caught
by the tower adjacent to the pedestrian gate, where a large
telescope mounted on a tripod is trained on you and on the path
from the small building that houses the allied military guard. At
the pedestrian gate on the East German side of no man's land,

you are met by two East German soldiers, one of whom requests passports. The soldier looks at the picture in the passport, stares at you for the purpose of comparing your face with the picture, places a small slip of paper in the passport, passes it back to you, and points you in the direction of a nearby wooden frame building. In the building, you wait in line at what resembles an old-fashioned teller's cage at a bank. When you reach the front of the line, the soldier behind the bars requests your passport. He studies the pages of the passport, checks the picture, and when satisfied, places the passport on a small conveyor belt that carries it to a separate room located behind the teller's cage. At this point, the man in the cage issues an application blank that requires standard personal information: your residence in Berlin, the amount of money you are carrying, and a list of articles you will be taking into East Berlin (a camera, for example).

After a fairly lengthy wait (five to ten minutes, depending on the number of people crossing the border at a given time), a second soldier, adjacent to the one who took your passport, calls out the names of countries. When he calls out your nationality, this is the cue to go to the counter to retrieve your passport. At the counter, the second soldier opens the passport to the page with your picture so that you can identify your passport and retrieve it. When your picture appears, you are required to submit your completed application form to the soldier who holds your passport. The soldier then inspects your application, compares it with the information in the passport, and compares the picture in the passport with you. When he is satisfied, he gives your passport back to you along with a *Transitivism*, a travel pass to East Berlin.

After the passport control routine, you move to the other end of the small frame building for customs declaration and inspection. This line moves fairly quickly, but only one person at a time can be inspected, and the next person in line must stand at a distance of about fifteen feet. The soldier at the customs inspection point first requests your passport, then asks for your travel application, which he or she keeps, and then looks through any bags that you may be carrying. When the inspector is satisfied, he returns your passport, after the customary comparison of picture with face, and sends you to the next small frame building, where the foreign currency exchange is located.

The two women in the teller's cages do not appear to be part of the military; they wear civilian clothes. The line here is relatively short, but because of the lengthy routines that precede it, even small delays can be annoying. Regardless of whether or not you intend to buy anything in East Berlin, it is necessary to exchange a minimum of 6 marks 50 pfennigs (about $2.50). If you exchange the minimum and if you spend nothing in East Germany, you must return the 6 DM 50 Pf to the currency exchange at Checkpoint Charlie on your return to West Berlin. Whether you spend any money in East Berlin or not, the East German government receives the equivalent of 6 DM 50 Pf in foreign currency each day for each visitor to East Berlin. The system is also devised to keep all East German currency in East Germany. For the visitor, it makes no sense to try to take currency out of East Germany, since the West German currency exchanges will not buy East German marks.

After the currency exchange, you head for the pedestrian gate at the far end of the East German border control area. In a small enclosure adjacent to the gate, an East German soldier once again requests your passport, stamped visitor's pass, and currency exchange slip. He looks at the picture in the passport and compares it once again with your face. If everything is in order, he signals a second soldier to open the gate and let you pass. You are now in East Berlin.

The entrance to East Berlin from Checkpoint Charlie is about six blocks south of Unter den Linden, a broad tree-lined boulevard that runs east from Brandenburger Tor (Brandenburg Gate) to Marx-Engels Platz, Alexander Platz, and Karl Marx Allee. The Alexander von Humboldt University (the old University of Berlin) is located on Unter den Linden just a short distance from the intersection of Friedrich Strasse.

As I walked north on Friedrich Strasse, I could see on my right the bombed-out ruins of a large neoclassic building in the massive architectural style favored by Hitler and Kaiser Wilhelm II—ruins that I presumed were intentionally neglected, perhaps to serve as a reminder of the horrors of the recent past. But unlike the ruins of the Kaiser Wilhelm Memorial Church, which stand in majestic spotlighted splendor in the central junction of West Berlin as a carefully maintained commemorative monument, these were off the beaten path. Crumbling and decaying, the roofless building was overrun by small trees, wild vines, and bushes. Whatever the reason for the neglect, the ruins were a powerful and chilling reminder of the fall of Nazi Germany.

I came to learn that such ruins were not commonplace in East Berlin, but that the city was, nonetheless, shoddy by comparison with West Berlin. All the visible cultural symbols of East Berlin contrasted sharply with West Berlin. The people on the streets were poorly clothed in ill-fitting, outmoded styles; the relatively small number of cars on the road were old and unattractively designed; stolid-faced people stood in long lines outside drab shops, waiting to purchase goods produced in inadequate numbers. The buildings and streets were shabby and gray; indeed, almost everything seemed gray, including the green linden trees of the broad thoroughfare that ran through the heart of East Berlin—the showcase of East Germany, the mecca to which school children and workers from all parts of the country came on holiday. The colossal buildings of Marx-Engels Platz and Alexander Platz did not relieve the feeling of vapidness. If anything, the gigantic scale on which the structures and streets were built left me feeling small and inconsequential.

The area in which the university is located is the heart of the cultural center of East Berlin. From the map, it can be seen that this area, which contains a number of both new and old buildings (the opera house, the national archives, museums, memorials, governmental administrative offices, etc.), protrudes from the otherwise straight north-south border that separates the two Berlins, East from West. That is, the border between East and West Berlin is linear and fairly smooth except for the East Berlin "lump" that sticks in the side of West Berlin. If the border followed a straight line, the Alexander von Humboldt University and the National Archives would be in West Berlin.

*   *   *

At the entrance to the large lobby of the university, two young men, presumably students, were seated at a table; it was their job to check the identification cards of every person who entered the building. After I identified myself and explained that the purpose of my visit was to obtain permission to use the archives of the university, one of the young men called someone on the phone. After a brief conversation, I was told that someone would be down to see me shortly. While waiting, I strolled around the lobby and came upon a display of books, one of which was entitled *Die Kaiser-Wilhelm-Gesellschaft 1911-1914: Zur Anatomie einer Imperialistischen Forschungsgesellschaft (The Kaiser Wilhelm Institute 1911-1914: On the Anatomy of an Imperialistic Research Organization)* by Günter Wendel. I was quite excited to discover that the East Germans were interested in the function of the Kaiser Wilhelm Gesellschaft—known as the KWG—immediately before World War I. It was my hope that I could uncover some link between Köhler and the anthropoid ape station and the KWG.

After about fifteen minutes, I was greeted by a man who identified himself as Alfons Sommers, director of foreign relations. I introduced myself, gave him a copy of my résumé, and explained my purpose for visiting the university. Sommers was cordial, pleasant, and relaxed; most important, he expressed interest in the project, and said that he would do everything he could to help me. I told him of my interest in the book about the KWG and asked him if Wendel lived in Berlin. He told me that Wendel was a member of the staff of the university and that he would try to get in touch with him for me, that I should return to the university the next morning at ten o'clock.

After my meeting with Sommers, I walked west on Unter den Linden to the university book store where I purchased a copy of Wendel's book. I scanned the index but could find no references to Köhler—or to the anthropoid station, or to the meteorological observatory, or to the sanitorium, or to Tenerife. Perhaps Wendel had information that he did not include in his book.

* * *

The next day, on my arrival at the university, I was greeted by the two student guards, who directed me to the table where Sommers and I had chatted previously. After about half an hour, Sommers appeared and informed me that Dr. Kosack, the director of the university archives, was very busy and would not be able to see me. He then told me that Wendel was on leave and couldn't be reached. I had the feeling that Sommers had changed his mind about helping me, or that someone had changed his mind for him. I decided to give him more information about the project—information about those aspects of the project that might be most interesting to East Germany, namely, my theses that Köhler may have been an agent of the German military, that the anthropoid ape station may have been a cover for his activities, that the KWG may have secretly underwritten Köhler's work in Tenerife, and that it may have been Germany's long-range plan to take control of the Canary Islands from Spain following World War I.

Sommers appeared to be very interested in this new information, and said that he would try again to help me, that it might be possible for him to reach Wendel, and that I should return to the university the next day at the same time.

* * *

The next morning, Sommers informed me that he was able to reach Wendel and that he had arranged a meeting for the following Monday morning. He told me to be at the entrance to the lobby of the university at ten o'clock. At this point, it occurred to me that I hadn't been beyond the lobby of the building, and I had the feeling that I wasn't going to get beyond it.

In the afternoon I returned to West Berlin and called Dr. Neuhaus, director of the new Berlin archives of the Max Planck Institute. After explaining my purpose, Dr. Neuhaus told me that the new archives in Berlin were to become the central archives of the Max Planck Institute, but that at the present time, the archives were not functional because all the documents from the various Max Planck Institutes throughout West Germany had not yet arrived in Berlin.

Dr. Neuhaus mentioned that he did remember hearing about the observatory in Tenerife in connection with the KWG, but that he had no specific data and did not know of any source to which he could refer me. This small bit of information had some value since it helped to confirm the statement by Jacob

Ahlers that attributed the financing of the meteorological observatory to the KWG.

* * *

The next day, I called on Dr. Ekkehart Vesper, director of the State Library for Prussian Cultural Possessions. After a lengthy discussion of the project, I was informed that during the 1930s, the Nazis were not concerned with maintaining old documents. As a consequence, many of the archives were moved from Berlin to other cities of Prussia. Therefore, East Germany was now in possession of most old documents, specifically, documents pertaining to the KWG and the Prussian Academy of Science. A quick search of the records revealed that the only information the library had that pertained to Wolfgang Köhler was a list of the books he had written.

An assistant archivist called the Secret Federal Archives (Geheimes Staats Archiv) and put me in touch with Frau Dr. Lowenthal-Hensel. We arranged to meet the following day.

* * *

At the appointed time, I met with Frau Dr. Lowenthal-Hensel, who said that the archives' files dated back only to 1928, that earlier records were in East Germany. She indicated, however, that they did have an index of the names of people who corresponded with the KWG.

Frau Dr. Lowenthal-Hensel checked the index and found Köhler's name. Only a single piece of Köhler's correspondence was addressed to Dr. Friedrich Schmidt-Ott, a member of the Presiding Council of the KWG, the last minister of culture in Germany, and past president of the Emergency Organization of German Scientists, a society formed during the early years of the Nazi government for the purpose of keeping politics out of science. Dated July 2, 1934, the letter expressed Köhler's regret that Dr. Schmidt-Ott had resigned his post as president of the emergency committee to keep politics out of science. Schmidt-Ott apparently realized that the Nazis could not be kept from taking control of the scientific and academic communities, and so had resigned his post in protest.

The same file also contained a letter from Wilhelm Köhler, Wolfgang's brother, informing Schmidt-Ott that he was resigning his post as director of the State Art Collection in Weimar and taking a post at Harvard University. It is interesting to note that in July of 1934, Wolfgang Köhler was scheduled to present the William James Lectures at Harvard for that fall. It is also important to note that as of July 2, 1934, Köhler was still director of the Psychological Institute at the University of Berlin. This corroborated Hans Wallach's statement that it was not Köhler's intention to leave Germany when he went to the United States in the fall of 1934. According to Wallach, Köhler stayed in the United States after he received word in the spring of 1935 that the Nazis had removed him from his post as director of the Psychological Institute. Wallach also said that Köhler had earlier turned down the offer of a post at Harvard, and that by the spring of 1935, when Köhler changed his mind, the post was no longer open and Köhler thus sought the post at Swarthmore.

* * *

On Monday morning I went to Humboldt University. The same student guards greeted me and motioned for me to sit at the table next to the entrance where Sommers and I had met the previous week. After about ten minutes, two men in open-collar short-sleeved shirts arrived; the shorter one, who carried a large black briefcase, extended his hand to me and introduced himself as Günter Wendel. Wendel, who appeared to be in his late thirties, had a pleasant, eager smile that suited his energetic bearing; he and his companion, who appeared tired or uninterested or perhaps both, were historians at the university. Wendel specialized in the history of science, his companion in the history of chemistry.

Wendel suggested that we have some refreshments while we talked. We walked for about four or five blocks in the direction of Checkpoint Charlie until we came to a fairly nondescript restaurant. Wendel did not have a clear understanding of my reason for wanting to see him except that I was interested in the topic of his book—the KWG from 1911 to 1914.

In order to allay any suspicions Wendel might have concerning my interests and to enlist his help, I emphasized my thesis that Köhler may have been an agent of the German military, and that the anthropoid station may have been a cover. I also told him I suspected that the KWG may have sponsored Köhler and the anthropoid station as well as the meteorological observatory and sanitorium. Wendel said that my thesis was not only tenable, but highly probable, and went on to explain that the Prussian Academy of Science, as well as the KWG, provided the means through which the German government could further its goal of colonial imperialism. He said that there was a great deal of evidence which proved that German scientific expeditions in foreign countries were established primarily for the purpose of gaining political influence.

I also explained my larger thesis, that it may have been Germany's intention to take control of the Canary Islands from Spain. He agreed that this thesis was highly probable, too. Unfortunately, however, he did not know of any evidence that was directly relevant to my theses. He said that if such data did exist, they would be found in the *Zentrales Staatsarchiv* in Merseburg, the *Zentrales Archiv der Akademie der Wissenschaften* in Berlin, and the *Zentrales Archivverwaltung* in Potsdam, all of which were in East Germany. Unlike archives in England, West Germany, and the United States, where I was able to obtain permission for their use on the same day as my application, permission for the use of archives in East Germany would require a letter of request several months in advance of their use. There was no way in which I could gain access to archival documents during my current stay in Berlin.

Wendel emphasized the importance of going through the formal procedure for obtaining permission, that I should write a letter to each of the three archives plus two other letters, one to the *Ministerium für Hoch- und Fachschulwesen* in Berlin, East Germany, and the other to the *Ausweisenministerium* in Berlin, East Germany. The letters, said Wendel, should include a summary of the project and a statement of the purpose for which the archives were sought. He explained that the data for his book were obtained from the archives in Merseburg and Potsdam, and added that the Max Planck Institute probably had more documents than it was willing to admit, that it had documents on both World War I and World War II. He felt this was true even though an official publication of the history of the Kaiser Wilhelm Gesellschaft and Max Planck Institute (*50 Jahre Kaiser-Wilhelm Gesellschaft und Max-Planck Gesellschaft zur Förderung der Wissenschaften, 1911-1961*) made little or no mention of the activities of the organizations or scientists who were sponsored, and no mention whatsoever of the years of World Wars I and II!

The meeting with Wendel was interesting and informative. Although I didn't find what I had hoped to find when I set out for Berlin, I did learn the location of potentially relevant information and the means by which this information might be obtained. My respect for historians continued to grow; those discourses on the problems of historical research with which I was familiar centered primarily on the analysis of data, not the more fundamental problems of locating and retrieving them. There was nothing more I could do in Berlin at this time; it would be necessary to return after permission for use of the East German archives had been granted. I would request permission as soon as I returned to Albany.

14.

Cambridge in the Fall

S oon after my return to Albany, I applied for permission to use the East German archives recommended to me by Günter Wendel. My plan was to visit Tenerife during the December-January break between semesters, and resume my research there. If my formal applications for the use of the archives were approved, I would fly to Berlin from Tenerife before returning to Albany in January.

In preparation for the trip to Tenerife, I made arrangements with the Peabody Museum at Harvard University to photograph the Hooton collection of Guanche relics sent there by the late Alexander Baillon. Austin Baillon, Alexander's son, was curious to see what his father had smuggled out of the island, a curiosity shared by Luís Diego Cuscoy, director of the Museo Arqueológico in Tenerife. I wanted to combine the trip to Cambridge with a meeting with Hans-Lukas Teuber at the nearby campus of the Massachusetts Institute of Technology, but I decided not to make my visit contingent on an appointment with Teuber for fear that I might lose the opportunity to photograph the Hooton collection before my departure for Tenerife in December. I called Teuber on Tuesday, November 2, two days before my visit to the Peabody Museum, but was unable to reach him.

On the morning of my scheduled visit, I remembered that Richard Held, a professor of psychology at MIT, was closely associated with Köhler. I called Held, and we made an appointment for lunch that same day. I would visit the Peabody Museum in the afternoon and return to Albany in the evening.

I left immediately for Cambridge and went to Held's office, where he greeted me and told me that he had heard about me and my interest in Köhler. He made it clear that he was not going to talk about Köhler until he knew in some detail what my business was, and until I answered to his satisfaction questions concerning my reasons for wanting information about Köhler. Although the interview I had planned became a rather one-sided discussion in which I did most of the talking, I was pleased that he was interested enough to take the time to hear my story. Held's directness made it easy for me to respond in turn with a succinct summary of the research I had done and the hypotheses I was entertaining. Held listened closely as we walked to the dining room of the faculty club, and continued to listen closely except for brief intermittent interruptions of my narration to ask questions—questions which revealed that he was a faithful friend and stout defender of Wolfgang Köhler.

Held's concern centered on Köhler's reputation. He seemed a bit more relaxed when I made it clear to him that I was neither a hostile critic nor a muckraker, that if it were established beyond chance that Köhler had been an agent of the German military during the years of World War I, this fact would in no way tarnish his reputation or reduce the importance of his contributions to science and scholarship. I was pleased to have the opportunity to tell Held this because there had been a time during the first few months of my research when I had felt that Köhler's integrity might be put to question by what seemed to be a conflict in his values. That is, as a scientist and humanist, Köhler dedicated his life to the pursuit of truth and the encouragement of humanistic values; if he had been a secret agent of the German military, however, his activities would have been dedicated to subterfuge and the discouragement of humanistic values. I came to realize, however, that the conflict I had created for Köhler was no different from that with which any humanist is confronted in a time of war. Köhler was a German patriot, but he was not a fascist.

Held told me that it was shortly after his discharge from the United States Navy at the end of World War II that he first met Köhler. Held enrolled in the Master's Degree program at Swarthmore for the purpose of studying with Köhler. Although Held returned to Columbia University, where he had taken his B.A., to continue his graduate studies for the Ph.D., he maintained the friendship that had grown between Köhler and him, a friendship that began with Held's respect and admiration for Köhler, and later grew into an affectionate relationship like that between a father and son.

Held didn't describe Köhler as dramatically as Henry Gleitman had, but it was clear that Held shared many of Gleitman's feelings, especially the feeling that Köhler was a special person. It was also clear that Held was on far more intimate terms with Köhler than was Gleitman, although the depth of the intimacy might have been relatively shallow by common standards. Köhler was not a warm and affectionate person, certainly not demonstrably warm and affectionate. Köhler was cool. Held remembered the time he and his wife visited Wolfgang and Lili Köhler at their summer cottage in Maine. It was a warm day, and Köhler suggested that they go for a swim in the ocean. Held was unfamiliar with the temperature of Maine's coastal waters (about 50 degrees Fahrenheit) and readily accepted the invitation. When the two men stepped into the water, Held almost literally froze in his tracks, but Köhler slowly waded into the frigid water without a moment's hesitation until the water was well above his waist; then he plunged headfirst into the surf. Held shook his head in the amazement that he still experienced as he reminisced about Köhler's apparent indifference to the numbing pain of the icy water. After Köhler had had his swim, he waded ashore with the same nonchalance with which he had waded into the water. Everyone who had known Köhler had a Köhler story to tell; this was Held's.

Held talked about Köhler's work toward the end of his career, especially his lack of success in establishing neurophysiological evidence for Gestalt principles of perception, and his failure to construct a comprehensive theory of the direct connection between perceptual experiences and corresponding electrical activity in specific locations in the brain.

Held was unable to add any new information about Köhler's years in Tenerife, and agreed that Mary Henle and Hans-Lukas Teuber were the persons who might be knowledgeable. I told him about my correspondence with Henle and my problem of trying to meet with Teuber. Although I had not hoped that he would help me to get information from Henle, I had hoped that he might be able to help me meet personally with Teuber. Held told me that Teuber was a very busy person.

*   *   *

After lunch, I drove directly to the Peabody Museum, where I photographed a representative sample of about fifty boxes of skeletal relics from the Hooton collection. By the end of the afternoon I had taken all of my pictures.

*   *   *

During the second week of November, I flew to St. Louis, Missouri, where I presented a paper at the annual meeting of the Psychonomic Society. The late William Battig, who was then a professor of psychology at the University of Colorado, also presented a paper, a summary of some recent research findings on verbal memory closely related to my own research interests. After his presentation, we met and chatted. He mentioned that a German graduate student who had been studying with him in Colorado had recently returned to Munich, a fact that led to a discussion of my research on Köhler. Bill asked me if I had been in touch with Michael Wertheimer, the son of Max Wertheimer and a professor of psychology in Bill's department. I told him I hadn't, but that I intended to. On my return from the meeting in St. Louis, I wrote to Battig to remind him to ask Wertheimer for information on Köhler.

Meanwhile, I received word that my formal applications for the use of East German archives in Berlin and Potsdam had been approved. I would leave for Tenerife on December 19 and fly from there to Berlin the week before my return to Albany for the beginning of the spring semester.

15.

Tenerife in the Winter

I t was still morning when I arrived at the Los Rodeos airport in Tenerife on Monday, December 20. Although I was eager to resume my search, I had anticipated that the Christmas holidays might slow my progress. There were, in fact, several social events for which I had to prepare. The Baillons had invited me to dinner on Christmas Eve; Lady Abercromby had invited me to dinner on Christmas Day; and Jack and Christine Stableford, friends of the Baillons, had invited me to a Boxing Day party on the twenty-sixth, where the guest of honor was to be Her Royal Highness, Princess Margaretha of Sweden, sister of King Carl XVI Gustaf, the reigning monarch.

With an all-work-and-no-play-makes-Jack-a-dull-boy spirit, I picked up the shiny new Spanish Ford Fiesta rental car that Austin Baillon had reserved for me, and drove directly to his house.

On my arrival, my spirits were dampened by the news that Manuel González y García had died a month earlier. Austin didn't know the details surrounding Manuel's death except that it had been the result of natural causes. Austin said that a few months earlier, he had met with Manuel and showed him a copy of Köhler's *The Mentality of Apes*. Manuel couldn't read English, but he was delighted with the pictures of the apes, and identified each animal by name.

After lunch, I visited the Hotel Tigaiga to inquire about the circumstances of Manuel's death. Tomas Viere-González, Manuel's nephew and a gardener at the hotel, told me that Manuel had developed a circulatory problem that led to a swelling of his leg, symptoms that sounded like phlebitis. Manuel ignored the discomfort until the condition became so severe that he could no longer walk. At this point he was taken to the hospital, but it was too late; he died a few days later, a month before his ninetieth birthday.

*   *   *

On the morning of Boxing Day, the British holiday on which the remnants of Christmas celebrations traditionally were boxed and distributed to the poor, I decided to drive to the Cañadas and visit the observatory in Izaña.

When I arrived, I was greeted by Fernando Molina-Herrero, the man responsible for the television relay station adjacent to the observatory. Fernando remembered me from my earlier visit and was happy to show me around both the present observatory and the old prefabricated building that had served as Kaiser Wilhelm's hunting lodge in equatorial Africa. I was disappointed to discover that the furnishings left there by the German expedition that had inhabited the building at the beginning of World War I had been removed, but was delighted to discover that a second prefabricated building, which accompanied the hunting lodge in the basin of the Cañadas, still existed and was located just a short distance away. I remembered that there were two concrete platforms at the site of the German observatory in the Cañadas, but for reasons that I cannot explain, I had not previously inquired about this second building.

As we walked from the lodge to the second building, Fernando explained that the lodge served as living quarters, while the second building was used for equipment storage and utility purposes. When we arrived and Fernando unlocked the door, he remarked on how well preserved the contents of the building were; owing to the extremely dry air of the mountains, nothing rusted.

As I walked through the entrance onto the concrete floor of a brightly lighted high-ceilinged room, I saw on the side opposite from me a very large antique diesel-powered dynamo. I was surprised by the sight of the generator, and mildly astonished by its size. The flywheel, which was about five feet in diameter, was located about twelve feet from the casing that enclosed the armature; the two components were connected by a twelve-inch-wide leather belt.

I marvelled at the flawless condition of the machine and asked Fernando where it came from and what it was used for. He told me, matter-of-factly, that it was part of the equipment brought with the German observatory from its location at La Grieta in the Cañadas, and that it was used to provide electricity for the observatory.

The size of the dynamo made me question him. I told Fernando that the generator appeared to be large enough to supply sufficient electrical power for a small town rather than a small observatory. He agreed with me, but insisted that this was the generator installed by the German scientific expedition at La Grieta. He added that the electrical output of the generator could have easily supplied sufficient electrical energy for the entire population of the town of Orotava during the years of World War I.

As I inspected the apparatus more closely, I noticed markings on its base which indicated that it had been manufactured in Liverpool, England. I was reminded of the document from the British Foreign Office files for 1914, which stated that Mr. V.B.D. Cooper, a British engineer in the Canary Islands, reported that he had been requested by the German observatory ''to quote for the supply of certain electric plant [materiel] to the observatory and that the plant required, amongst other apparatus, consisted of a *three-phase dynamo* [italics mine], transformers and a battery of cells.''

Since the document was sent to the Foreign Office just a few days after Britain's entry into World War I, the materiel to which Cooper alluded was requested some time before the war, but how long before the war could not be determined. Nonetheless, it seemed certain that the dynamo I was inspecting was the same one reported by Cooper. Although I had no way of determining the exact amount of power the dynamo could generate (it was still operative), there was no doubt that it was more than that required for the day-to-day needs of a small expedition, nor was there any question that it was capable of powering a long-distance radio.

* * *

The weather was bright and clear on Tuesday morning, an ideal time to visit the peak of Teide. I left for the Cañadas immediately after breakfast and arrived at the cable car station in time for the first run of the day. Although it was warm when I left Puerto de la Cruz, I took a heavy sweater, lined gloves, and a hooded storm coat with me. The weather was still fairly warm when I boarded the cable car, but by the time it reached its terminus, the sweater, coat, and gloves felt comfortable. The walk from this point to the peak was only a fraction of a mile, but the thin air at twelve thousand feet forced me to stop and rest several times along the way.

From the peak, I was able to see the entire outline of the island of Tenerife plus the adjacent islands of the archipelago. The peak also provided an excellent view of the sea. On a small flat area about fifty yards from where I stood, there were several steel I-beams and a number of bolts embedded in the rock surface. The high winds on the peak would require that even a small building have a solid footing in a firm foundation. Because the I-beams were shiny and completely free of rust, my immediate impression was that they had been recently shipped there for some forthcoming construction. But when I inspected the area where they lay, it became clear that they had been there for some time, that the moisture-free air at this altitude would not support oxidation, and that the high winds blew particles from the granular terrain against the steel I-beams with a velocity that polished the steel. The I-beams were the footing for the building constructed by the German research team that had worked in the Cañadas more than sixty years earlier. This must have been the site where the German meteorologists and astronomers made their telescopic observations.

*   *   *

In the afternoon of the following day, I drove to Sauzal, a coastal town northeast of Puerto de la Cruz and the home of Dr. Christine Jordan. Dr. Jordan, a German agronomist, came to Tenerife in 1961 on a mission sponsored by the West German government, a mission designed to research and develop plants grown in Germany. Dr. Jordan explained that Tenerife was ideally suited for agronomical experimentation because of its unique location and topography: small fluctuations in illumination from season to season, relatively constant temperatures and humidity at sea level, and variation of climatic conditions offered by the differences in temperature and humidity at the different altitudes of its mountains.

I asked Dr. Jordan to tell me what she knew about the old German meteorological observatory. She said she had last been to Izaña in 1961, but that she did recall seeing German meteorological instruments from the old observatory which indicated that they had been purchased by the Kaiser Wilhelm Gesellschaft, a fact that supported Jacob Ahlers' contention that the old weather station at La Grieta was sponsored by the German government.

Dr. Jordan was friendly with the German community on the island and was well acquainted with Enrique Talg, the owner and builder of the Hotel Tigaiga and the son of the man who managed the Hotel Taoro during the years of World War I. I told her I would be very interested in meeting with Talg. She called him, and a rather lengthy conversation ensued in which she told Talg about my interest in Köhler.

After their conversation, she summarized what Talg had told her. She said that Talg knew about Manuel and his relationship with Köhler, that there recently had been several people interested in knowing about Manuel's work with Köhler, and that *Köhler had been sent from Tenerife by the Spanish government under threat of force.*

I asked Dr. Jordan if she was certain that Talg had said that Köhler was "forced" to leave Tenerife. She said she was. She added that Talg had also told her that that was all he knew, and that there would be no need for me to visit him.

* * *

On Thursday, I drove to Santa Cruz and met with Dr. Luís Diego Cuscoy, director of the Museo Arqueológico, at his office. Cuscoy was effusive in his thanks for the slides and pictures of the Peabody Museum's Hooton collection I had sent to him. He laughed quietly as he told the story of how Alexander Baillon managed to ship Hooton's Guanche relics to Boston, but bore a serious demeanor when he expressed his thanks to Hooton for having protected the collection from potential destruction by souvenir hunters.

According to Cuscoy, the first person to note the similarity between the Guanches and the present inhabitants of Tenerife was Eugene Fischer, a German anthropologist. Cuscoy mentioned several other German scientists who had worked in Tenerife, chief among them Oscar Burckard, a leading German botanist during the early part of the century, and father of one of Cuscoy's boyhood friends. Burckard, who established the first experimental garden in the Canary Islands, was influential in shaping Cuscoy's interest in science. Cuscoy said that since 1900, most anthropologists, archaeologists, botanists, and geologists who worked in the islands were German.

I asked Cuscoy if he knew anything about German spies in Tenerife. He smiled as he told me that there had always been spies in Tenerife, both in World War I and World War II, that in World War I there were a number of German ships held in anchorage in Santa Cruz, and that many of the seamen of these ships married Spanish women and remained in Tenerife.

As for the German meteorological observatory in La Grieta, Cuscoy knew only that it had been established by Germans, but added that the man who was best informed about the history of the observatory was Pedro Rodríguez García Prieto, a meteorologist who had been stationed for many years at Izaña and was at present working at the observatory of Los Rodeos airport.

Cuscoy knew little about the sanatorium in the Cañadas; his understanding was that the project had been given up before the hospital had been completed, that although the two buildings there (a physician's residence and a staff residence) were occupied from time to time, they never housed any patients.

* * *

The next day I drove to Orotava in search of records of the construction of the sanatorium. A building permit or a deed to the land, which should be on file in Orotava, would contain the names of the persons who built the buildings and the dates that they were constructed.

Both the secretary of the government of Orotava and the mayor were on hand when I arrived, and were free to see me. They told me with certainty that the buildings at the site of the sanatorium were constructed by Germans, but they regretted that there were no official records that would give me the specific information I sought. It was true that the land where the sanatorium was to be built belonged to the town of Orotava, but, according to the mayor and the secretary, no one at the time of the buildings' construction cared whether or not anyone built anything at that site, because the land was remote and worthless. Thus, an official deed to the property was not registered. This may well have been the case, but I was a little disturbed by the fact that the mayor stated this without consulting the records of the town. I also found it difficult to believe that anyone would undertake the construction of a staff house, a physician's residence, and a hospital without having a deed to the land.

* * *

The next afternoon, I visited Cecil Bellamy at his home in Santa Cruz. Mr. Bellamy, who was born in Las Palmas in 1894, was, at the time of the outbreak of World War I, working in Gomera on a farm that grew tomatoes and bananas. He joined the British Army shortly thereafter and served as a second lieutenant in a cavalry division. When he told me that he had seen action at the Battle of the Somme, I was a bit surprised. At eighty-two years of age, it is somewhat rare to be in such good health, as Mr. Bellamy appeared to be, but even rarer to have survived the Battle of the Somme, probably the bloodiest battle of World War I. The battle was initiated by a British offensive drive in June 1916, and continued through the summer and fall until November, when the attack slackened off and the Allies dug in to protect the two or three thousand yards they had gained. The introduction into warfare of Britain's new secret weapon, the tank, the carefully guarded secret vehicle so called as a code name to disguise its production in England, had little or no effect on the outcome of the battle. The combined losses (British, French, and German) totalled more than one million, or about five thousand lives per yard. Mr. Bellamy suffered mustard gas poisoning and was discharged from the army and told that he had but three months to live. He consulted a specialist who told him that he should not expect to live more than two months; that had happened sixty years before, and was an event that Mr. Bellamy enjoyed talking about.

In 1915, shortly before leaving the islands to serve in the British Army, Mr. Bellamy made a trip on mule to the peak of Teide. Although he did not meet any Germans in the mountains, he recalled being told by his native Spanish guides and by the Spanish meteorologists at Izaña that there was a wireless station in the Cañadas and that Kaiser Wilhelm's hunting lodge and the sanatorium were both manned by Germans. Mr. Bellamy did not recall a house on the peak, but he did remember an apparatus that he described as a "tripod with a cover over it."

Mr. and Mrs. Bellamy both remembered visiting the Hotel Martiánez, run at that time by a man named "Trinkel," and seeing the "monkeys." Mr. Bellamy was a reliable source of information, but his participation in World War I limited his knowledge of German activities in Tenerife during those years. I was not surprised to learn that many of the older generation of German residents of Tenerife were Nazis—colonials often become super patriots—but this information made me wonder if perhaps some of the uncooperative attitudes I had encountered recently were motivated by suspicions that I was seeking information that might prove embarrassing to present-day German residents of the island. There was no question that the Germans of Tenerife had a greater economic impact on the island than any other national group. While the British had recently closed their consulate in Las Palmas, the German government had recently opened a full-time professional consulate in Santa Cruz. The simple fact was that the strength of political influence is directly correlated with economic wealth. There would be little point in helping me if my work might lead to the embarrassment of a valuable business associate.

* * *

On Friday morning, January 7, I drove to the old airport terminal building at Los Rodeos for the appointment I had made two days earlier with Pedro Rodríguez García Prieto, the meteorologist about whom Luís Diego Cuscoy had told me.

Prieto, who was forty-nine years old, prided himself on his good memory. He explained that his knowledge of the history of the observatory was a consequence of his thorough reading of all the documents and books at the new observatory's archives and library during the twenty years he and his wife and children had lived there. During that time, he had served as a meteorologist following his training in chemistry at the University of Salamanca and his study of meteorology at the University of Madrid. In case I wasn't familiar with Izaña, Prieto made it clear that there had been plenty of free time for reading and studying during those twenty years.

In answer to my questions concerning the history of the observatory, Prieto told me that the first observatory in the Cañadas was built in 1904 by a group of German scientists under the direction of a meteorologist named Benger. The observatory consisted of two buildings located in the basin of the Cañadas near the sanatorium. From 1904 to 1912, the Germans used the observatory while they conducted studies on solar radiation.

In 1909, Mascart, a French astronomer, came to Tenerife for the purpose of observing Halley's comet, which would be observable from earth in 1910. Mascart brought a telescope with him and built a small observatory on the peak of Teide. The Germans built another post on the peak, on a flat area adjacent to Mascart's observatory.

Prieto said that the Germans had a seismograph as well as a telescope in their observatory at the peak, that they divided their observatory into two parts—one for meteorology, and the other for astronomy. In 1912, the Germans gave control of their observatory in the Cañadas to a team of Spanish meteorologists, but maintained the one at the peak. In 1913, Spain began construction of an observatory at Izaña, and on January 1, 1916, the observatory was functioning. For two years, meteorological observations were made from both stations—the new one at Izaña, and the old one in the basin of the Cañadas. In 1919, the two houses in the Cañadas were moved to Izaña, their present location.

Prieto said that in World War I, Allied ships were being sunk by the German Navy in waters near the Canary Islands. Observations of the activities of the Germans on the peak of Teide revealed that they had their telescope trained on the sea, that the Germans on the peak were watching Allied ships and sending information concerning their type, number, location, direction, etc., to German ships. Britain told Spain to stop the Germans from engaging in these espionage activities. As a consequence, the Spanish government sent troops to the peak, where they confiscated the telescope, which is now at the observatory in Izaña. Prieto told me that information concerning the history of the observatory was contained in a book written by two Spanish engineers while stationed at the observatory (the book was in either the archives or the library at Izaña), but that his information concerning German activities in the Cañadas during the years of World War I came from Alejandro Hernández Bethencourt, the carpenter responsible for moving the two German buildings from the basin of the Cañadas to Izaña. Alejandro, who came from Orotava, as did all the staff at the observatory, was well known by the people in the area; he had died about five years ago.

According to Prieto, the Germans who worked in the Cañadas lived in La Paz, a fact which reminded me that Köhler, too, lived in the environs of La Paz. La Costa, the location of the ape station and Köhler's residence, was the first plantation next to the town of La Paz, and La Paz could not have been inhabited by more than a few hundred people at that time. It was inconceivable that Köhler and these German scientists did not know one another.

In answer to my questions concerning spies in Tenerife during World War I, Prieto said that there were lots of Germans in Tenerife during the war, that he had heard of one German spy, a physician, who was making observations in Güimar. He did not recall his source of information, but suggested strongly that I seek additional data at the meteorological observatory in Santa Cruz.

* * *

When I arrived at the Observatorio Meteorológico in Santa Cruz later that day, I explained that Pedro Rodríguez García Prieto had suggested that I consult the staff of the observatory for information from their archives concerning the history of the meteorological observatory in the Cañadas, and that I request *La Memoria del Observatorio Meteorológico*, the book purported to contain the history of the observatory at La Grieta, the book from which Prieto had obtained much of his information. Two of the staff members said they knew about the book, but did not know where it was located. However, Señor Zalote, the sub-director of the observatory, said that he knew about the German scientists in the Cañadas in World War I. His story was essentially the same as the one told to me by Prieto, namely, that the Germans on the peak of Teide were using their telescope for the purpose of observing the passage of Allied ships in the seas around the islands.

Zalote said that the Germans had a radio transmitter in the Cañadas, and that they used it to send messages to German ships operating in the adjacent waters. He added the interesting bit of information that the code used was based on a conventional meteorological system designed to convey weather information (barometric pressure, temperature, wind velocity, wind direction, and precipitation). The code consisted of five digits, each of which represented a dimension of one of the five weather variables measured. For example, the first digit might represent temperature, with the range of the temperature being expressed by a number from zero to nine; the second digit might represent barometric pressure, with the range expressed by a number from zero to nine; and so forth. Through use of this simple method, meteorologists were able to transmit brief and clear messages concerning five separate variables by transmitting one five-digit number—except that the information which each digit conveyed pertained to the location, direction, speed, type, or number of Allied ships. Zalote claimed that the British detected the transmission of these messages and realized that the numbers did not contain meteorological information because they made no sense. That is, using the meteorological convention for their interpretation, the weather data were impossible for the region from which the messages were coming.

* * *

The following Tuesday, I drove to Izaña to try to locate the book Pedro Rodríguez García Prieto said contained the history of the observatory at La Grieta. I was met by Fernando Molina Herrero, who led me to the library. Since there were only a few hundred books in the library, it didn't take long to find that the book I was seeking wasn't among them. There were, however, several that proved interesting.

The most interesting book was entitled *Trabajos Efectuados en la Isla de Tenerife Durante los Años 1914 a 1917 (Studies Done on the Island of Tenerife During the Years From 1914 to 1917)*, written by H. Dember, W. Buchheim, and M. Uibe. The introduction gave a brief bit of biographical information about the authors of the articles contained in the book: Dr. Harry Dember, Professor of Physics, Technical School Superior of Dresden and Adjunct of the Physics Institute; Martin Uibe, student of physics at the University of Leipzig; Walter Buchheim, Leonardville, Kansas, United States, student at the Technical School, Dresden. The introduction, which was written by J. Galbis in Madrid on April 1, 1919, also gave a brief historical sketch of the events that took place during the course of the research cited in the book.

According to Galbis, Dember, Uibe, and Buchheim—members of a scientific expedition sponsored by the "Academias de Ciencias Alemanas" (the German Academy of Science) and headed by Dr. Dember—arrived in Santa Cruz on August 1, 1914, three days before Britain entered World War I. From Santa Cruz, Dember and his wife, Uibe, and Buchheim set out for the German meteorological observatory at La Grieta in the Cañadas because the observatory at Izaña was not yet complete. The casetas (the prefabricated houses donated by the Kaiser) were attended by three Spaniards.

The German expedition stayed at La Grieta for six days before setting out for the peak of Teide. On August 12, they established their camp at a point just beyond Altavista, a camp site on a trail located on the eastern slope of the mountain—the least steep path of ascent. The camp was positioned 1,452 feet from the peak, 12,226 feet above sea level. The expedition lived and worked there until September 8, 1914, and then returned to the observatory at La Grieta for three days before leaving for Orotava, where they arrived on September 13. From Orotava, Buchheim returned to the United States, while Dember and Uibe remained in Tenerife, being prevented from returning to Germany by the outbreak of the war. (I later learned that Dember's wife was able to leave Tenerife and return to Germany.)

According to Galbis, Dember and Uibe spent the duration of the war in the towns of Güimar and Vilaflor, respectively. However, the first study in the collection was written by Dember, who stated in the last sentence of his article that the study was written in Santa Cruz on April 4, 1915, a date that probably indicated the day on which the manuscript was completed. It appeared, therefore, that before Dember and Uibe went to either Güimar or Vilaflor, Dember moved from Orotava to Santa Cruz.

The second article, coauthored by Buchheim and Dember, was dated Güimar, October 28, 1915. Since Buchheim was the first author, the dateline suggested that he did not return to the United States from Orotava in 1914, unless it was Dember who wrote the article and gave Buchheim the first authorship because of his larger contribution to the study. The third article was coauthored by Dember and Uibe and dated Güimar, December 18, 1916. The remaining four articles, all coauthored by Dember and Uibe, were dated Güimar, December 18, 1916; Güimar, February 13, 1917; Güimar, June 1917; and Güimar, August 1917. Since Güimar is a relatively large town a short distance down the coast from Santa Cruz, and Vilaflor is a very small town located high in the mountains in the southwestern part of the island, Dember and Uibe may have chosen to live in Güimar, but to make the necessary observations for their research in Vilaflor, the town with the highest altitude (4,620 feet) of any in Tenerife, a town located outside the restricted region of the Cañadas Mountains. The second-to-last paragraph of Galbis' introduction indicated that Dember and Uibe were refused permission to return to the provisional observatory at La Grieta or the new observatory in Izaña following its opening on January 1, 1916:

It would have been our pleasure to allow our guests [Dember, Uibe, and Buchheim] to live in the provisional observatory, and later, after the inauguration on January 1, 1916, in the observatory at Izaña, since they would have assisted our scientists and contributed to their research. But it was the desire of the Spanish government during the duration of the war not to give even the slightest motives for anyone to doubt our strict neutrality; and for this reason, lodging was not offered them, nor was collaborative research permitted, although kindly offered by the gentlemen.

Documents from the British Foreign Office files, the Tenerife newspaper article found in the German military records, and the information contained in Galbis' introduction made it clear that Dember, Uibe, and Buchheim were the men, or part of a larger group of men, suspected of having installed a radio antenna on the peak of Teide and a wireless station at the observatory at La Grieta. These men were the same German scientists to whom Zalote, the subdirector of the meteorological observatory at Santa Cruz, referred when telling the story of how the German scientists on the peak used the five-digit meteorological code for the purpose of disguising wireless messages to German ships. Zalote had said that the Germans on the peak were both scientists and spies.

It was also interesting to note that Prieto had heard of a German spy who was making observations from Güimar, the town where Dember appeared to have spent almost all his time in Tenerife after he was forbidden to visit the observatories in the mountains. Güimar is located very near the coast (two and a half miles from Puerto Güimar), about twenty miles south of Santa Cruz. From a cliff about one and a half miles from Güimar, you can see the entire coast of Tenerife from Puerto Güimar to Santa Cruz; the location provides an excellent spot for observing ships entering and leaving the harbor of Santa Cruz. The other important port in Tenerife during World War I was Puerto de la Cruz; Dember was in Güimar, a good location for observing the port of Santa Cruz, and Köhler was in La Paz, a good location for observing the port of Puerto de la Cruz. Both men were trained in physics and thereby had the technical skills necessary for building and maintaining a radio.

Considering the nature of the research reported in the book (ultraviolet rays of the sun in the atmosphere, light polarization in the sky, the distribution of illumination in the sky, and the daily ionization curve on the outer layers of the upper atmosphere in relation to solar radiation), the introduction was a curious one. It read like a disclaimer, a statement that denied that the Spanish government had anything to do with the work of Dember, Uibe, and Buchheim. The introduction was written in 1919. I wondered how it might have read if Germany had won the war.

* * *

On my return from Izaña, I received word from Dr. Christine Jordan that she had arranged an appointment with Francisco Sanchez, professor of astrophysics, director of the Institute of Astrophysics, and vice-rector of the University of La Laguna, for the following day.

* * *

I met Dr. Jordan on the appointed day at her laboratory in El Sauzal. From there, we drove together to La Laguna to meet with Sanchez.

Sanchez, who spent seven years at Izaña, during which time he read everything there that was to be read, was able to add little to what I already knew. He did mention, however, that while browsing through the files of the archives, he came across a document that made reference to a letter written in 1913 by the Spanish ambassador in Berlin to the Spanish government in Madrid, in which the ambassador indicated that he suspected that the German astronomers at the Cañadas observatory were spies. Sanchez said that he did not know where the archives were now. He added that he was at the observatory in Izaña fifteen years ago and recalled that the archives weren't there then, that many documents were lost in a fire.

* * *

The next day I confirmed my reservations for a flight to Berlin on the following day. The bits and pieces of information I had gathered during the past several weeks were difficult to sort out. Some questions had been answered, at least partially; other questions remained; and some new questions had been raised. Still other questions would forever stay unanswered—if Manuel González y García knew more than he had told me, it would never be known. I was eager to visit the archives in Berlin; I hoped that data from these records would help to tie some of the loose ends together. Köhler must have been associated with the German expedition in the Cañadas.

16.

East Berlin Archives

West Berlin was dark in winter. The northern latitude, which provides such long days of sunlight during the summer, had the opposite effect in January; not only were the hours of daylight short, but the oblique angle of the sun lighted the city dimly and cast long shadows even at midday. The cold and gloom, coupled with the absence of vacationing visitors, made the streets barren by comparison with the busy activity of the summer. This was especially true of the usually bright and noisy Kurfürstendamm, which now seemed subdued, like a holiday resort out of season.

Not to put too fine a point upon it, East Berlin was simply grayer than West Berlin, partly the result of the low illumination of winter, and partly the result of thick clouds of acrid coal smoke. The tiny particles of soot, which rained from the sulphur-flavored clouds, reminded me of New York after dark, late at night when trash is incinerated.

When I arrived at the archives of the Prussian Academy, my expectation for discovering significant documents was not high. Thus, I was delighted when the attentive and cooperative staff produced in short order the records of the Tenerife anthropoid ape station from its inception in 1912 to its dissolution in 1920.

Here at last were authentic documents that gave a side of the story I sometimes feared I would never learn.

1912

The earliest document in the records—the minutes of the first meeting, February 29, 1912, of the Board of Trustees of the Albert Samson Foundation—stated that the Kaiser had approved the establishment of the foundation on January 20, 1912, with an endowment of approximately 950,000 marks. The minutes of the board's meeting of October 31, 1912, which mentioned that Nobel laureate Max Planck has been appointed secretary of the Prussian Academy of Science, stated that the foundation's funds came from the estate of Albert Samson, who died on September 6, 1908. The minutes also contained the first reference to the anthropoid ape station in Tenerife:

> Five thousand Marks are made available for the year starting November 1, 1912 to the committee responsible for the observation of anthropoid apes which are kept in Tenerife. These observations are carried out for the study of physiological and particularly psychological animal behavior. . . .

The anthropoid ape station was the first project to be funded for the initiation of research. At its last meeting of 1912, held on December 12, the board approved the appointment of E.L. Teuber, a doctoral candidate, to direct the station in Tenerife starting January 1, 1913. The minutes made it clear that the ape station was funded through the Prussian Academy of Science, not the Kaiser Wilhelm Gesellschaft. However, the origin of the foundation's funds was the estate of Albert Samson, a patriot who bequeathed part of his personal fortune to his country with the responsibility for its disbursement left in the hands of the Kaiser. It was almost four years after Samson's death that the Kaiser approved the establishment of the foundation. Presumably, the Kaiser's approval was based on the recommendation of Friedrich von Schmidt-Ott, the minister of culture, who in turn made his recommendation on the basis of Professor Rothmann's request. Although a few other research projects were funded by the foundation, the bulk of the foundation's funds was claimed by the ape station, a fact which suggests that the foundation may have been created for the primary purpose of underwriting the ape station.

The date of the establishment of the foundation coincided closely with the first documents from the British Foreign Office files that indicated Britain's recognition of the strategic importance of the Canary Islands. The fact that Germany also recognized the strategic importance of the Canaries was made clear in the German military records, which included a summary of the work of the Las Palmas Etappe from August 1 (the first day of Germany's engagement in the war) to August 26, 1914. The summary reported on the Etappe's efforts to maintain encountering lines for supplying German ships in the Atlantic off the northwestern coast of Africa. Whatever the connection between the establishment of the scientific expeditions in the Canary Islands and the Etappes, there can be no doubt that the German Foreign Office was well aware of the military importance of the islands when it approved the establishment of the expeditions.

1913

The earliest relevant information for 1913 was an item contained in the minutes of the board's meeting of October 30, which stated that the chairman was "authorized to apply for the transport of orangutans to Tenerife with the government of the Netherlands, and to conclude the contract with Dr. Köhler, who will take Mr. Teuber's place in Tenerife."

The first document from Köhler was a letter to Privy Councillor von Waldeyer. Dated November 20, 1913, the letter had been written in Neu-Isenburg, a small town located a few miles south of Frankfurt, Köhler's place of residence during his tenure at the University of Frankfurt:

> I thank you for the requested 800 marks which I received. I was still able to book a cabin in time and we shall be sailing from Barcelona on the 15th of December. . . . As we are leaving Frankfurt on the 10th or 11th of December, I would recommend that the sum [travel expenses] be sent by the 5th of December. . . .

I would also like to advise you that my wife and I have decided to take our older boy, whom we originally thought of leaving behind with relatives, to Tenerife. As I negotiated with you without taking into account this possibility, I fully understand that the traveling expenses and stay for this child are my own responsibility. . . .

May I request your reply regarding the requested sum. With the expression of my highest esteem, I remain, W. Köhler.

Köhler's letter established the time and date of his departure from Frankfurt for Tenerife, but it also contained the curious fact that he and his wife had originally planned to leave their older boy behind with relatives. Köhler was twenty-six years old in December of 1913. I wondered what the reason was for their initial decision to leave their older child behind. Whatever the reason, mention of an "older" child indicated that there was a younger child, and thus confirmed Manuel's recollection that Köhler and his wife arrived in Tenerife with two children, at least one of whom was a boy.

A note written in the margins of Köhler's letter, presumably by Waldeyer, gave Köhler's temporary residence in Tenerife as the Hotel Martiánez, Puerto de la Cruz, Orotava: "Write Köhler that he should get in touch with Teuber and to write what he requires, namely for the keeper [presumably Manuel González y García]."

1914

The first two documents for 1914 were letters to Waldeyer from Köhler at Puerto de la Cruz. In the first letter, dated January 4, Köhler reported on his good relationship with Teuber and his early association with Manuel González y García: "Mr. Teuber suggests that from now on the keeper's [Manuel's] salary should be 125 pesetas per month. *I have satisfied myself about this man being indispensable at the moment and would therefore recommend the same amount* [italics mine]."

The second letter, dated January 6, confirmed Isidoro Luz-Carpenter's statement that there was no electricity at La Costa when he and his family left there, and Manuel González y García's claim that Köhler had electricity throughout his stay at La Costa: "We shall probably buy our electricity for lighting and projectors and possibly also a small motor from the electrical power station in Villa Orotava....We are presently consulting with the power station and a very competent English technician whose acquaintance I made in the hotel."

Although Köhler did not give the name of the competent "English technician," it is quite likely that he was Mr. V.B.D. Cooper, the man who on August 26, 1914, reported to the British Admiralty information concerning the alleged German wireless station in the Cañadas, and the request for electrical supplies presumably connected with the construction of a radio.

* * *

The next document, a letter to Waldeyer from Eugen L. Teuber, dated Santa Cruz de la Palma (an island of the Canary Archipelago located northwest of Tenerife), January 18, established the fact that Teuber had left Tenerife more than six months before the war began, summarized the transition of the directorship of the station from Teuber to Köhler, mentioned the plans for the installation of electricity at La Costa, and indicated that Köhler had been introduced to significant people on the island: "I also went with him visiting at Dr. Pérez [a Spanish physician], Melchor Luz [the owner of La Costa], Dr. Burckard [the German botanist-meteorologist], amongst others."

* * *

A letter to Waldeyer from Köhler, dated March 7, included the first informal report on research at the station. The historical importance of this report should be noted, first because it marked the first of a series of similar reports that provided the data for *The Mentality of Apes*, and second, because it may have been the first scientific report of systematically controlled observations designed to demonstrate the cognitive processes of reasoning and problem solving in anthropoid apes.

   ...Dr. Rothmann probably reported also how wonderfully Tschego, a chimpanzee, is developing, and that he

can even be used for tests. Photograph 1 shows how
from out of his running area he angles with a stick for
bananas and bread. All I did was put a few pieces of
wood in his cage and his food outside beyond his reach.
To use the sticks as tools he arrived at by himself when he
became hungry. He is very skilled at it. Another test
which I couldn't photograph for technical reasons went
like this. All sticks had been removed, but a whole part
of a tree totally unsuitable as a tool, because the
branches wouldn't go through the fence, was put in his
running area. After Tschego tried for a long time to force
the tree through the fence, and other "ideas" didn't get
him closer to his aim, he suddenly charged toward the
tree, broke off a branch and used it to fetch in his feed.
This is obviously a good demonstration of tool production. Picture number 2 shows an experiment with Chica.
Sokolowsky tells how a chimpanzee from the Hagenbeck
Circus succeeded in climbing over a high wall by getting
hold of a rope dangling from the ceiling. Allegedly, he
pushed himself harder and harder, until he would reach
the upper edge of the wall. Some do not believe that it
could have happened in this manner. Therefore, I attached a rope to the top of the fenced-in area and let one
end fall freely and tied to the other end, a basket with
bananas. The basket cannot be reached from the
ground, but the rope is within two meters reach. Chica is
led into the cage, soon discovers the rope, gets hold of it,
and with a mighty vault, swings to the basket with the
fruit. The photo shows this particular moment. We have
made the same test with other animals, without their
having seen it performed of course. (Imitation will be
treated separately.) Today I captured this test with a
movie camera to provide proof for the skeptics. I hope it
will turn out well. The cranking noise of the movie camera no longer disturbs the animals. We got them used to
this noise by continually cranking the camera without
film in it. It will be a good thing to use the movie camera
for the most important experiments because nobody
knows any more what to believe and what not in animal
psychology. . . .

I recently visited Consul Ahlers in Santa Cruz and
am very pleased to have had the opportunity to make the

acquaintance of such a charming and interesting gentleman. I am enclosing Don Melchor Luz's receipt.

Respectfully yours, Wolfgang Köhler

* * *

In Köhler's next letter to Waldeyer, dated April 19, Köhler discussed his proposed budget, indicated his desire to publish the results of his research to date, and gave a brief description of some recent research findings. The most interesting bit of information contained in the letter, written more than three months before the beginning of World War I, was Köhler's report that "certain Englishmen . . . take us for German spies, and are even so kind as to spread the rumors in confidence that the animals are just a pretext."

The basis for the allegation that Köhler was a spy was not given. Even if the allegation were only a suspicion, the fact that it was made several months before the outbreak of the war suggested the imminence of war. Whatever the reason for the allegation, it was clear that Köhler and his family lived in jeopardy almost from the moment of their arrival in Tenerife.

* * *

The last letter from Köhler before the war was a cover letter of July 23, which accompanied his first semiannual progress report, a report that summarized some experimental findings: the general health of the animals; some problems with the animals (ill-tempered behavior, coughing and runny noses, coprophagy); an attack on Mrs. Köhler by several of the animals (an anecdote told to me by Manuel); sexual development of the animals; death of an animal; problems of measuring performance of animals independent of contamination caused by early social experiences; attempts to accustom the animals to the conditions of social isolation; speculation on the relationship between cerebral development and intelligent behavior; distinction between intelligence and behavior based on conditioned responses; plans of new tests of intelligence; plans for publication of research; formulation of the concept of ''insight''; thoughts on the origins of intelligent behavior; plans for comparative psychological research; new research on vision in the chimpanzee; speculation on the importance of research on perceptual processes as leads for research on physiological processes; and the pressing need for an adequate library of books and journals at the station. The report was impressive. The rather long and comprehensive summary provided an outline of the book to come—*The Mentality of Apes.*

The cover letter told Waldeyer that Köhler had no definite news on the transportation of new animals from the Cameroons to Tenerife, but that Köhler had recently bought a young male chimpanzee in Santa Cruz which he was keeping in his house.

Acting on one of Köhler's requests in his letter of April 19, Waldeyer wrote to the minister of foreign affairs on July 25 and recommended that Mr. Ahlers and Dr. Pérez receive official recognition for help on behalf of the ape station.

*   *   *

Köhler's first letter to Waldeyer after the outbreak of the war was written on August 10:

> I hope this missive will reach you via Professor von Monakow of Zurich whom I am asking to forward it to you. I went to Santa Cruz on August 3 because there was talk of German mobilization. As a reservist, in the event of war I have to return immediately to the Empire. Unfortunately, it had already become impossible to leave the island because German steamers naturally remain in the neutral port and neither Spanish nor Italian ships are prepared to take one aboard for fear of trouble on the parts of French and English warships. Thus, not one of about 60 persons liable for military service could get away, and it is unlikely that the sea shall be clear for the duration of the war; I shall have to stay here. If by chance I should be able to get away, my wife will take over things during my absence; with the help of the *absolutely reliable keeper* [italics mine], she could do this without any trouble until my return or a substitute would be sent out by you. . . .

Köhler's statement that he went to Santa Cruz at the outbreak of war, presumably to the German Consulate there, to
report for military duty, implied that he was not sent to Tenerife
as an agent of the military. However, since Ernst Groth, the head
of the Tenerife Etappe, was also the German consul in Tenerife
during the war, it was only reasonable that he should use consulate information to take stock of German residents of the island
for the purpose of enlisting the services of patriotic nationals
willing and able to serve their country. Moreover, considering
the strong nationalistic spirit of the time, young men with special
skills who were unable to serve in the military in Germany very
likely felt a strong obligation to volunteer their services to the
Etappe.

* * *

Köhler's last letter to Waldeyer from 1914, dated October 19,
described the trying conditions under which Köhler worked and
some of the important things he discovered:

> ... The other animal that died is little Konsul, who was
> always far behind Koko. This death is not quite as seri-
> ous for the station because apart from occasional obser-
> vations, his record of results remained almost nil because
> it was impossible to isolate him. Three weeks ago he
> gradually stopped eating—he always ate a lot less than
> the others anyway—and showed symptoms of stomach
> pains. He was then immediately isolated, also because he
> was sufficiently apathetic (p.s., little Koko was never put
> with the other animals, therefore, transfer of the tape-
> worm is out of the question). Then he passed bloody
> mucus. As he continued not eating, we force fed him for
> two weeks with Nestle's baby cereal to keep him alive.
> Unfortunately with insufficient success because he
> brought up most of it either immediately or an hour
> later. After this, the keeper, my wife, and self kept him
> upright for several hours after feeding him. However, as
> soon as he was put down, he started writhing on the
> floor with pain and still vomited almost everything. He
> must have had a severe stomach condition, although the
> evacuation of the intestines was normal. . . . The day be-

fore yesterday, the pain the animal was suffering became too much for me. He squirmed and convulsed on the floor and cried bitterly, so I gave him a strong morphine injection and slit his carotid artery. . . .

The remaining animals (six), I am glad to say, are very well, except for the coprophagy. The optical experiments I'm involved in at present require particular effort and patience on my part because the animals are not particularly interested in them. However after a month of experimenting, I have finally succeeded in answering the first question; that in one essential respect, the brains of the animals are equally highly developed as those of human beings. As a consequence, it became obvious that if one trains a bright chimpanzee (such as Sultan) to do something, the usual associative process does not occur as in other animals, where a gradual imprint upon their memory takes place; but rather at a certain moment, all of a sudden, the maximum output is given without any previous reaction at all having been shown.

The significance is clear. There is no underlying conditioning taking place; rather, from a certain point on, the animal *realizes* what it is all about, and from this moment on the resultant behavior is of course perfect. (Perfect, that is, as long as the animal at that moment does not hear a cock crow, see a car passing by, have a cold, or something else on its mind, whereupon his performance drops to zero. Such distractions very often put my patience to the test. But punishment makes it all the worse.) . . .

Respectfully yours, W. Köhler.

1915

The first document for 1915 reminded me that the German military records for that year contained a file giving detailed evidence that the German consulates in Tenerife and Las Palmas worked cooperatively with their respective Etappes. The military records also showed that Alfred Baeger (Bäger), a German spy, was sent from the Las Palmas Etappe to Tenerife, where he worked closely with Ernst Groth, the German consul for Tenerife and a high-ranking agent of the Tenerife Etappe. A possible connection between Köhler and the Tenerife Etappe was suggested by Köhler's letter to Waldeyer, dated March 12, in which Köhler revealed his association with Dember and Uibe, the German scientists who were forbidden by the Spanish government to conduct research in the Cañadas:

> ...Mr. Martin Uibe, a doctoral student in physics from Leipzig working under Privy Councillor Wiener, arrived in Tenerife with Professor Dember on the day the war broke out. They came here on behalf of the Saxon Academy of Science for the purpose of making astronophotometrical tests on top of the mountain [Teide]. When Uibe came down from the mountain, I brought him here and, with his assistance, used his instruments to make measurements... (during the two and a half months he was here).

The letter indicated that Köhler's association with Dember and Uibe, the alleged spies accused of sending coded radio messages from a secret wireless station, began as early as September 13, 1914, the date that they arrived in Orotava (the region of La Paz) after being expelled by the Spanish government from the observatory in the Cañadas. Furthermore, the association appeared to have been a fairly close one since in addition to collaborating on Köhler's research, Uibe lived at the ape station with Köhler and his family for two and a half months on this occasion.

There seemed to be no doubt that Dember and Uibe were the Germans who Manuel told me were living in the mountains when they were captured by the Spanish military and had their radio confiscated. In this connection, it was also interesting to note that in the same letter in which first reference was made to Dember and Uibe, Köhler also revealed additional information that contributed to Manuel's credibility: "Perhaps the keeper could be given a small increment, and if he stays on, after a while, a medal or some form of recognition. He is always decent, modest, and industrious."

*   *   *

Köhler's semiannual report for the last six months of 1914 summarized his work and the problems at the station that were, for the most part, mentioned in his earlier letters. In his discussion of the deaths of Koko and Konsul, Köhler indirectly indicated that Manuel had been with the animals since their first year in Tenerife: "According to the Keeper, this animal [Konsul] had once before been given up during the first year of the station's existence." In connection with the deaths, Köhler also alluded to anti-German sentiment among some of the local physicians, one of whom was likely the Englishman who, according to Manuel, tried to cause trouble for Köhler.

The report did contain encouraging information concerning the improved health of the animals, which Köhler attributed primarily to his increased knowledge of a more suitable diet, one that contained a supplement of locally grown herbs. He again mentioned his observation of Tschego's sexual maturity and signs of her cyclical menstruation, and indicated his concern for Sultan's adolescent innocence. "I will give exact details of the menstrual cycle after further observations have eliminated the last uncertainties. Tschego and Sultan may have to be separated in the future so that the big female animal does not ruin the little male by frequent coitus."

Köhler's semiannual report for the first six months of 1915 dealt primarily with the animals and with research at the station. The report contained some interesting remarks on the problems of motivating subjects for participation in psychological experiments, remarks that will strike a familiar chord with anyone who has used college students as subjects in research:

> . . . for them, being with the others and at liberty means so much . . . that they refuse to go along with the test, and rage and cry. If they have learned something during a test and the experiment lasts longer than they would like, their performance, which for a while has been excellent, will deteriorate from day to day and can, after weeks of tiring work, become so bad at the decisive moment, that all invested efforts will have been in vain. This shows that tests made without taking the [subjects'] mood into account, in a mechanical fashion according to

a set program, render essentially negative results. If one doesn't have to work under these pressures, but is able to observe the [subjects] calmly, one will of course recognize the higher organization of this unreliability. . . .

The report continued with a discussion of some preliminary findings on the question of whether animals other than humans have a concept of self, a question that, in conjunction with attempts to teach sign language (and other synthetic forms of non-oral language) to anthropoid apes, is at the center of current research and debate among comparative psychologists:

The observation that chimpanzees after several tests with a mirror retain lasting interest in everything reflective, that they examined every piece of glass, even the smallest, for reflections, looked at their own images in rain puddles, and finally, immediately after urinating on the concrete floor of their rooms, bent their heads back and forth to stare at the changing reflections lead to the question of whether or not these animals recognize pictures which are even further removed from the originals than mirror images, with their colors, their mobility, their stereoscopic effect, etc. It was proved that the chimpanzee will still recognize photographs with, for him, interesting subjects if these are reduced to about a tenth of their original size. This question will be pursued still further.

The last part of the report told of new charges of espionage leveled against the station by an unidentified Englishman:

The station during this report period was not, as previously, spared political troubles. An Englishman of the local colony—whom I don't know—denounced the station to the English consul in Santa Cruz: we allegedly supplied German submarines with petrol and food, also installed a station for wireless telegraphy to make contact and appointments with the U-boats. The consul wrote a letter containing the same allegation to the Governor of the Province of the Canaries. The result was an almost daily visit by the constabulary patrols, but without molestation. The governor further passed the English indictment letter to the local authorities with a request for particulars. The authorities, without checking, declared the supicions as unfounded and although the English consul repeated his accusations, nothing was undertaken against the station. The constabulary visits became rarer too, and this matter seems to be closed now.

Köhler's remarks in the last part of his report corroborated Manuel's statement that "soldiers of the Spanish National Guard visited Köhler to search his home almost every week" and that their visits were prompted by the British consul. I was reminded, too, of Manuel's amusement when he related that a friend had alerted him in advance of the coming searches and that he told Köhler who, in turn, concealed his radio and ordered his servants to have food and coffee ready for the soldiers on their arrival. My confidence in the reliability of Manuel's memory and in the veracity of the events he recalled increased.

* * *

In a letter to Waldeyer dated August 3, Köhler announced the birth of a third child, a boy, and discussed matters pertaining to work at the station:

> Would you please excuse me for answering your two letters only briefly? I am rather overworked, for the birth of a son (on July 31) and last, but not least, uninterruptible experiments are making great demands on my strength. Such an infant—if the mother is still confined to bed, and servants don't know anything about hygiene—naturally becomes the object of care of the father, without mentioning that the household too has to be run by this layman. Thus, the new report and the second article will be delayed a little . . . .
> Mr. Uibe and my wife agreed to the way the title page to the treatise is set up—to be known as "Frau Th. Köhler" rather than "Frau Dr. Köhler."

"Th. K." were the initials of the artist who drew the frontispiece of the German edition of the The Mentality of Apes. Although Thekla Köhler's name would not appear in either the

German or English versions of the book, it was her drawing that confirmed Manuel's recollection that Köhler had at La Costa the electricity necessary to power a radio transmitter and receiver.

* * *

On September 13, Waldeyer wrote a response to Köhler's letter of August 3. The response contained, among other things, the explanation of how the spelling of Köhler's name was changed from "Koehler" to "Köhler."

> The title page of your paper reads according to your wife's wishes, that is "Frau Th. Köhler." Unfortunately, however, everywhere was printed "Köhler" instead of "Koehler," which I regret to say cannot be changed now. In connection with future publications, we will pay special attention to the proper spelling. It was impossible to mail you the corrected proof of your paper because we could not delay printing it.

* * *

The last document for 1915 was a letter to Waldeyer from Köhler, dated December 5, in which Köhler told of the problems he was having in writing his "intelligence paper," the paper that would later be expanded upon and published as a book, *The Mentality of Apes.* He revealed that the major problem centered on difficulties in formulating a satisfactory theory to account for his observations. The resolution, to which Köhler alluded in the letter, would be the presentation of his findings without the theory he sought. The letter also contained information about conditions at the station, and more on the allegations of espionage:

> ...I did mention briefly the submarine story in my report. That is how things go and there is nothing we can do about it, as long as this country England exists. (Even in the midst of peacetime did these people do their damndest to have the observatory on Pico Teide—half a gift from the Emperor as far as I know—closed down, because of espionage.) As long as this matter was still

acute, I pretended not to know anything about it. I installed conducting wires on this piece of land and a battery for experiments because they happened to become necessary at that point. But the gendarmes gloomily stared at everything but didn't say a word. Now nobody thinks of this matter any more, and since the Serbian campaign, the German has risen in the Spaniard's esteem. They still take it amiss, however, on the basis of a very naive notion, that the Franco-English front has not been broken. But the captain of a Spanish cruiser was dismissed because his crew, when catching sight of a German submarine near Gibraltar, broke out into a resounding ''Long live Germany!''

1916

The records contained very few relevant documents for 1916—a few letters, and the minutes of the meetings of the Board of Directors of the Samson Foundation.

One brief letter to Waldeyer from Agnes Dember, dated July 14, announced the arrival of the orangutans in Tenerife.

Today I received a postcard from my husband, dated June 18, in which he writes that I should advise you on behalf of Dr. Köhler that the anthropoid station has received two new orangutans.

Thanking you once again for the kindness you showed toward me, I remain yours sincerely, Agnes Dember.

Perhaps more important than the news of the arrival of the orangutans was the fact that Mrs. Dember gave Charlottenburg, a city of Germany, as her home address. In spite of the outbreak of the war, it appears that Mrs. Dember was able to escape from Tenerife and return safely to Germany.

* * *

The minutes of the meetings of the Board of Trustees contained routine information, except perhaps for the minutes of the November 16 meeting, which confirmed receipt of Köhler's long-promised paper on intelligence tests ("A manuscript by Dr. Köhler concerning intelligence tests on anthropoids is submitted and turned over to Mr. Stumpf for scrutiny"), and the minutes of the December 14 meeting, which mentioned the ironic fact that one of the two long-sought-after orangutans sent by the Netherlands died shortly after its arrival in Tenerife.

1917-1919

There were no significant documents for 1917, and except for an announcement of the birth of another son, the only document for 1918 was the minutes of the board's October 24 meeting, its last meeting before the end of the war. The one item of interest was a statement that "there was a danger of the grounds of the station being sold to an English company," a curious statement, because the copy of the record of the purchase of La Costa that I had obtained from Anthony Yeoward stated clearly that the land of the plantation and all the buildings on it were purchased from Melchor Luz y Lima on July 18, 1918. Perhaps the discrepancy between the dates of events in Tenerife and the dates of the minutes of the board's meeting simply reflected the lag in communication created by the wartime postal system and less frequent meetings of the board.

The exact date of Köhler's move from La Costa to El Ciprés could not be determined from the minutes of the meeting, but the minutes of the board's meeting of March 27, 1919 announced the fact that "Dr. Köhler had found new grounds in Tenerife and that the station's inhabitants had taken well to their new surroundings." Whatever the exact date, the important fact was that Manuel's claims that La Costa was purchased during the war and that Köhler was pressured to move during the war were corroborated by the minutes.

* * *

Although the minutes of the June 18 meeting of the board indicated that the postwar plans for the continuation of the ape station included the appointment of Max Wertheimer as Köhler's

successor ("In the case that Dr. Köhler should resign as director
of the anthropoid station, Dr. Wertheimer shall be given primary
consideration as his successor...."), the minutes of the July 24
meeting stated that "Dr. Köhler expresses his desire by mail to
remain director of the Tenerife station until next spring, and
possibly longer," and indicated that the board readily agreed to
approve his request. However, postwar plans came to an abrupt
end just a few months later, when at the November 6 meeting,
the board agreed to end its support of the ape station:

> The Samson Foundation's Board of Trustees in their
> meeting of November 6, 1919, decided to dissolve the
> anthropoid station due to the strong decline of the
> currency.
> The undersigned chairman [v. Waldeyer-Hartz] was
> authorized to take the necessary steps. He informed Dr.
> Köhler by registered letter of the Board's decision and
> followed it up with another letter of the same content.

The minutes of the board's meeting of December 18 gave
more details concerning the dissolution of the ape station, and
revealed that an attempt was made to sell the station to the
government of the Netherlands. The minutes also revealed the
board's recognition of Köhler's exemplary performance in
Tenerife and its wish that he be well provided for on his return to
Germany:

> The trustees agree that the station be dissolved as
> quickly as possible and that first of all an attempt be
> made to sell it to the government of the Netherlands. A
> minimum selling price of 10,000 pesetas is set. The un-
> dersigned [v. Waldeyer-Hartz] is authorized to take over
> negotiations with the government of the Netherlands. It
> should be attempted in this connection to secure a job at
> the station for a German.
> After his return, Dr. Köhler is to receive out of foun-
> dation funds, an amount that will make his and his fami-
> ly's subsistence secure until he can find a position that
> will sufficiently ensure him a livelihood.
> For defrayal of printing costs of one of Dr. Köhler's
> manuscripts, "Die Gestalten," the printing company of
> Fr. Vieweg & Son in Braunschweig requires a subsidy of

1500 marks. An attempt is to be made to get this money from the Academy. In the event that the Academy declines, the Samson Foundation will pay the amount.

1920

The minutes of the board's meeting of April 8, 1920, gave more information concerning the disposition of the station and revealed the additional fact that Köhler made an *urgent* request in March to be recalled from Tenerife for unspecified reasons said to be related to his health or the health of his family:

> Finally, Dr. Köhler, in a letter dated March 25, urges to be recalled. The owner of the site where the station is located should be informed as to what is to happen to the station; in any event, the rent has to be paid until December 1, 1920. He also required a completely new wardrobe and consequently is afraid that his account will show a small deficit.
>
> In view of the fact that for health reasons one could no longer detain Dr. Köhler and his family in Tenerife and because the Foundation's capital could no longer be decreased, it was decided: (1) To cable Dr. Köhler to start his homeward journey at the beginning of May; that he should pay the rent until December 1, 1920, and to come to an arrangement with one of the keepers to look after the animals until further notice. (2) To write to Prof. Kraepelin that we are prepared to turn over to them, or rather to the Psychiatric Institute of Munich and the Institute for Experimental Therapy, the station, under the condition that they reimburse us for the equipment. It is to be left to both institutes to come to an understanding with Holland. Dr. Köhler is to be advised of this.

Köhler's urgent request to be recalled reminded me of Enrique Talg's statement that Köhler's departure from Tenerife was not voluntary, that he was requested by the Spanish government to leave, and of Manuel's description of Köhler's sudden departure. Although unspecified health reasons often proved a convenient excuse, there was no immediate way to determine whether Köhler's urgent request to be recalled was prompted by the Spanish government or by reasons of health. There was, of course, the possibility that neither explanation was false; perhaps illness coincided with the Spanish government's request. Whatever the explanation, Köhler and his family did depart from Tenerife in May, and the minutes of the board's meeting of July 8, 1920, indicated that Dr. W. Köhler attended the meeting and was given the responsibility for finding a new home in Germany for the apes:

It was decided to dissolve the station on Tenerife and to bring the animals—six chimpanzees—to Germany. A request was produced from Prof. Vosseler, Director of the Hamburg Zoo, to give the animals to the Hamburg Zoo, where they would find the best possible shelter in the new monkey house and would, like up to now, be available for scientific observations and tests. The chairman proposed that the request be granted, to let the Hamburg Zoo have the animals free of charge, on condition that they should be at the disposal of the Prussian Academy of Science for scientific tests; also that the Zoo should be responsible, technically and monetarily, for the transport of the animals to Hamburg.

After a thorough discussion in which, apart from the chairman, mainly Messrs. Kreiss, Köhler, Rubner, Stumpf, and Panok took part, it was decided to go along with the Chairman's recommendation, but to negotiate first with the director of the Berlin Zoo to see if he would not take the animals on the same conditions. Dr. Köhler is instructed to negotiate first with Prof. Heck in Berlin and then also with Prof. Vosseler in Hamburg and to examine the respective facilities for the lodging of the animals. After Dr. Köhler's report is at hand, a definite decision is to be made.

Thus ended the documented history of the anthropoid ape station. Aside from the interesting information directly related to Köhler and the history of the station, the documents revealed a close association between Köhler and the alleged German spies accused of operating a secret wireless station—Dember and Uibe. The documents also confirmed Manuel González y García's contention that Köhler was harassed by the British and that the Spanish authorities were lax in their investigation of the espionage charges made by the British consul.

Manuel's credibility continued to grow, but the documents did not reveal Köhler with a smoking gun in his hand. As I reflected on the correspondence between Köhler and the Samson Foundation, it occurred to me that my desire to find substantive evidence may have been encouraging my expectations. Perhaps it was naive of me to expect that either Köhler or the foundation would have revealed any information that might compromise Köhler. Virtually any written communication puts the communicants in jeopardy of discovery, especially during times of war. Was it reasonable to expect that Köhler might give so much as a hint that he, Dember, and Uibe were operating a concealed radio? If they were, as Manuel claimed, the evidence that could confirm this might never be found in the form of written documents.

With this thought in mind, I turned my attention to some leads provided by the documents, most important of which was the fact that Köhler had with him on Tenerife three sons and a daughter from his first marriage, the eldest of whom would now be about sixty-five years old. If these children were alive, they might have relevant information concerning their days in Tenerife. Surely Lili Köhler, Wolfgang's widow, would know something about the children born to Köhler's first wife. It was important that I talk to Lili Köhler.

17.

Lili Köhler

The day after my return to Albany, I went to my office at the university and found, among the letters that had accumulated during my absence, one from Michael Wertheimer dated December 15, 1976, a reply to the letter I had sent to Bill Battig in November. Wertheimer urged me to write to Professor Mary Henle, who, he said, was presently engaged in the process of writing a biography of Köhler and was the one person who might have the information I requested. Wertheimer mentioned the names of two other people who might be able to help me, and also suggested that I get in touch with Lili Köhler.

Wertheimer knew little about Köhler's years before he came to the United States and did not know the names of the children from Köhler's first marriage.

* * *

In March, I learned that Hans-Lukas Teuber was dead. It seemed that while vacationing on an island in the Caribbean Sea, Teuber waded into the ocean for a swim and was never seen again. Since his body was not found, the presumption was that he either drowned or was eaten by a fish. Although I was shocked by the news of his death and by the strange circumstances surrounding it, I felt a little ashamed that this news suggested the urgency of reaching Lili Köhler. The opportunity to meet with Mrs. Köhler arose just a few months later.

* * *

On June 1, I drove to Philadelphia to visit the American Philosophical Society, whose archives contained the personal papers of Wolfgang Köhler. Mr. Murphy D. Smith, the director of the society, introduced me to Jim McClellan, a manuscript librarian, who would help me to locate the documents I wished to see. Smith and McClellan explained that all the materials in the collection were available to me, but that if I wished copies it would be necessary to obtain permission from Mary Henle, that although the papers had been donated by Lili Köhler, it was Henle who was responsible for the restrictions put on them. A "Memorandum of Understanding," which I was required to read before I could see the papers, stated that "the American Philosophical Society would not undertake to deny access to the materials, but will notify Miss Henle who asks to use them." McClellan said that this arrangement was rather unusual.

When the documents were finally retrieved, a quick review of them led me to believe that they would be of little interest to me. A relatively small portion of the material antedated Köhler's departure from Germany for the United States; the bulk had been written during the later years of his career.

Among the correspondence, there was but one item from Köhler's first family—a letter dated September 3, 1947, from his son Martin, the second child born to Wolfgang and Thekla on Tenerife. The letter, which was typed on stationery from the Neurological Clinic of the University at Tübingen/Neckar, stated that Martin had waited for Köhler's recent return to the United States from Sweden to thank him for "all your care for us" (presumably Martin, his wife Barbara, and their children). In September of 1947, Germany was still in a severely devastated state; the Marshall Plan, which would lead to the economic recovery of Germany, had been instituted only two months earlier. The bulk of this long letter presented a somewhat confusing array of ideas on the biological origins of schizophrenia and the neurophysiological bases of mental disorders. Martin, a recent graduate in psychiatry who was working on the effect of electric shock on depression, admitted that "all this is very diffuse and unclear."

In the last part of the letter, Martin's purpose in writing to Köhler was stated: "In November of 1948 I will finish with Kretschmer [Prof. Dr. E. Kretschmer, the Director of the Clinic] and I will be required to leave here. Naturally I would like to associate with psychophysiology or psychopathology, but would be willing to work in neurology. I would like to know if you would have me as your successor in your work?" There was no indication in the papers what Köhler's response was to Martin's request, but I would soon learn that Martin remained in Germany where, in 1967, he died.

I requested copies of about a dozen documents: a letter from the Kaiser Wilhelm Gesellschaft dated February 8, 1932; a letter from Friedrich Schmidt-Ott, dated October 14, 1933; several letters from Carl Stumpf from the years of 1928 to 1936; and a brief note from Edward L. Thorndike, dated April 14, 1929. (The brief note from Thorndike, the American psychologist whose trial-and-error theory of learning was so vigorously opposed by Köhler and the Gestalt school, stated: "Thank you for your courtesy and thoughtfulness in sending me your *Gestalt Psychology*. I have read every word of it, and with profit." It is difficult to estimate the amount of profit Thorndike gleaned from reading Köhler's book, but Thorndike did make a number of revisions in his theory in the 1930s, one of which, the concept of belongingness, may be a concession to Gestalt psychology.)

Based on the sample of documents I had read, my impression was that they had been carefully selected to present a favorable profile of Köhler. The papers revealed nice things that Köhler said and flattering things that were said about him. The nature of the papers made me realize a basic problem in the evaluation of historical data, namely, the difficulty of determining the extent to which a set of papers is a true representation of a person or a slanted one, either favorable or unfavorable, biased by the person who selected the papers to be made public.

At the end of my day at the archives, McClellan asked me if I had met Mrs. Köhler. I told him I hadn't but that it was my intention to try to reach her that day. McClellan simplified my task by giving me the telephone number of her residence in nearby Kennett Square, Pennsylvania. I went directly to the telephone at the archives and called. Mrs. Köhler answered and offered an enthusiastic invitation to visit her the following day. I must emphasize the enthusiasm of her response, because it surprised me. Enthusiasm is a sign of health and well-being, qualities I did not expect to hear in Mrs. Köhler's voice.

I was, of course, delighted by her invitation; at last I would have the opportunity to talk with the woman who knew Köhler best, the woman who was intimately associated with Köhler for more than fifty years. If there were any keys to Köhler's past, Lili Köhler held them.

* * *

Kendal at Longwood was a very attractive retirement home, a well-kept and expensive-looking complex of buildings constructed around a central edifice that contained a restaurant, a store, recreational facilities, health facilities, etc. The "home" was located in the country, about four miles from the town of Kennett Square. The atmosphere was bright and pleasant, and matched the mood of the wealthy retirees who lived there. In spite of the advanced ages of the residents, the atmosphere of the place was more like a resort hotel than an "old folks home."

Mrs. Köhler met me at the switchboard near the entrance to the central building. Although she was seventy-eight, her beauty was still apparent; she was, as Henry Gleitman described her, a handsome woman. Although the retirement home offered a great deal, it was obvious that she was eager to meet and chat with an interested visitor.

We left the central building and walked to her apartment, which was located on the ground floor of one of the dozen or so large two-story frame buildings that appeared to be composed of strings of town houses. Mrs. Köhler's apartment was comfortable and decorated in good taste. The living room was functional; it was straightforward and predictable. It was also a bit cold.

I explained to Mrs. Köhler that my interest was in the early years of her late husband's career, the years from his graduation from Berlin to the time he left Germany to take up permanent residence in the United States. She was happy to know that I was not interested in the same period in which Mary Henle was. Mrs. Köhler did not indicate that she knew of me through Mary Henle, and I did not raise the topic of my earlier correspondence with Mary, although I did tell her that I knew Mary.

Mrs. Köhler (née von Horlemann) was born in Sweden to a family of the aristocracy. She said that she attended school in France in the early 1920s and then returned to Sweden, where she expressed an interest in psychology. She was advised that the center for the study of psychology was Berlin, and that the man to see there was Wolfgang Köhler.

Mrs. Köhler's episodic memory was poor. She couldn't recall which year she arrived in Berlin. She was very aware of her faulty memory, and cautioned me to "check everything I tell you." Examples of her poor memory popped up throughout our conversation.

I asked Mrs. Köhler about her late husband's early years in Berlin and about his years in Tenerife. She told me that he had fond memories of Tenerife, that he often talked about the beauty of the island and how he would like to return some day, but that he never did.

I mentioned Wolfgang's first wife, and the frontispiece she had drawn for the German edition of *The Mentality of Apes*, a pencil drawing of an ape initialed "Th.K." Mrs. Köhler got the book and turned to the frontispiece; she gave me the impression that she hadn't been aware of the fact that this drawing had been done by the first Mrs. Köhler. She knew that Thekla was an artist, primarily a sculptress, and told me that she had met Thekla and Thekla's children on one occasion before Thekla and Wolfgang were divorced—shortly before they were divorced, she added. She remembered that Thekla was very sad. In a very matter-of-fact way, she told me that Thekla did not want the divorce; it was Wolfgang who left her. She pointed out quickly that Wolfgang supported the family financially, but had nothing to do with Thekla or his children thereafter.

Mrs. Köhler seemed to think that there were three children, two boys and a girl—she remembered Charlotte and Martin, but couldn't remember the other child's name, and she did not know where either of the boys were today. She explained that since Wolfgang had nothing to do with his children, she knew little about them.

Mrs. Köhler knew very little about Thekla, but did remember that she had died a long time ago. She was, however, in touch with Wolfgang's daughter from his first marriage, Charlotte Dietrich, a resident of Edsvalla, Sweden, who was divorced and the mother of Wolfgang Dietrich, a recent Ph.D. in physics from the University of Uppsala. Mrs. Köhler told me that she had helped Charlotte to settle there after the war; Mrs. Köhler had worked with the Friends' Field Service Commission in the relocation of refugees. It may have been this charitable act that kept Charlotte in touch with Mrs. Köhler. There was nothing to indicate that Wolfgang made any attempts to keep in touch with his children. In fact, it was quite the opposite—Mrs. Köhler confirmed Metzger's statement that Wolfgang completely severed his relationship with his ex-wife and the children of his first marriage.

In her discussion of Wolfgang's first marriage, she mentioned parenthetically that she must remember to include Charlotte in her will. She said that Charlotte was a nice person, a thoughtful person. Mrs. Köhler gave me the address of Charlotte, who would know the addresses of her brothers.

Mrs. Köhler retrieved some photo albums and showed me a picture of Wolfgang taken shortly after his return to Germany from Tenerife. There were three children in the picture with him—a girl and two blond-haired boys. There were many other pictures, snapshots that Mrs. Köhler had taken while she and Wolfgang vacationed. Mrs. Köhler said that Wolfgang loved the outdoors, and that she and he traveled extensively on foot, on bicycles, and in roadsters: "Wolfgang never owned anything but an open car." There were a number of pictures of him and of him and Lili in Sweden and other countries of northern Europe. These summer vacations were taken between the time that Köhler left Thekla (about 1924 or 1925) and the time that he married Lili (1927 or 1928—Lili wasn't sure which year).

Lili said that Wolfgang was opposed to marriage, that he saw it as an imposition on his freedom, that he felt everyone should be free to do as he liked, that this was the reason for his leaving Thekla. I didn't ask Mrs. Köhler why it was then that Wolfgang married her, but she did say that she and Wolfgang were comrades.

Later on, Mrs. Köhler mentioned that her daughter, Karin, was born in Sweden in 1927 or 1928—Mrs. Köhler wasn't sure which year. She said that Wolfgang "was never a family man, he never liked being a family man, he never liked marriage: Wolfgang thought everyone should be free—responsible but free."

She told me that Wolfgang paid a considerable amount of money to Thekla for the care of their children, and that Wolfgang's family life with Thekla was poor, that Thekla was the one who took care of the children. She mentioned again that Wolfgang felt strongly that people shouldn't be tied down to someone else, but added that she did not know the details of their separation, because Wolfgang would never talk of such things.

We talked about the difficulty of leaving Germany in the early 1930s. Mrs. Köhler showed me a picture of the house where she and Wolfgang lived after their marriage, a small house in the country outside of Potsdam. Since they were both Lutherans, it wasn't necessary for them to leave Germany. She added that she and Wolfgang were nominal Lutherans, not practicing Lutherans, that Wolfgang did not adhere to any formal religion, but that he was interested in the Quakers (the Society of Friends). She hastened to point out that it was not the religion's opposition to war that attracted him—"Wolfgang was not a pacifist"—but rather the religion's service, the silence that characterized the service, not the philosophy of the religion.

Mrs. Köhler remembered that they were in the United States the academic year before their final decision to leave Germany (1934-1935). Köhler gave the William James Lectures at Harvard in the fall of 1934, and was at the University of Chicago in the spring of 1935. In the summer, they returned to Germany to settle things, and in the fall of 1935 they returned to the United States, where Köhler took a post at Swarthmore. Mrs. Köhler mentioned that they were not allowed to sell their house; it was confiscated by the government.

Mrs. Köhler confirmed the fact that Wolfgang came from a German family in Estonia, where his father was the director of a school in Reval, a major port on the northern coast, renamed Tallinn after the Russian annexation following World War II. She mentioned that Wolfgang's brother Wilhelm had been a professor at Harvard, and that another brother was an economist. Wolfgang was the youngest of five children; he had two sisters. Mrs. Köhler said that Wolfgang and his brother Wilhelm were very close. At the time of Köhler's divorce from his first wife, the German bourgeoisie led very conservative family lives—leaving one's wife and children was uncommon behavior within this group. Köhler's actions seemed to be quite daring for his times.

I asked Mrs. Köhler what had motivated Wolfgang to accept the post as director of the anthropoid ape station in such a remote spot as Tenerife. She smiled fondly as she told me that Wolfgang was an "adventurous romantic"; it was the adventure that led him to accept the post at Tenerife. I indicated that I was a little surprised to hear this. Mrs. Köhler went on to explain that Wolfgang had a public self and a private self, and that with the exception of close friends, people knew only his public self. She said that Wolfgang had a zest for life that was little known to others because they saw only the public self, that Wolfgang was a great scholar who enjoyed the good life as well: the outdoors, mountain hiking, bicycling, travel, dancing, swimming, drawing, music, food, wine, and good conversation, conversation in which he could learn something. He enjoyed doing everything; although he may not have been expert at many of the things he did, he enjoyed doing them nonetheless. Music was probably his favorite pastime; she and Wolfgang played four-handed pieces for the piano with about equal proficiency. His favorite composer was Brahms.

Mrs. Köhler explained that Americans don't understand people like Wolfgang, people who have two sides to their personalities—a public self and a private self. Americans are usually one way or the other. That is, an American who is a serious-minded scholar would be a serious-minded scholar all of the time; there would not be another side to his personality. Thus, many Americans may never have thought that Wolfgang was ever anything but a serious scholar. They certainly would not have guessed that he was an "adventurous romantic."

When the time came for me to depart, Mrs. Köhler was clearly disappointed when I told her that I would be unable to dine that day; her invitation was sincere, not perfunctory. She seemed pleased when I told her that I regretted waiting so long to get in touch with her. She told me that she hoped to talk to me again.

* * *

The day after my meeting with Lili Köhler, I wrote to Charlotte Dietrich and told her about my interest in her father. I asked for permission to meet with her in Sweden, and requested the addresses of her brothers. Her swift response of June 7 arrived about a week later. She indicated interest in my project and offered her help, but warned me that all she knew about Tenerife came from tales told to her by her mother, that she was born in 1923, several years after her parents returned from Tenerife. Charlotte told me that she was in touch with her brother Dr. Peter Koehler and gave me his address. She also invited me to visit her in Sweden.

On June 18, I wrote to Charlotte Dietrich to accept her invitation to meet with her, and to her brother Peter to request a meeting with him, and to ask him for his brother Martin's address. Charlotte answered my letter on June 27, and gave me her telephone number and directions to her home in Edsvalla.

Dr. Peter Koehler wrote his reply on July 1. Dr. Koehler, who was born in Tenerife in 1915, also warned me that he knew little about Tenerife except for stories told to him by his mother—he was five years old when he and his family left for Germany. He also mentioned that his brother Martin, who was three years younger than he, died in 1967.

His letter did, however, contain some encouraging information. He said that he had visited Tenerife on a holiday journey in 1971 and met Dr. Ernst Groth, the German consul during the years of World War I. He added that Groth took him to El Ciprés and introduced him to Manuel González y García, a name he remembered well from stories told to him by his mother. According to Peter Koehler, Manuel recognized him instantly because of his resemblance to his father. Dr. Koehler said that he would be glad to meet with me in Germany and invited me to his home in Kronshagen, a village not far from Kiel.

I was delighted with the cordial responses from Charlotte and Peter, but Peter's mention of his meeting with Ernst Groth in 1971 came as an exciting surprise; not only had Groth been the German consul in Tenerife during World War I, but the German military records listed him as a high-ranking agent of the Tenerife Etappe! Doubtless, Groth could confirm Manuel's story. More important, Groth would know the details of Köhler's work for the Etappe.

On July 8, I wrote to Peter Koehler to tell him that I would call him later in the month, after my arrival in Europe, to set a date for our meeting. On July 9, I wrote to Charlotte Dietrich and gave her the same message.

18.

Peter Koehler

I was eager to meet Peter Koehler, but it was necessary that I first go to the American college in Switzerland in Leysin, where I would discuss a professional matter with some members of the faculty
and administration. During my stay there, I called Dr. Koehler
and made arrangements to meet with him in Kiel on July 28.

After my business at the college was concluded, I returned to
Geneva on the morning of July 27, and boarded a flight for
Hamburg, where I would spend the night. I knew little about
Hamburg besides the fact that it was a very large industrial
inland port on the Elbe River, about fifty miles from the North
Sea. My hotel, the Graf Moltke, was situated adjacent to the rail
station, only a short distance from St. Pauli, the most notorious
red-light district of Germany, if not all of Europe. Like most New
Yorkers, I knew what the Forty-Second Street area was like; and
in a visit to Amsterdam, I had strolled through the streets of the
red-light district adjacent to the university; but St. Pauli was
more than I had expected. Like the Alps, which in reality far
exceed their best publicity, St. Pauli's reputation was vastly un-
derstated. Its size and gaudy thematic displays that promised
whatever sexual delights one could desire, gave it a fantasy-land

quality. It reminded me of Disney Land. An hour's stroll left me less foot weary than jaded.

* * *

The following morning I took a train to Kiel, where I was met at the railroad station by Dr. Peter Koehler, the son of Wolfgang and Thekla Köhler. Dr. Koehler greeted me cordially; his conservative suit, tie, and white shirt matched his greeting and his somewhat formal demeanor. His smile was narrow as opposed to broad; I was reminded of Henry Gleitman's remark that Wolfgang Köhler's response to humor was a smile, not a laugh.

From the railroad station, Peter drove me in his wife's new Volkswagen to a nearby hotel where he had made a reservation for me. After I checked in, we drove to Peter's home, a small two-story single-family brick house on a short, quiet street in a residential suburb of Kiel. Like the other similar houses on the street, Peter's house was neat, well maintained, and surrounded by shrubs and flowers. Peter has a keen interest in gardening and expressed pride in his handiwork.

When we entered the house, we were met by Mrs. Koehler. The interior of their house complemented the exterior; it was clean, functional, and conservative. I was invited to sit in a large, comfortable chair, and was given coffee. Peter then requested that I present my credentials. I gave him a copy of my curriculum vitae, which he studied for several minutes before giving his approval for the interview.

Peter told me that he was born July 31, 1915, in Puerto de la Cruz, Tenerife, the second of Thekla and Wolfgang Köhler's four children: Marianne, born July 3, 1913; Peter; Martin, born August 30, 1918; and Charlotte, born March 2, 1923. He said that his mother had an illegitimate child, Claus Köhler-Achenbach, in March 1912, and that he was not certain who Claus's father was, but that he thought he may have been a Czech composer from Prague. Although Claus, now a professor of graphic art at the Kunstakademie in Düsseldorf where he taught painting, was born before Thekla and Wolfgang married, Wolfgang gave his name to the child. Thus, Claus was raised in the same family as his two half sisters and two half brothers. Peter Koehler explained that while his father changed the spelling of his name from "Koehler" to "Köhler," all of his children from his first marriage kept the old spelling except Claus.

As I jotted down the addresses of Marianne and Claus, I remembered the letter Köhler had written to Waldeyer shortly before departing for Tenerife, in December of 1913. In the letter, Köhler mentioned that he had changed his mind and that he and his wife had finally decided to take their older boy, whom they originally thought of leaving behind with relatives, with them. If Köhler were not Claus's natural father, this might help to explain why Köhler had originally planned to leave Claus behind. I wondered about the effect, if any, Claus had on the marriage.

Peter's mother was born November 22, 1889, in Hamburg, and died October 12, 1964, in the same city. She did not reside in Hamburg during the years before her death; her reason for being there was to receive therapy at a hospital that offered a special program for the treatment of cancer. Thekla's father was Max Alvary Achenbach, an opera singer and the son of a popular German neo-romantic painter. Her mother was Thekla Thomas Achenbach. Peter said that Thekla married Wolfgang in either 1912 or 1913; he was not certain of the year.

Peter Koehler was a physicist. He studied at the University of Kiel, and since his graduation had worked in Kiel as an industrial physicist. From 1939 to 1940 he served in the German Army. Following his discharge, his skills as a physicist were required for a special project, namely, the development of a means of propelling torpedoes that would not leave a traceable track in the water. Peter explained that until 1941, torpedoes were powered by small steam engines that burned oil and compressed air. Since the torpedoes traveled close to the surface of the water, the exhaust smoke and residual steam left a trail that allowed ships under attack to detect the presence of the oncoming torpedo and thus change course to avoid being hit. Furthermore, the trail of the torpedo revealed the location of the submarine, and thus put the submarine in jeopardy of counterattack. Peter developed an electric motor, powered by wet-cell batteries, to propel torpedoes, thus eliminating their telltale exhaust trails. He showed me an award he had received from the government for his work—a silver formée cross with a swastika in the center. The box from which the cross was taken contained a number of photographs from Peter's military service. I expressed interest in seeing them, and although Peter initially seemed enthusiastic about discussing the war years, he rather abruptly changed his mind, put the award in the box, closed it, and said he did not wish to show me the pictures or discuss the war.

Peter told me that during his student days at the University of Kiel, he had worked on a project involving the eardrum's adaptation to changes in loudness of sound, and that this work was an outgrowth of his father's research at the University of Frankfurt. According to Peter, no one at the University of Kiel knew of his father's earlier research. Peter believed that his father may have been the first person to discover this adaptive characteristic of the eardrum.

Peter was born in a hospital in Puerto de la Cruz. The family was living at La Costa at this time, but Peter was not aware of the fact; he seemed surprised when I told him that his family did not move to El Ciprés until 1918. Apparently, Groth had not told him about La Costa when Peter visited Tenerife in 1971. Peter made a second visit in 1974, at which time he learned that Groth had died the year before. The purpose of this second visit was to explore the feasibility of returning to Tenerife or Las Palmas to retire. Peter had had a heart attack recently and planned to retire soon if he could afford it. All his children were grown and lived apart from him—two children from his first marriage in 1939 (he was divorced in 1948) and a daughter from his second and current marriage. Peter remarked that he and his siblings had something in common with their father in that they all had been married and divorced.

Peter's only memories of Tenerife were of the garden at El Ciprés. Thinking back to the time when he was four years old, he was able to remember the odors and colors of flowers at the spot in the garden where he had fallen and cut his chin. It was necessary for Thekla to close the cut with several stitches; he showed me the scar. He did not remember Manuel from his childhood, but he did remember his mother's frequent mention of Manuel during the years after their return to Germany. Peter also remembered a portrait of Dember that his mother had painted in Tenerife. The painting was last seen at his mother's flat in Berlin, but he didn't know its present location. He said that Dember was doing research on light refraction, a topic that was of special interest to Peter's mother because of its relevance to her painting. Thekla was also a sculptress; she had done a life-size statue of one of the apes. In Peter's house, there were several paintings and a piece of sculpture by her, a two-and-a-half-foot angel with outstretched arms. The paintings and the sculpture showed technical skill as well as a light and delicate touch. Thekla Köhler was more than a weekend artist.

Peter's brother Martin, who was born at El Ciprés, died of an embolism of the brain at his home in a town near Stuttgart in 1967. Martin, a psychiatrist, was educated at the universities of Berlin and Tübingen. He was married twice, and had two daughters and a son. Although Martin would not have had any memories of Tenerife, Peter said that Martin's widow might have belongings left to Martin by his mother. Peter mentioned that shortly before his death, Martin had decided to move to Berlin and establish a practice there.

According to Peter, Thekla gave birth to Martin in the kitchen at El Ciprés. It was not explained why she didn't go to the hospital in Puerto de la Cruz, where Peter had been born, but it was made clear that it was not an accident—that is, Thekla intended to give birth at El Ciprés. Perhaps she felt it was unsafe to leave her home.

Peter's sister Charlotte Dietrich was born in Braunlage, a small town in Harz, about 120 miles southwest of Berlin. This was the family's second residence after their return to Germany from Tenerife. Their first residence was located somewhere in the Black Forest; they remained there for one year in 1920 and 1921. In 1921, the family moved to Braunlage, where they stayed until 1923 or thereabouts before moving to Berlin. Housing was difficult to obtain in Berlin in 1920.

According to Peter, Wolfgang and a friend of his, a military doctor, were present at the time of Charlotte's birth. They were "caught in a snowstorm on the highest peak in Harz." At the time the physician was called to assist in the delivery, Wolfgang and the physician had been playing chess and drinking cognac—so much cognac that after the child was delivered, the physician reported that it was a boy.

After Peter's joke, he told me that Charlotte tried to change the negative attitude of her brothers towards their father. Peter remembered Thekla's complaints that Wolfgang was too engaged with his science. From the beginning of the interview, it was clear that although Peter had great respect for his late father, he had no love for him. Peter appeared to have been strongly attached to his mother and to have identified with her. Like Thekla, Peter felt abandoned when his father left the family. In discussing Wolfgang's last visit with the family before leaving for the United States, Peter said bitterly, ''He had no time for us in 1935.'' Thekla, who did not remarry, was ill with cancer for ten years before her death. Peter was sad as he told me that he was with her during the last few days of her life. Peter was not a man who expressed emotions freely, at least not the tender emotions. The fact that he conveyed these feelings to me attested to their depth.

Peter said that the men in his father's family for several generations were academicians. His paternal grandfather, Franz Koehler, was a school director in Reval, Estonia (his paternal grandmother's name was Girgenson—Peter couldn't remember her first name); and his uncle Wilhelm was a professor of art history at Harvard. Although he never met Wilhelm, he did meet his uncle's widow—as well as Lili Köhler, who accompanied Wolfgang—at a meeting in Boston in 1960.

In 1923, shortly after Charlotte was born, Thekla and the children left Braunlage and joined Wolfgang in Berlin. They lived together only a short time before Wolfgang left. It must have been during this brief period in 1923 or 1924 that Lili von Horlemann met Thekla and the children. Lili had said that Thekla was very sad on the occasion of their meeting: ''Thekla didn't want the divorce, Wolfgang left her.''

Peter Koehler said that his mother was very depressed for a long time after the divorce. According to Lili, she and Wolfgang were married in 1927 or 1928, and their daughter Karin was born at about the same time. The important point is that Wolfgang knew Lili before his separation from Thekla. Whatever negative feelings Wolfgang may have had about Thekla, the children, or marriage in general, part of his reason for leaving Thekla was based on the positive feelings he had for Lili. Peter Koehler made it quite clear that he believed that Lili was the cause of the separation, and that this is what his mother believed as well. However, romantic interests may not have been Wolfgang's sole or primary concern. Peter explained that Wolfgang's father had been poor. It had been necessary for the children in the family to help each other raise money for school. Typically, the eldest son had his education paid for by his father. After he completed school, he was obliged to work and to pay for the education of his younger brother who, following graduation, would in turn work and pay for the education of his younger brother, and so on. So it was in Wolfgang's case. After his marriage to Lili, he would never have to worry about money again.

Thekla and the children lived in their flat in Berlin from 1923 to 1935, the year that Wolfgang, Lili, and Karin left Germany and moved to Swarthmore, Pennsylvania. During this time, Thekla and the children were financially supported by Wolfgang. It is likely that Hans Wallach's story that Wolfgang used his salary from the University of Berlin to support Thekla and the children was accurate. It is also likely that Lili used some of her money to support Wolfgang and herself. Lili mentioned that she and Wolfgang spent their summers as well as long holidays traveling. Whatever the arrangement, Peter made it clear that Thekla and the children lived on money from Wolfgang.

In 1935, Thekla gave up the flat in Berlin and moved to Niehagen, a small town about 125 miles north of Berlin on the Baltic Sea, where she remained until some time after the Russian occupation. Except for Charlotte, the children had finished school and were more or less on their own. Thekla chose Niehagen because she liked living in remote places and because there was an artist colony there. Peter indicated that Thekla's depression during the years immediately following the divorce was severe to the point that it prevented her from working. As Peter talked about the sad years in his mother's life and her penchant for remote places, the frontispiece of the *The Mentality of Apes* came to mind. I pictured Thekla in happier days in the remote town of La Paz on the remote island of Tenerife sketching the little farmhouse at La Costa, sketching all the details that made the house unique, details such as the pole that supported the electrical power supply to the house.

In Niehagen, Thekla resumed painting and sculpting. Peter said that his father made a brief visit there in 1937, his last visit before the war, a visit prompted by the necessity to make financial arrangements with Thekla. It was not a social call, and Wolfgang spent little time visiting with the children. Wolfgang paid for the university education of his sons Peter and Martin, but he did not pay for Claus. Peter told me that Thekla did not like Claus, that she favored Peter and his brother Martin.

*　*　*

In the early afternoon, Peter, his wife, and I drove to the shore of the Baltic Sea, to a restaurant in a marina constructed for the 1972 Olympics. In the large dining room of the restaurant, we sat at a table next to a window overlooking the yacht basin and the sea.

During lunch we chatted about Tenerife. Peter told me that he knew nothing about the naval history of Tenerife in World War I. I told him about my research at the British Imperial War Museum and the London Public Records Office, about the problem the British Navy had in locating German ships, and about the complaints made to the Spanish government by the British concerning coded wireless messages sent by Germans on Tenerife and intercepted by the British at sea. I emphasized how frustrated the British were in their attempts to stop the Germans from sending their messages. The Koehlers were very amused by this story. In a somewhat boastful manner, Peter commented on the high quality of the communication network that the Germans had: he said that when he was in Tenerife, *Groth told him that throughout the years of the war, Groth and Peter's father were in constant radio communication with Nauen, the town west of Berlin that served as the center for German military intelligence.*

I am not sure whether I successfully concealed the rush I felt in response to this information. Here at last were words, second-hand though they might be, of a high-ranking member of the Tenerife Etappe talking about radio communication between Tenerife and Germany, words that confirmed the validity of Manuel's story.

I asked Peter whether he was certain about the story Groth had told him. I said that I could understand how messages could be sent from Germany to Tenerife, but was not certain how messages could have been sent from Tenerife. Peter insisted that they were able to send radio messages directly to Germany from Tenerife. I reminded him that it was only a few years earlier that

Marconi had sent the first wireless message across the Atlantic from Ireland to Newfoundland. Peter appeared a bit frustrated as he continued to insist that it was technically possible to send messages to Germany from Tenerife, that they had an "extreme long-wave transmitter." I asked Peter where they got the power to run a transmitter capable of reaching Germany. Without answering my question, Peter raised his voice and chopped the table top with his hand as he heatedly insisted that he knew that Tenerife was in radio communication with Germany because "Groth told me with his own mouth!" As soon as he said this, he became aware of his heightened emotions, and what it was that he had said. There was a long, tense pause, and then Peter said in a quiet and even voice: "I don't think my father was political."

I wanted to continue to ask Peter about the radio in Tenerife and about other things that Groth had told him, but it was apparent that Peter felt he had already said too much. The subject was dropped at lunch, but later that afternoon, near the close of the interview, I would ask Peter again about the radio.

Shortly after we returned to the Koehler home, Peter went through his files and pulled out some pictures taken in Tenerife. I was especially interested in one taken on a lawn tennis court in 1917. It showed Peter on his mother's lap sitting next to Wolfgang, Marianne, and Claus. There were two other couples in the picture, as well as several other children; one couple was Dr. and Mrs. Groth. Peter allowed me to borrow the picture to have copies made. He also lent me a color slide of Ernst Groth taken by Peter during his visit to Tenerife in 1971.

As we chatted about Tenerife, Peter told me that when he went there in 1971, he had stopped at the office of the German consul, Jacob Ahlers, to inquire about the location of his childhood home, El Ciprés. He said that Ahlers called Groth and introduced them. I told Peter that I had met Ahlers in 1975, two years after Groth's death, and that Ahlers did not mention having met Peter. (Since there can't be very many people who inquire about the location of the ape station, surely Ahlers remembered meeting Peter. As I thought back on our meeting, I recalled that Ahlers did not tell me anything I did not already know, or anything that was not a matter of public record.)

When Groth took Peter to meet Manuel, Peter did not learn anything from Manuel, because Peter does not speak Spanish and Groth did not translate for him. Peter said that the meeting with Manuel, which took place in front of the Hotel Tigaiga, was rather brief because Groth was in a hurry. On the occasion of their visit to El Ciprés, where Peter took the picture of Groth, Groth told Peter that the animal cages had been at El Ciprés, but didn't mention La Costa. I asked Peter if Manuel gave him any pictures or documents relating to his father's days in Tenerife. He said that Manuel did not. (In my first meeting with Manuel, I remembered that he mentioned having given some pictures and papers to a foreigner who visited him a short time before I did. Apparently, this person was not Peter.)

Although Peter remembered very little about his days in Tenerife, he did recall things his mother had told him. His impression was that Thekla worked very closely with Wolfgang in his research with the apes. I told Peter that I believed that his impression was correct, that among the documents from the archives in East Berlin was a letter from Wolfgang to the Samson Foundation of the Prussian Academy of Science, in which Wolfgang said that if it should be necessary for him to leave Tenerife, Thekla was capable of managing the station by herself. He also said that he wanted Thekla to be the coauthor of his research on the mentality of apes, and that her name should be listed separately, not as Frau Dr. Wolfgang Köhler. However, when the book was finally published, Thekla Köhler's name did not appear.

As Peter thought about Tenerife and his early years, he remembered a story his mother had told him concerning Konsul, an ape who "was in love with my mother." It seems that Wolfgang and Thekla sometimes worked together in the cage with the apes. On one of these occasions, Konsul expressed his jealousy of Köhler by striking him on the face. Peter was told that an imprint of four of the ape's fingers was visible on his father's face for some time afterwards. According to Peter, this jealous act illustrated that apes knew the difference between men and women.

Peter recalled a newspaper article concerning the apes in which it was reported that they were required to learn to clean their cages. They learned to do this, and in fact did clean their cages for a while, but finally decided that the work was not good enough for them, and quit. Peter said that the German press gave his father the nickname, ''Ape Köhler.'' Peter did not like the name.

Among some old pictures that Peter showed me was one of Wolfgang, Max Wertheimer, A. Gelb, and Peter with his brother Claus and sister Marianne. Peter said the picture was taken in about 1922, which meant it was probably taken in Braunlage by Thekla. Peter pointed out that Gelb, a psychologist who had also studied with Stumpf in Berlin, was a colleague of Wolfgang's at Frankfurt. It was Gelb who introduced Thekla to Wolfgang. It seems that Gelb was living with Thekla's sister when Wolfgang and he were fellow Dozents at the University of Frankfurt. Another picture, which appeared to have been taken the same day, showed Thekla standing next to Wolfgang, with Peter at their feet. Peter said that he remembered meeting Wertheimer in Berlin some time in the 1920s, that Wertheimer was a very nice man, and that Wertheimer liked Wolfgang. Peter showed me a picture of Thekla that was taken in November 1940. Thekla was a handsome woman.

Towards the end of the afternoon, we moved to the garden, where Mrs. Koehler served pastries and coffee. Peter talked about his sister Marianne; he said that she had trained in operatic singing, but married just before the war and did not pursue a career, and that she had two daughters, one of whom lived in Denmark. I told him that I was very pleased to learn about Marianne and that I planned to visit her after I met with Charlotte. Peter said that I might not be able to locate her at her home because she was probably spending her summer with her daughter in Denmark; he said that he did not know the daughter's address, and added that Marianne did not have a telephone. (I was left with the strong impression that Peter did not want me to meet with Marianne.)

Peter appeared to be getting a bit weary, and so I decided to inquire again about Groth and the radio before taking my leave. I asked Peter if he could describe in more detail the type of radio used in Tenerife to communicate with Nauen. He said he did not know the exact English words, but that they used a ''spark'' transmitter and a ''fritter'' type of receiver. Before I could ask another question, he stated firmly that he did not want to talk

further about this. Then, as an afterthought, he said that he may
have been mistaken about what Groth had told him.

I didn't pursue the matter further, but I did ask Mrs. Koehler
if there was anything she could add to what had already been
said. (Earlier in the day, she had participated quite freely in the
conversation.) She closed her eyes as she shook her head, and
when she opened her eyes, she glared at Peter and said: "I know
nothing."

*   *   *

With Peter Koehler's statement that his father and Ernst Groth,
the head of the German espionage ring in Tenerife, were in
constant radio communication with Nauen, the central command post for German military intelligence, part of my quest
was completed. That is, the story told to Peter by Groth was
consistent with Manuel's claim that Köhler operated a concealed
radio from his house at La Costa. Although Peter was too young
to remember events during his childhood in Tenerife, his sister
Marianne and half brother Claus might. If Claus was born in
1912 and Marianne in 1913, they would have been six and five
years of age respectively during 1918, the last year of the war.
My eagerness to talk with them grew. Was there a chance that
they might be able to provide firsthand information in the form
of recollections of events that would corroborate Manuel's claim
and the story that Groth had told to Peter? After I met with
Charlotte, I would try to reach Marianne and Claus.

19.

Charlotte and Marianne

O n the morning of July 29, I returned to Hamburg and boarded a flight for Copenhagen. From there I would travel overland to Karlstad, Sweden, a large town on the northern shore of Lake Vaner, about 150 miles west of Stockholm, and the nearest rail station to Charlotte's home in Edsvalla.

* * *

On Monday morning, I called Charlotte Dietrich from Karlstad. Later that afternoon, we met at my hotel and then drove to her home, where we would dine and talk.

Charlotte was very different from her brother Peter. Her firm handshake and broad smile gave me the feeling I was greeting an old friend rather than making a new acquaintance. Her open, informal manner and animated expressions matched her relaxed posture and springy gait. She appeared strong and athletic; if I hadn't known she was a nurse, I might have guessed she was a teacher of physical education.

Charlotte's ingenuous nature was reflected in her home, an old frame farmhouse that she was in the process of renovating.

217

The freshly painted house with its bright trim, the colorful flowers that encircled the house, and the whitewashed trunks of the trees that dotted the emerald grass of her garden contrasted starkly with the somewhat drab and sparsely populated country-side of Edsvalla, and gave a fairy-tale quality to the setting. It seemed perfectly natural that a small barn, located a short dis-tance from the house, should now be an aviary.

Charlotte explained that friends and neighbors often left pet birds in her care while on holiday, and then neglected to retrieve the birds on their return. Thus, Charlotte began a collection of tropical birds. She abhorred the idea of keeping the birds in cages and decided to provide them with greater space and free-dom by converting the little barn into a birdhouse. As she ex-plained how she built the double-door entrance that permitted her to move in and out of the aviary without allowing the birds to escape, how she replaced a section of a wall with a large window to provide more daylight, how she installed an electric heater to protect the birds during the cold winter, how she sus-pended large tree-limb perches from the ceiling, and how she added plants to give the interior an outdoor-like setting, the dozens of colorful little birds—parakeets, canaries, and parrots—chirped and sang as they flew around and about our heads.

The birds delighted Charlotte, but her favorite pets were two dogs: a very large Alsatian-wolf and a very tiny terrier. Their barking seemed to increase in intensity as we chatted in the aviary, and so Charlotte decided we had best visit them so that they might meet me and quiet down.

I thought that Charlotte's description of her Alsatian as part wolf was hyperbole, but when I met him, I realized that she meant what she said. The dogs seemed friendly enough, except that the Alsatian-wolf had the disconcerting habit of taking my hand in his mouth whenever I stopped petting him. The pressure of his enormous jaws was light, and the warm saliva that he exuded on my hand didn't bother me so much as did the sight of his glistening-white two-inch-long canines. Charlotte assured me that the Alsatian-wolf would not harm me, but she came to realize that it was rather difficult for me to take notes, even though it was my non-preferred left hand that was the animal's ruminant object. She admonished the dogs and took them to another room.

As Charlotte prepared dinner, she recalled anecdotes her
mother had told her about the apes in Tenerife: how one of the
apes lifted her brother Martin's diaper to see if the baby was
male or female; how a mother ape put large leaves on the head of
her infant to shade it from the sun; how one of the apes climbed
upon her father's shoulders to reach a bunch of bananas suspended from the ceiling, while the other apes scampered about
searching for boxes with which to build a platform; how
Wolfgang kicked an ape, and the ape in turn bit Thekla; how the
female apes decorated themselves with beads and feedbags, and
then flirted with Wolfgang—"the female apes were jealous of my
mother."

After dinner we retired to the sitting room, where Charlotte
served coffee and lighted a bundle of scrap wood in the fireplace.
Although it was now late evening, and the sun had set, the sky
along the horizon to the north would remain an indigo blue
throughout the night. The day had been warm, but now there
was a chill in the air; the fast-burning wood warmed the room
quickly. As we sipped coffee and stared at the fire, Charlotte told
me that like her four siblings, she too was divorced, that her ex-
husband, the father of the child she bore in 1946, had been with
the German Army on the Russian front. She did not describe his
behavior, but she did tell me that he returned from the war a
different man from the one who had left.

I asked Charlotte if she remembered anything her mother
had said about military operations on Tenerife. She told me that
she remembered hearing that there were many ships in the seas
surrounding the island, but nothing else. When I mentioned the
names of Uibe and Dember, she said that they were very familiar
to her, that her mother had told her that the two men often
lectured to each other as a means of passing the time. Charlotte
also remembered the name Groth; she said that Thekla painted a
portrait of him, and mentioned him often in her stories of
Tenerife.

As for the reason for her brother Martin's birth at El Ciprés
rather than the local hospital, Charlotte had no explanation, but
she was able to provide the additional fact that Martin's birth
was unattended by either a physician or a midwife. Charlotte
was not at all fond of her mother (she admitted quite frankly
that they did not get on), but she did express admiration for her

boldness. She told me that Thekla was ingenious and far more colorful than Lili, that Lili was very direct—''she knew what she wanted and went after it.''

Charlotte disdained Thekla's upper-class snobbishness and exalted her father's humility and financially impoverished origins: ''My father's family was very poor—they almost starved in order to study.'' She explained that there were seven children in Wolfgang's family, that in addition to his two brothers, he had four sisters: Regina, Irmgard, Elizabeth, and Walburg, the youngest and Wolfgang's favorite. All became teachers except for Regina, who became the head nurse for the Red Cross in West Germany. Thekla, on the other hand, came from a wealthy family, and knew nothing about poverty or poor people—''the lower classes.'' Charlotte pensively wondered aloud why her father ever married Thekla, and, with a shrug of the shoulders, concluded, *''l'attraction des poles,''* opposites attract.

Since Wolfgang and Thekla divorced shortly after Charlotte's birth in 1923, Charlotte had no recollection at all of her father during the early years of her childhood. She told me that when queried by a teacher at school as to the whereabouts of her father, she answered that her father was dead. Her response led her to ask Thekla where her father was, and thus, for the first time, Charlotte learned that her father was living in the United States. Since Wolfgang and Lili did not take up residence in the United States until the fall of 1935, this meant that Charlotte was at least twelve years old before she knew her father was alive.

Charlotte recalled meeting her father for the first time in 1937, at the art colony on the Baltic Sea where Thekla and the children took up residence after their departure from Berlin. It was just two years later that Charlotte left home, and a year later, at age seventeen, that she began her studies to become a nurse. Charlotte talked about her poor relationship with her mother and about her mother's absorption in herself. Thekla admonished Charlotte for leaving her in 1939: ''You are the same as your father, you deserted your mother and her sons.''

In 1948, Charlotte met her father in Germany for the second time in her memory, but she then met him more regularly during his and Lili's frequent visits to Europe. From these early postwar years until 1959, Charlotte worked as a nurse with the United States army intelligence unit in West Germany. From 1959 to the present, Charlotte had lived in Sweden, where she now worked as a public health nurse assigned to a large rural territory surrounding Edsvalla.

The last time that Charlotte saw her father was in June of 1967, the week before his death. She showed me a copy of a Swedish newspaper dated June 1, 1967. The front page contained a large picture of Wolfgang Köhler in academic regalia, complete with laurel wreath, taken on the occasion of his receipt of an honorary doctorate from the University of Uppsala. This may well be his last picture. Charlotte said that he complained about being very tired, that he was eager to return to his home in Enfield, New Hampshire, to rest. Köhler returned to New Hampshire where he died in his sleep on June 11.

It was well after midnight when we left for Karlstad. As we prepared to leave, I asked Charlotte if there was anything else that might be of interest to me, anything that she could add to what she had already told me. She thought for a moment, and then remembered that in 1935, shortly after her father's departure from Germany and his relocation in the United States, he received a personal letter from Adolf Hitler inviting him to return to Germany to resume his post at the University of Berlin. I told her that such a letter was not part of the documents contained in her father's papers at the archives of the American Philosophical Society. Charlotte seemed a bit surprised, and then surmised that the letter must still be in the possession of Lili Köhler.

* * *

On Tuesday afternoon, August 2, I left Karlstad for Stockholm. There I would spend a few days before flying to Munich to search for Marianne Winneberger (née Koehler), the first-born daughter of Wolfgang and Thekla Köhler, and the elder sister of Peter Koehler and Charlotte Dietrich.

* * *

On my arrival in Munich on Friday, I tried several times to reach Claus Köhler-Achenbach in Düsseldorf, but no one answered his phone. I would try again before leaving Germany, but without success.

Early Saturday morning, I took a train to Peissenburg in search of Marianne Winneberger. The address I had been given by her brother Peter was a private residence of a family with whom Frau Winneberger stayed when she visited Peissenburg from time to time. Her official residence was in Obersöcheringen, a hamlet in the rural farmlands of Weilheim, where she was employed as a companion by an elderly widower.

I called Marianne's number in Obersöcheringen, explained my purpose for calling, and asked to see her that afternoon. I was surprised to learn that she was expecting to hear from me, that her brother Peter had visited her just the day before for the first time in three years. She agreed to see me and gave me directions for finding her residence in Obersöcheringen, directions that were complicated by the fact that there was no public transportation that went directly to her village, that it would be necessary to take a bus from Peissenburg to Weilheim, and then a cab from there to Obersöcheringen.

I was delighted to have located Marianne and to have obtained permission to interview her, but as I walked to the stop to await the bus for Weilheim, my thoughts centered on the fact that Peter had visited her the day before. It seemed odd to me that just a week earlier, when I talked with him in Kiel, he said nothing about plans to see her, and that several times during our meeting he had strongly implied that it would be a waste of time for me to try to reach her because she was most likely not at home, that she would be visiting her daughter in Denmark.

Obersöcheringen, located in the south of Germany just a few miles from the Austrian border, and Kiel, located in the north of Germany on the Baltic Sea coast, are about as far apart as two places in West Germany can be. Somehow, I could not believe that Peter's visit was for social reasons. The children of Wolfgang and Thekla were not close; they were not in the habit of meeting frequently. And it had been three years since Marianne and Peter last met.

If Peter had been in touch with Charlotte after my visit with her in Edsvalla on Tuesday, he would have known of my intention to seek Marianne after my visit to Stockholm. Assuming he talked with Charlotte on Wednesday, the day after my visit with her, and left for Obersöcheringen the next day, the long drive (about six hundred miles) would have taken most of the day, which meant he could not have driven to Obersöcheringen any sooner than he did, unless he drove through the night. If his trip had not been prompted by my visit, what was the reason for it? Whether urgent or not, I felt certain that his trip was connected with my visit. Did Peter have something to hide that Marianne knew, or did Marianne have information about her father that Peter did not want her to reveal?

During the long wait for the bus, and during the long ride to Weilheim, I thought back on my meeting with Peter and what he might have said that would account for his urgent action, action that seemed especially out of keeping for a sixty-two-year-old man who had recently suffered a heart attack. It was obvious that Peter regretted his remarks concerning the spark-gap radio transmitter. Since Marianne was two years older than Peter, she should have some firsthand recollections of events in Tenerife. I wondered what her response would be to my questions concerning the radio.

When my bus arrived in Weilheim, I secured a cab and made arrangements with the driver to return to Obersöcheringen three hours after my arrival. In order to return to Munich that night, it would be necessary to catch the last train from Weilheim. Obersöcheringen consisted of little more than a few dozen houses, several shops, and one rustic restaurant that served beer, wine, bread, wurst, and cheese, the odor of which resembled closely the scent that permeated the air of the town, in which the number of cows exceeded the number of human residents.

I had no trouble locating the house where Marianne Winneberger lived. She greeted me at the door, led me to the tidy downstairs parlor where she introduced me to her elderly employer, and then took me to her equally tidy quarters on the second floor, where she had prepared coffee and pastries in anticipation of my visit.

Marianne reminded me of her brother Peter, both in physical appearance and in her somewhat shy demeanor. She was not at all like her sister Charlotte, whom she had last seen in 1957. As for her brother Claus, Marianne said that she hadn't been in touch with him since 1950, that Claus's wife wanted him to break off his relationship with his brothers and sisters. The reason for the breach in the relationship appeared to center on the issue of Claus's parentage: Claus insisted that Wolfgang Köhler was his lineal father, while his siblings disagreed. Except for the recent visit from her brother Peter, Marianne had last seen him in 1974, in Kiel, when she stopped on her return from Denmark to visit one of her two daughters. The other daughter, whom she saw more frequently, lived in Munich.

Marianne told me that each of her siblings was very different from the others. Part of the reason for the differences could be attributed to inherited factors, but it was clear that Thekla's self-centered grief following her separation from Wolfgang forced her children to fend for themselves at a time in their development when they needed strong parental support. Marianne talked about the very hard time her mother had following the separation, that "after the separation, my mother retreated from the children," both psychologically and physically. In 1926, the year in which Marianne said her parents divorced, Thekla left the children in Germany and returned to Tenerife, where she painted a portrait of Ernst Groth. Marianne wept as she talked about these sad years in her childhood. She openly expressed bitterness towards Lili Köhler, the person she felt was the cause of the divorce. She said that her sister Charlotte and Lili's daughter Karin were born the same year.

The implication of Marianne's remark was clear, but I questioned the accuracy. Charlotte had told me she was born in 1923, whereas Karin, according to Lili Köhler, was not born until 1927 or 1928. Although Lili Köhler admitted to having a poor memory, it was conceivable that Marianne's recollection was colored by her hostile feelings towards Lili.

The sad events of Marianne's youth did not end with her parents' divorce. Marianne, who was gifted with an operatic voice, won a fellowship at the Berlin Academy of Music, where she studied voice along with fellow student Elisabeth Schwarzkopf. Whereas Marianne was thought to have one of the best voices of any of the students at the academy in many years, Elisabeth Schwarzkopf was discouraged by their professor from continuing at the academy. Ironically, when Wolfgang Köhler resigned his post at the University of Berlin and left Germany for the United States, Marianne consequently lost her fellowship at the academy, while Schwarzkopf continued her studies, and subsequently achieved international recognition.

After losing her fellowship, Marianne moved to Mecklenburg where she lived with her mother. In 1953, she left East Germany for West Germany, where she lived in a relocation camp for several years, during which time she visited her mother, who had moved to Frankfurt. It was during this visit, in 1957, that Marianne last saw her sister Charlotte. Although it was not until seven years later that Thekla died, Marianne said that her mother was very nervous, and looked very old.

Marianne's story was difficult for her to tell, but when I began to ask her about her days in Tenerife, she showed the signs of relief that an emotional catharsis brings. As she struggled to regain her composure, she smiled faintly, and prefaced her reminiscences of her earliest years with: "Tenerife was the best period of my life." She clearly remembered Manuel González y García: "He took care of the apes; he was good at handling the animals. The apes were never mean to Manuel. Manuel was a simple man, but very handsome; he had a beard, and looked older than his years. My parents didn't spend much time with the children, but there were many Spanish maids who took care of us. Claus was always climbing trees. My father was very angry with him. Sometimes Manuel had to take care of us; he used to pretend he was sleeping. My father often chased me around the garden, but I was too fast for him. We were never allowed to leave the compound; I often wished that I could play with other children."

In answer to my question of why the children could not leave the compound, Marianne's initial response was: "We were such wild children that my parents would not allow us to leave." Then, after a few moments of thought, she said: "When the war broke out, our family was not allowed to leave the compound; we were forbidden by the Spanish government. There were many English in Tenerife." Marianne explained that during the last years of the war, her family was essentially interned in their house, that supplies were brought to them by Manuel and the maids. During the early years of the war, she remembered playing with the Stritters' children (Herr Stritter was a member of the German Consulate), but later on, she and her brothers could play with no one.

I showed her the photograph her brother Peter had lent me, the picture of her with her family and two other couples with young children, a picture taken on a tennis court in Tenerife. She remembered that there was a tennis court at the Hotel Martiánez, and identified one of the other families as Dr. Groth, his wife Toni, and their children. Marianne said that her mother had told her that her father was very interested in Mrs. Groth. She remembered, too, that there was another psychologist from Berlin in Tenerife at that time, a Dr. Max Friedermann. She said that Friedermann was very fond of her mother, that in 1933, Friedermann asked Thekla to marry him and move to Switzerland. Thekla refused, and Friedermann left Germany and took up residence in Basel. "Friedermann loved her, even in Tenerife."

According to Marianne, Thekla played a significant role in Wolfgang's research. She said that Thekla, who was very fond of the animals, did most of the work: "She was his inspiration, the one who pressed to continue the work during times when things were going poorly. My mother was very interested in science, far more so than most women of her time. When other scientists were around, she participated in the discussions. She was an intelligent woman, capable of catching on quickly in conversation."

Marianne added that her mother had studied at the Kunstakademie in Düsseldorf, and that in addition to her painting and sculpting, she was interested in photography, that it was she who took the pictures used in *The Mentality of Apes*.

The names of Uibe and Dember brought immediate recognition; Marianne recalled that they were doing work on the peak of Mount Teide. In response to my question concerning a wireless set that her father was alleged to have built, she told me that Uibe and Dember had worked with her father at La Costa in an attempt to build a radio "to find out the news from Germany," but added, *"it never worked."*

Marianne's claim that the radio did not work was not consistent with what Ernst Groth had told her brother Peter. I wondered if perhaps Peter had told Marianne to tell me this.

Marianne went on to explain that the "team" (Köhler, Uibe, and Dember) used a room on the second floor of the house at La Costa where they worked on the radio: "Everyone was forbidden to use the room except for the 'team.'" She didn't know why the family left La Costa to move to El Ciprés, but she did remember that there was also a room at El Ciprés that was set aside for the concealment of the radio.

Since the children were forbidden to enter the room where the radio was concealed at both La Costa and El Ciprés, Marianne's report that the radio did not work could not have been based on firsthand knowledge. Understandably, she and her siblings never had direct contact with the radio; any knowledge they had would have to come from those who did, namely, members of "the team" and Groth. The important bits of information that Marianne had given me were: one, that Köhler and Groth were personal friends; two, that she remembered that there was a team composed of Köhler, Dember, and Uibe; three, that the team worked on a radio; four, that the radio was concealed in a room that the children were forbidden to enter; and five, that rooms were set aside for concealment of the radio at both La Costa and El Ciprés.

I thought about confronting Marianne with the contradiction between her story that the radio didn't work and Groth's story that he and Köhler were in constant radio communication with the German military intelligence center throughout the years of the war, but decided against it. The interview had been difficult for her. Besides, if she had been led to believe that the radio did not work, why should she be expected to explain Groth's story. And if she had attempted to mislead me, why confront her with a contradiction that might prove embarrassing and still give me no additional information?

My meeting with Marianne was brought to a close by the arrival of my cab, which took me to Weilheim where I caught the last train for Munich. As I sat in the nearly empty car and looked through the window at the dark countryside, I began to feel the weariness of a long day's journey into night.

* * *

Shortly after my return to Albany and the university, I got in touch with Jack Dugan, an electronics engineer and military history buff who was especially interested in the development of radio. Jack lent me a copy of a small book entitled *Wireless Telephone Construction*. Written in 1909 by Newton Harrison, the book claimed to be: "A comprehensive explanation of the making of a wireless telephone equipment. Transmitting and Receiving stations fully explained with details of construction sufficient to give an intelligent reader a good start in building a wireless telephone system and in operating it." I learned from Jack that the materials for such a radio would have been readily available in 1914, even in a remote place such as Tenerife, and that a team of physicists trained in German universities would have knowledge and skills far beyond those required to build a transmitter with which to send radio signals from Tenerife to Germany, and a receiver with which to decode radio signals sent from Germany to Tenerife. It was inconceivable that Köhler, Uibe, and Dember should be unsuccessful in their attempt to build such a radio.

20.

Claus
Köhler-Achenbach

lthough I was satisfied that the information given to me by Peter Koehler and his sister validated Manuel's story, I did not experience the feeling of completion I had anticipated. There was still Claus Köhler-Achenbach to be heard from, as well as the children of Ernst Groth, who might live in Tenerife now.

* * *

I departed for Tenerife in mid-December. On my arrival in Puerto de la Cruz, I met with Austin Baillon who took me to the home of Don Isidoro Luz-Carpenter, where Austin had made arrangements for me to stay during my visit. It seems that Don Isidoro's house was in fact a complex of separate but connected buildings all constructed at different times. Two of the old buildings, one of which served as my quarters, had been the family's house and barn when they first moved from La Costa in 1913. Through the years, as the family's wealth increased, Don Isidoro's father added a new house, several times the size of the old building, which served now as the residence of the Don and

Doña, their children, and their servants. It took almost no time at all to become acquainted with Sugar, a friendly Dalmatian with a strange but comical expression caused by the absence of teeth. Sugar was at times somewhat aggressive, but there was no question that his bark was worse than his bite.

* * *

A few days after my arrival, I called the Arcano Histórico de Tenerife to set a date to visit the archives and study the files of the Hamilton Company for the years of World War I. I was especially interested in the correspondence and other papers of the late Robert Cary Griffith, the ex-partner in the company who served as vice consul for the British government during the years of the war. It was rather surprising to learn that the archives had not yet received any documents from the Hamilton Company, that they were still awaiting delivery.

On Christmas Eve, I dined with Austin Baillon and his family. When I told Austin about my difficulties in trying to locate the Hamilton Company records, he said he would call Carlos Ramón Pérez-Hamilton, a relative of the manager of the company.

* * *

Several days later, I visited Isidoro Luz-Carpenter to ask him if he knew the whereabouts of Ernst Groth's children. He said he did not, but thought that Enrique Talg might. Don Isidoro called Talg, who in turn gave him the address and telephone number of Ernst Groth's daughter. Talg explained that she was in a rather poor state—her daughter had committed suicide just a month earlier. With this caution in mind, I called Señora Susana Groth-Iglesia de Ascañio, who agreed to meet with me at her home that same afternoon.

* * *

It was only a few hours later that I arrived at Doña Susana's residence in the heart of La Laguna, a cold and damp town in

December when heavy clouds cover its mountain setting and shade it from the sun. Although the house was a large old Spanish colonial, the interior appeared more German than Spanish; the Christmas decorations looked familiar. Doña Susana smiled cordially when she greeted me, but the smile did not conceal the signs of strain that showed in her face.

We chatted briefly about her late daughter before I answered Doña Susana's questions concerning the nature of my research, and assured her that my interests were limited to the period of World War I. She seemed to be a bit guarded, but I wasn't certain whether her attitude was an expression of a defensive posture or a manifestation of her emotional state.

Susana Groth-Iglesia de Ascañio, who was born in Tenerife on November 3, 1923, remembered well her parents' frequent mention of their close friendship with the Köhlers. I showed her a copy of the picture Peter Koehler had lent me, the picture of Peter, his parents, his brother and sister, and two other couples with children on the tennis court of the Hotel Martiánez. Doña Susana identified one of the couples as her parents, and guessed that the infant at their feet was her brother Berend Groth, who was born in Tenerife in June of 1917 and who now resided in the United States. As she looked at the picture, she remembered that the manager of the Martiánez during the years of the war was a man named "Trinkle," a fact that agreed with the recollections of Mr. and Mrs. Cecil Bellamy.

According to Doña Susana, her father was born in Pinneberg—a town on the outskirts of Hamburg, Germany—on February 2, 1887, just twelve days after Wolfgang Köhler's birth. Ernst Groth came to Tenerife in 1909 as an employee of the Jacob Ahlers Company, for which he worked throughout his entire career. He returned to Germany in June of 1914 to marry Toni Preister, a resident of Hamburg and the woman who would bear Susana Groth, her brother Berend, and her sister Brigid, who now lived in West Germany. Shortly after the newlyweds arrived in Tenerife in July of 1914, Jacob Ahlers took his family to Germany for a summer holiday, but with the outbreak of the war in August, was forced to remain in Germany for its duration. Thus, Ernst Groth was given the responsibility for managing Jacob Ahler's business and for heading the German Consulate in Tenerife for the years of the war.

Doña Susana showed me a number of pictures taken during the early years of her parents' marriage. Among them was one of her father and the staff of the German Consulate: Herren Peiplemann, Witt, Groth, von Sternenfels, and Alfred Baeger, a man whose name struck a familiar chord. (Baeger's name was mentioned frequently in the German military records, and was listed among the men who received commendations for their service to the German espionage ring in the Canary Islands during World War I.)

I didn't mention anything about Ernst Groth's activities in the Tenerife Etappe, but I did ask Doña Susana if she recalled anything her father might have told her about his work with the German Consulate during the years of the war. She said that she did not. I told her about my meeting with Peter Koehler and about what he had told me concerning his meeting with her father—namely, the story about daily radio communication between Tenerife and Germany during the war—and asked her if her father ever mentioned anything about this to her. She said that he did not, that her father never talked about such matters. Her matter-of-fact response reminded me of Peter Koehler's wife, who answered a similar question by closing her eyes while she shook her head and told me that she knew nothing.

As for personal papers and other documents left by her father, Doña Susana said that they were in her possession, but that they were not accessible because she had not yet sorted through them to assess their content.

At the outset of our meeting, it had been my intention to make the interview brief, and so I thanked Doña Susana for seeing me. It was difficult to determine the extent to which the tragic event of her daughter's death had affected her, but my feeling was that if I had spent additional time with her, I would not have learned more than what she had already told me.

* * *

The following morning, I met Carlos Ramón Pérez-Hamilton at his office in Santa Cruz, where we chatted briefly about my interest in the Hamilton Company records before departing for the company's offices. When we arrived, we were greeted by

Charles Hamilton, the man who first told me that Robert Cary Griffith, the British vice consul during World War I, was a partner in the Hamilton Company. As Mr. Hamilton thought more about Griffith's work with the company, he said he doubted that the company's records would contain anything related to Griffith's post as vice consul. That same morning, after an examination of a reasonable sample of the records, I learned that Mr. Hamilton was correct. The documents for the period of interest to me were almost exclusively legal contracts pertaining to the company's business.

* * *

Carlos and I lunched at a nearby restaurant before our meeting with Antonio Martí, a journalist, co-editor of a German language magazine in Tenerife (*Teneriffa Woche*), and author of a recently published book, *70 Años de la Vida de un Hombre y de un Pueblo (70 Years in the Life of a Man and a Town)*. Carlos had called Señor Martí and made an appointment for us to meet with him at an outdoor café across the street from Martí's apartment in the center of Santa Cruz. Señor Martí arrived at the café just moments after we did and greeted Carlos with an exuberant expression of welcome accompanied by gestures that emphasized the enthusiasm of his words.

Martí, who was born in Santa Cruz in 1901, extended his friendly greeting to me and expressed his delight in meeting a foreigner who shared his interest in Tenerife. We chatted briefly about his book; Martí explained that it was not intended as a historical treatise so much as an account of one man's life through the years of dramatic change in Santa Cruz.

When I told Martí that my interests were in the years of World War I, he related his personal observations of German submarines sailing off the coast of Santa Cruz. He said that he and some of his young friends would climb the roofs of their houses at night where they could clearly see the German submarines, that the submarines would surface at night for the purpose of charging their batteries. He added that it was his understanding that German ships refueled somewhere in the area of

Güimar. (Güimar was the town where Uibe lived after he left La Costa.)

In answer to my question concerning the year he first saw German submarines, Martí said that it was 1915, certainly no later than 1916, and added that he remembered seeing a German ship sink a British ship just outside the bay of Santa Cruz. He did not recall the names of the ships or the date. I wondered if he had this sinking confused with the publicly witnessed sinking of the *Kedivi* by two German submarines off the southern coast of Gran Canaria in December of 1916. He said he did not, that the sinking he witnessed was outside the bay of Santa Cruz.

Except for Ernst Groth, Martí did not recognize the names of the German residents of Tenerife during World War I, and in the case of this one exception, it was not until after the war that Martí met Groth.

* * *

During the next two weeks, I attended several parties, where I renewed my acquaintance with the many people I had met on earlier visits. During this period I also managed to follow up on some leads, but nothing of substance resulted.

Since my work in Tenerife took less time than I had anticipated, I decided to leave for London. There, I would once more check the British Foreign Office files for information that I might have overlooked on my first inspection, and for information that might now be useful in view of my increased knowledge of pertinent people and events. Furthermore, because the distance from London to Düsseldorf is only a few hundred miles, it would be possible for me to meet Claus Köhler-Achenbach on short notice—if I could reach him. I left for London on January 10.

* * *

On Thursday morning I left my Hampstead Heath flat and walked to the Belsize Park underground station, where I took a train to the Public Records Office on Portugal Street. In a city whose charm is based at least in part on a strong feeling of tradition and immutability, I was surprised and disappointed to discover that the archives had been moved to a new building in Kew Gardens, a village in southwest London on the second-to-last underground station of the District Line.

I spent Friday going through the index card file looking for references to names of the many people and places I had learned about since my first visit to the Public Records Office in 1975, but found no specific reference to these people or places under any of the headings for each of the five years of 1914 to 1918. I then rechecked the index card file under some of the headings I had used during my first visit to the Public Records Office. Since the new retrieval system limited the number of volumes that could be requested at a given time, I had to be somewhat selective so as not to waste time waiting for useless documents.

* * *

On Saturday morning, January 14, I called Düsseldorf and reached Claus Köhler-Achenbach at his home. After I identified myself and told him about my lack of success in trying to reach him, he explained that he had suffered a stroke several months ago and had only recently been released from the hospital. He said that he would be happy to meet with me, but that he could not see me until after the nineteenth. I told him that I would go to Düsseldorf on the twentieth and call him when I arrived. He warned me that he was still convalescing, and that he could meet for only a brief interview, but that he still remembered his days in Tenerife.

I was excited with the prospect of finally meeting with the eldest child of Wolfgang Köhler's first family, and thus the one who should have the best recollection of Tenerife. My lack of success in finding new documents of interest among the British Foreign Office files made the days of the following week pass slowly.

When Friday finally arrived, I left London for Düsseldorf. By the time my flight landed and I made my way from the airport via the S-Bahn to my hotel in the commercial center of the city, just a few blocks from the Bahnhof, it was already mid-afternoon. I called Claus Köhler-Achenbach, who said that he had some business at the Düsseldorf Kunstakademie (School of Art) early Saturday, but that he would be free to see me there at ten in the morning.

*   *   *

On Saturday morning the weather was bright, sunny, and unseasonably warm when my cab arrived at Eiskellerstrasse 1. Before I had paid the driver, I saw a man standing at the front door of the Kunstakademie who I thought must be Claus Köhler-Achenbach. He was about the same height and had the same stocky build as Peter Koehler, and bore a strong resemblance to both Peter and his sister Marianne. But there was something about the expression on his face that surprised me: he looked like a man who smiled quickly and often. And there were other aspects of his appearance that did not match the image I had formed: his thick, close-cropped white hair was a bit tousled, not neatly combed as I had expected; his skin was tan and healthy looking, not wan and sickly; and his costume was not a neat conservative business suit, but a casual combination of royal blue trousers and a light tan bulky-knit turtleneck sweater beneath an unbuttoned fur-lined suede jacket.

As I stepped from the cab, the thought occurred to me that perhaps it was a coincidence that a sixty-five-year-old man who bore a resemblance to Peter Koehler should be standing at this place at this time. But a moment later, the man extended his hand and smiled broadly as he introduced himself as Claus Köhler-Achenbach, and introduced me to his companion, an attractive, red-haired woman of about thirty, who identified herself as Professor Köhler's assistant. Claus may have physically resembled his brother Peter and sister Marianne, but it was Charlotte who came to mind as we talked. I wondered if he shared her attitudes.

After we exchanged greetings, Claus invited me to his studio on the second floor of the building. As we started up the staircase to the doors leading to the foyer, I became aware of the effects of the stroke suffered by Professor Köhler: his left arm hung loosely at his side, and although he could support his weight with his left leg, he could lift himself up the stairs only by means of advancing his right leg one step at a time. After we entered the foyer, we walked slowly to the door of the elevator. While we waited, Claus seemed to anticipate my thoughts by explaining that although his condition was still quite poor, it was much improved over what it had been just a few months before. His assistant confirmed that he had recovered considerably from the condition he experienced immediately following the stroke, that he had made a remarkable recovery, and added that it was unfortunate that I did not have the opportunity to meet him before the stroke. There was something about the way in which she said this that led me to feel that she may have wished to turn back the clock more for herself than for me.

The large freight elevator arrived and took us to the second floor. As we walked through the corridor to Claus's studio, we passed an assortment of curious objects not uncommon to schools of art: truncated Grecian columns with elaborate Corinthian capitals, plaster copies of classical sculpture, bits and pieces of discarded graphic art, some colorful posters, and a vast assortment of both common and curious objects used as subjects in still-life sketching and painting. By contrast, Claus's studio, a large circular room with a high ceiling, was empty—that is, there were no pictures on the walls, no materials on the tables, and no signs of any work in progress. Apparently, the studio had not been used since Professor Köhler's stroke, and it appeared that all his things had been cleared out.

Claus pushed a stool next to a low window overlooking the Hofgarten, a large park with lofty trees and gravel paths that twisted through well-manicured lawns to placid ponds dotted with ducks and swans. He explained that this was where he sat when he worked. I sat on a stool next to him. Although the sun was bright, it was low in the sky. Thus the branches of the tall trees were underlighted and cast long shadows on the green lawns; it was almost high noon, but the winter sun made it look like twilight. Claus gazed sadly at the scene so familiar to him. Since he was already sixty-five, the stroke precluded any possibility that he might remain at the Kunstakademie for a few more years. He would soon be leaving his studio, with its view of the Hofgarten, forever.

His assistant interrupted his reverie by reminding us that our meeting would have to be brief, that she would leave us to talk but would return in about an hour, when it would be time for

Professor Köhler to take his medicine and return to his home to rest.

I began the formal part of the interview by asking Claus about his lineage. He told me that he was born to Thekla Achenbach in Frankfurt, Germany, on March 18, 1912, the year before her marriage to Wolfgang Köhler. He said that it was not until he was sixteen years old that his mother told him that Wolfgang Köhler was his father. Presumably, until that time he believed that Wolfgang Köhler was not his father. In answer to my question of why his mother had kept this information from him for so many years, and why he had been led to believe that Wolfgang Köhler was not his father, he answered: "This is a mystery." Since a tenable solution to this mystery might prove embarrassing, I decided not to pursue the matter further, at least not at that moment.

Perhaps it was this mystery that reminded me of the curious event preceding my meeting with Marianne Winneberger, namely the visit by her brother Peter the day before our interview. I wondered whether Claus had heard from his brother Peter or from his sisters, so I reminded him that I had met Charlotte, Peter, and Marianne last summer, and asked him if any of them had been in touch with him recently. He told me that he had not been in touch with Peter or Marianne for several years, but that he had been in touch with Charlotte, whom he planned to visit soon for a six-month period of convalescence. This would be his first visit to Edsvalla, and so I described Charlotte's house to him and warned him that Edsvalla was a very tiny town in the hinterland of Sweden, and that he had better be prepared for a quiet life there. Charlotte would be very happy to have him stay with her.

Mention of Charlotte reminded Claus of a picture he planned to show me, a picture sent to him by Charlotte. The picture was a copy of the one that appeared on the front page of the Uppsala newspaper in June of 1967, on the occasion of the honorary doctoral degree given to Wolfgang Köhler for his contributions to humanity as well as to science. Claus elaborated on the story; he told me that the award was the "Vasen Order," a special tribute bestowed by the king of Sweden for Köhler's work in helping Jews to leave Germany during the early years of the Nazi regime. Claus cited Einstein, Wertheimer, and Gelb as examples. There was no question in my mind that Wolfgang Köhler was opposed to the Nazis, and I knew that after he had secured a post for himself at Swarthmore in 1935, he had tried to help Gelb; but I had never heard any stories of how he had helped Einstein or Wertheimer, both of whom left Germany before Köhler. If there was any evidence that Köhler had helped either of these men, I felt certain that Mary Henle would have made this information public.

The picture Claus showed me reminded me of the picture I had brought as a gift for him, the picture of Claus, Marianne, Peter, their parents, and two other couples with children taken on the tennis court of the Hotel Martiánez. Claus was delighted. He quickly identified himself, the other members of his family, and the Groths, but he did not know the third couple. As he stared at the picture, he began to recount his experiences as a child in Tenerife.

The first story he told was one that, like so many others I had heard and that Claus would subsequently tell me, demonstrated how clever Sultan was. According to Claus, who as a small child spent considerable time playing in and about the ape compound, there was an occasion in which he sat on one side of the bars unable to pull a banana through them because the banana was lying in a horizontal position with respect to the bars. When Sultan saw Claus's predicament, he reached down and turned the banana ninety degrees to a vertical position so that it could be slipped between the bars. Claus added that Wolfgang Köhler witnessed this and told Claus that Sultan was more clever than he. I laughed with Claus at his story, but I wondered to myself if this theme of the child's inferiority to the beast was not intended to demean the child as well as provide for an amusing anecdote.

In a somewhat indirect way, Claus confirmed my suspicion by telling a second story, one in which Köhler got his comeuppance. One day, Sultan took Claus up to the top of a tree. When Köhler saw this, he told Claus to come down, but Claus refused. Köhler was adamant in his demand, but Claus continued to disobey. When Claus finally came down, Köhler pulled down Claus's shorts and spanked his bare bottom. A short time later that day, while Köhler was busy working about the compound, Sultan quietly approached him from the rear, grabbed his trousers by the seat, and pulled them down to his ankles. Claus's eyes twinkled with impish delight as he told this Katzenjammer story.

Yet another Katzenjammer story dealt with Sultan's mischievous sense of humor. It seems that the children were customarily called to lunch when the maid beat a cooking pan with a stick. Sultan apparently learned what this sound meant, and on one occasion he went into the house and took the soup tureen from the dining room table and hid it in the garden.

Although these stories were similar to so many cute anecdotes about pet animals, they did agree with Manuel González y García's anthropomorphic attitude toward Sultan. Perhaps those experiments dealing with Sultan that Köhler reported in *The Mentality of Apes* were less typical of apes in general and more a description of an unusual individual animal; perhaps Sultan was an exceptional ape among apes.

Claus expressed his affection for Sultan in a story that concerned an Englishman who made regular visits to the animal compound. During these visits, the Englishman often teased and annoyed Sultan by poking him with a stick through the bars of the cage. On one occasion, Sultan managed to grab the man's hand and bite his finger. The Englishman fainted and was in a mild state of shock for a short time afterwards. In an effort to help the Englishman recover, Wolfgang Köhler mixed a brandy and raw egg drink and gave it to Claus to take to the Englishman. When Claus went to the shocked man sitting near the compound, instead of handing the drink to the man, Claus threw it on him.

I asked Claus who the Englishman was and why he made regular visits to the compound. Claus said that he was one of several Englishmen who kept Köhler and the station under surveillance, that the English suspected that Köhler was involved in espionage because of his association with the men at the observatory in the mountains. Although Claus said that he did not recognize the names of Dember and Uibe, these were obviously the men to whom he was referring.

Claus also mentioned that Wolfgang Köhler had built a radio and was successful in communicating with Germany. His story about Köhler and the men from the observatory, and about the radio they constructed, was consistent with his sister Marianne's story about the radio built by the "team" and hidden in a second-story room that the children were forbidden to enter. The essential difference between the two versions was that Marianne had said the team was not successful in their attempt to build an operative radio, whereas Claus had said they were, a statement that was consistent with Peter Köhler's insistence that they had been successful in building a radio—"Groth told me with his own mouth!"

When the family returned to Germany, they stayed with Wolfgang Köhler's mother in Enttlingen, a town near Baden-Baden. Claus said that it was not very pleasant staying there because Köhler's mother was very strict, and the children, having grown up in Tenerife, were very wild. As Claus talked about this period in his life, he was reminded of his relationship with his siblings, a poor relationship marred by rivalry and rancor that continued into adult years. Claus said that Peter and the other children were especially envious of him at the time he received his professorship, "something which neither Peter nor Martin were able to do." Claus said that his brothers and sisters told him, "You may be a professor, but you are not one of Wolfgang Köhler's children!" Claus remarked that Wolfgang Köhler had written a letter to his sister Charlotte in which he told her that he was very proud of Claus because Claus never asked him for help, whereas all of the other children did. This, plus the fact that Claus had earned a professorship, seemed to satisfy him that he was the favored son.

In keeping with the feelings of his siblings, Claus had great respect for Wolfgang Köhler and the fame he achieved. As a young man, he had hoped that he could accomplish just a fraction of what his father had: "He was a genius." Claus said that as he grew older and accomplished more, he had come to realize that he was only at the beginning of things. He was not a contented man, who, in the winter of his years, looks back with pride on his life's work.

As he reminisced about his accomplishments and those of his father, Claus mentioned that Wolfgang Köhler had built an organ made of glass; glass bottles of different sizes and different shapes cut in different heights were used as resonating chambers in place of the conventional metal organ pipes. Claus said that he remembered seeing the organ in 1933 or 1934 on display at the Reichstag. I reminded Claus that it couldn't have been 1934, because the Reichstag fire was in 1933, and if it was 1933, it had to be in the early part of the year because the fire was on February 27. Claus said that the organ was, in fact, destroyed in the fire. The question of the exact date was an insignificant one; the important fact was that Köhler had the intellectual capability and technical ingenuity to construct such a remarkable machine as the one described by Claus, and to construct it so well that it was put on display at the Reichstag.

Claus smiled sardonically as he told me that his mother used to tell people that Wolfgang Köhler could not have done the research in Tenerife if it had not been for her. He said that he thought Köhler resented this, and added that his mother should not have talked this way. When I told Claus about the letters Köhler sent from Tenerife to the Prussian Academy of Science—the letters in which he acknowledged Thekla's importance in his work and stated that she was capable of managing the ape station if it were necessary for him to return to Germany—Claus was surprised, but insisted nonetheless that his mother should not have said the resentful things she did. It was clear that Claus and Charlotte shared a lack of affection for their late mother.

I asked him again if he recognized the names "Dember" and "Uibe." His eyes turned upward and moved back and forth scanning the space above them as he searched his memory. He said that he did not recognize the names, but that he did remember that Köhler, oftentimes accompanied by the family, made frequent trips to Güimar to visit a German family that lived there. I was reminded that Dember lived with the Köhler family at La Costa during the time Uibe lived in Güimar. Perhaps this helped to account for the frequent trips that Köhler made to Güimar. Claus also recalled that Köhler made a trip from Güimar to the "peak of Tenerife" (Teide).

This information about the frequent trips to Güimar was especially interesting, because the route to Güimar from La Paz—the town nearest La Costa, which is northwest of Güimar—is not an easy one; it requires a steep climb to the crest of the Cañadas Mountains from Aguamansa, and a steep descent to the town of Güimar. If they took the less steep trail to El Portillo from Aguamansa, they would have passed within a few miles of the meteorological observatory at La Grieta, the station that the Spanish government forced Dember and Uibe to vacate because of complaints from the British government that the observatory was being used by its German residents as a radio station for the German military. Since the observatory was well supplied with electrical equipment, perhaps the trips between La Paz and Güimar were a means of stopping unobtrusively at the observatory to pick up electrical supplies and tools necessary for the radio that Köhler, Dember, and Uibe built at La Costa and maintained at El Ciprés. Considering the time and effort required to make the arduous trek up and down the mountains between La Paz and Güimar, it seemed very unlikely that Köhler frequently made this trip to socialize with German friends.

Another explanation for the frequent trips through the mountains might have been that the primary radio transmitter and long-wave antenna remained at La Grieta or in the area of La Grieta, while the broadcasting was initiated at La Costa. From there, the signal from a relatively low-powered radio transmitter was sent to the station of La Grieta, where it was amplified and beamed to Germany. Such an arrangement would have allowed several low-powered transmitters throughout the islands to use one central high-powered transmitter as a relay for long-distance communication.

In my research on the early spark-gap radio transmitters typical of those used about the time of World War I, I had learned that the long antennas required by these radios (three hundred to a thousand feet or more) were not mounted in a vertical position as are radio transmitter towers of today, but rather in a horizontal position like parallel telephone wires, except on short poles sufficiently tall to hold them off the ground. This precluded the need to build tall steel towers (which can be seen from many miles away) to support the antenna, and also made the antenna portable and simple to conceal. That is, after the direction in which you wished to beam a signal was determined, it was simply a matter of running out two lengths of wire sufficiently long to accommodate the transmitter. When not in use, the antenna could, in a matter of minutes, be dropped to the ground or wound on a spool. Thus, the reason for the frequent trips through the mountains may have been to maintain the primary long-distance transmitter and receiver. Even if maintenance requirements were minimal, the diesel-powered generator at the observatory would have required fuel from time to time.

Claus's assistant entered the studio to remind us that it was time for Claus to take his medicine and time for me to take my leave. Before we left the studio, I asked Claus if he would put me in touch with Nelli Gelb, Claus's aunt who lived in nearby Köln. Claus said that she had died a few years ago, and told me the story of how her late husband had died shortly before he was scheduled to leave Germany for the United States to join Köhler at Swarthmore College.

As we walked from the studio, I asked Claus if I could meet with him the next day. After a brief consultation with his assistant, he agreed to see me at his apartment at noon of the following day.

* * *

It was almost midday when I left the Kunstakademie, and so I decided to walk to the nearby Altstadt (the largest "Old Town" of any German city) to explore its market place and shops and to have lunch. Afterwards, I returned to the western entrance to the Hofgarten and strolled leisurely along its twisting paths to the Scholl Jägerhoff, an eighteenth-century hunting residence that now contains a magnificent collection of twentieth-century art, including works by Léger, Kandinsky, Chagall, Braque, Ernst, Miro, Pollock, and Picasso. The museum also contains an especially large collection of paintings by Paul Klee, who, I learned that afternoon, taught at the Düsseldorf Kunstakademie from 1931 until 1933, when the Nazis, who judged his work to be degenerate, forced him to resign.

* * *

Shortly before noon on Sunday, I took a cab from the Bahnhof to Claus Köhler's home, an apartment in a relatively new four-story building located in an attractive residential neighborhood, a short distance from the center of the city. When I entered the vestibule of his building, Claus called down to me from outside the door of his second-floor apartment. I climbed the stairs to his landing, where we shook hands before he showed me into the living room of his apartment. Although he apologized for the appearance of the room, it was in fact clean and neat except for a number of loose papers, drawings, and odds and ends that accumulate during the normal course of day-to-day living. It appeared that the living room was now serving partly as a studio; one wall was covered with a dozen or so colorful pastel drawings, the central theme of which was the sun.

As I studied the drawings, Claus explained that his technique for getting both the strong and subtle shading effects was to build several layers of color until he got just the shade he wanted. He went on to explain that he had a long-time interest in the effects of light refraction. I was reminded of my conversation with Claus's brother Peter, who remembered that Dember did research on light refraction when in Tenerife, and that his mother told him of her special interest in this research because of its relevance to her painting.

One of Claus's drawings showed a view of the sun as seen in a sirocco. I remarked that I was familiar with the scene, that I had experienced such a sandstorm when I visited Tenerife last, that the strong, hot, dry winds blowing from the Sahara Desert turned the sky yellow at midday and left a residue of fine brown dust everywhere. I was reminded, too, that Claus's sister Marianne recalled a sirocco she had experienced during her childhood in Tenerife, and that it was the cause of some concern on the part of her parents. Although it seemed obvious to me that Claus's current work was colored by his experiences in Tenerife, he claimed that it was not. I asked him again whether he remembered the names "Dember" and "Uibe." He said he did not.

In preparation for my visit, Claus had retrieved two newspaper articles. One, which was published in a 1953 edition of *Stadt Düsseldorf*, told a story about Claus's experiences with Sultan in Tenerife. The other, which did not contain the date or name of the paper in which it appeared, discussed Wolfgang Köhler and his part in the founding of Gestalt psychology.

I asked Claus when he last saw Wolfgang Köhler. I knew that Köhler had been detached from the children of his first marriage, but I was still surprised when Claus told me that the last time he saw Wolfgang Köhler was in the early 1930s, during the time that Claus was a student at the Kunstakademie in Berlin. It seems that Claus knew the train on which Köhler rode on his way to and from his home and his office at the University of

Berlin, a train that stopped momentarily at the Kunstakademie station. Claus would wait at the station for the train to pass through in hopes of catching a glimpse of the man his mother had, only a few years earlier, told him was his father. As Claus told me this story, his expression of sadness reminded me of his sister Marianne; it was the same expression she wore when she talked about the separation.

Claus said that he was about sixteen years old at the time of the divorce. He said that both parties must have been to blame for a couple with five children to divorce. Unlike Marianne, who made it clear that she believed that Lili was to blame for the divorce, Claus did not offer a clear and simple explanation; he certainly didn't blame Lili. He mentioned that Nelli Gelb, his aunt, had told him that "Lili was a wonderful woman." Since Claus was very close to Nelli Gelb, I'm sure he believed her. Whatever his beliefs, he expressed no hostility towards Lili.

As Claus thought back on his early years, he mentioned that Wolfgang Köhler had given Thekla money for his studies, but that Thekla gave the money to a girl friend, and thus Claus was forced to make his way on his own. He said that Thekla had been very jealous of him when he was accepted at the Kunstakademie because it was something she had not done but would have very much liked to do.

Claus said that he and his brother Peter were the only ones to attend Thekla's funeral, that it was a very sad affair—no words were said. "All her life she wanted to be known as Achenbach's daughter. She had many friends during her lifetime, but lost them all because she thought of herself as the best and therefore better than all others"—a sentiment that Claus shared with his sister Charlotte.

Claus told a story that was intended to contrast Wolfgang with Thekla. The setting was in Germany at a time when horses were still used to pull milk wagons. According to Claus, Wolfgang Köhler looked from the window of his house and saw a milkman beating his horse. This act so infuriated Köhler that he went from his house into the street and slapped the face of the milkman. Claus added that one can learn a great deal about a person on the basis of the person's attitude towards animals. I agreed with him, but I didn't specify what it was one learned about the person, nor did I offer the proposition that one could learn a great deal about a person on the basis of the person's attitude towards people.

Claus said that he could not have been so creative and as successful in his own life if it had not been for the personal tragedies he suffered, especially the one associated with his divorce. He said that he shared with his father the ability to turn tragic events into motivating forces, that his and his father's successful careers were motivated by similar marital tragedies.

I had not given much thought to Claus's life apart from his relationship with Wolfgang and Thekla; therefore, it surprised me to learn that Claus felt that this own divorce was more tragic than what he experienced when his parents divorced. It also surprised me to learn that Claus identified so closely with Wolfgang Köhler. Except for an occasional glimpse of Köhler as his train passed through the Kunstakademie station in Berlin, Claus never saw Köhler or received a written word from him after Köhler left Thekla and the children. Furthermore, although the period surrounding Wolfgang's divorce from Thekla may well have been a difficult time in his life, it was Wolfgang who initiated the divorce, not Thekla. Finally, while Thekla, who became the ex-wife of the director of the Psychology Laboratory at the University of Berlin, was left with five children ranging in age from about two to fourteen, Wolfgang, who did not lose his position at the university as a consequence of the divorce, was left with Lili von Horlemann, a young, beautiful, well-educated, wealthy aristocrat. Nonetheless, Claus chose to equate his marital tragedy with that of Wolfgang Köhler.

In answer to an open-ended question concerning his past marriage, Claus said only that he had a son and a married daughter from his ex-wife, whom he described as a spendthrift (the very word used by Wolfgang Metzger in his description of Thekla), and that following the birth of his daughter's child, his daughter had sent the hospital bill to Claus. Claus smiled and laughed quietly when he mentioned the hospital bill.

According to Claus, Wolfgang and Thekla first met at a party at Thekla's family's house on September 19, 1912, a date that is six months after Claus's birthday. I thought at first that Claus had made an error in the year, but he produced a document dated September 19, 1912, that contained the signatures of the guests to the party on that occasion. Perhaps I should have brought this discrepancy in dates to Claus's attention, but the fact of Claus's lineage was less important than the potential embarrassment for him. Perhaps the answer to the mystery of why Thekla waited until after the divorce to tell Claus that Wolfgang Köhler was his father was that Köhler was not on hand to contradict her.

Claus told me that at the time of Wolfgang and Thekla's first meeting, Thekla was friendly with an Austrian violinist who wanted to marry her, and that soon after the meeting, Thekla had to decide whether to marry the Austrian or Köhler. Claus said that Thekla chose Wolfgang because she felt that the Austrian was not very reliable.

Apparently, the Austrian violinist was the man who was thought to be Claus's father, the man whom Claus's brother Peter described as a Czech composer from Prague. Claus said that for the purpose of seeing what the man looked like, he had once attended a concert where the violinist played, and that after seeing him, he was convinced that the man was not his father. Whether or not the Austrian violinist was Claus's father was not so important as the fact that this story illustrated Claus's own feelings of uncertainty, that he did not firmly believe Thekla when she told him after the divorce that Wolfgang Köhler was his father. Perhaps, as Claus grew older, it became easier for him to incorporate the belief that Köhler was his father—in spite of evidence to the contrary—than to live with uncertainty. This is a fairly common psychological phenomenon, one that can be explained nicely by a fundamental principle of Gestalt psychology, *closure*, the innate mental process that imposes symmetry on asymmetrical figures, meaning on meaningless forms, resolution on unresolved chords, and harmony on the dissonant events of life. Claus found closure in Wolfgang Köhler. In "The Nature of Intelligence," Köhler himself explains this process: "Is it too bold a thought that an organization which is unclosed in a particular way tends to closure, in a way suited to its particular structure, by means of selective recall?"

I tried to change the tenor of the discussion by asking Claus if he had more recollections of days in Tenerife. He said that he did, and began by telling me a story about a very beautiful Spanish nursemaid named Candelaria, who lived with the family and took care of the children. It seemed that Candelaria, who was unmarried, had a baby every year, but was never sure which of her lovers was the father. Wolfgang Köhler told the girl that it was important that she should know who the fathers were. The girl disagreed, and told him that the only important thing was that the children should be beautiful. Claus said that the girl's lovers would often serenade her at night with singing accompanied by guitar playing. One night, Wolfgang became especially annoyed with this practice, and went quietly to the garden and turned a hose on the troubadour.

I asked Claus whether he remembered Manuel González y García. Without a moment of hesitation, he said that he remembered him well, that Manuel was a good man and a very modest man who was trustworthy, loyal, and very close to Wolfgang Köhler and the family. Claus's words lent additional support to the already high credibility of Manuel's word. If Manuel had any detractors, I neither met one nor heard of one.

I asked Claus if he knew why the family moved from La Costa to El Ciprés. He said that he remembered the move but did not know the reason for it. I then asked him if the radio that Köhler built was used to communicate by means of wireless telegraphy or radio telephony. He said that he did not know, but stated with certainty that the radio worked, that Wolfgang Köhler was successful in communicating with Germany.

Claus's assistant arrived and we chatted briefly before she helped him on with his coat; they had plans for the afternoon. Before I left, Claus gave me a copy of a program that accompanied a recent showing of pastel drawings by Claus Köhler-Achenbach. The show, entitled "Licht-Reflexion," was held at the Kunstmuseum Düsseldorf. A biographical sketch on the second-to-last page of the program stated that his mother took to painting and sculpture very early in life; that his grandfather, Maximilian Alvary Achenbach, a Wagnerian singer and architect, was a professor of music at the academy in Düsseldorf; and that his great-grandfather, Andreas Achenbach, a landscape painter, was also a professor at the academy. Claus indicated his pride in the family's long tradition of professional artists and professors of art. The program also stated that Claus's father was Professor Doctor Wolfgang Köhler.

21.

Conclusion

On Monday morning, I flew from Düsseldorf to Frankfurt, where I made a connection for a flight to New York. As the plane took off from Frankfurt, there was heavy cloud cover, so low that the earth was out of sight before my plane reached that critical altitude where one loses perspective of absolute size, and all objects on earth appear to be miniature models of themselves. When my plane passed through the clouds and attained its assigned altitude, I retrieved some notes from the shoulder bag beneath the seat in front of me. Among them was a newspaper clipping lent to me by Claus Köhler-Achenbach, the article that Claus had told me dealt with stories about his family and their experiences in Tenerife, especially anecdotes involving him and Sultan. The article didn't add anything to what I already knew except for one out-of-context sentence at the bottom of the second-to-last paragraph:

> During the first World War, when all connections to the homeland were cut, the orang-scientist Köhler built his own transmitting set which was, however, destroyed by the British.

As I thought back on our meetings, I realized that I had not asked Claus about what happened to the radio; it seemed unimportant. The fact that Wolfgang Köhler was under surveillance by the British during the war was well documented, and the fact that he built and operated a radio was adequately documented too, but the fate of the radio, an otherwise insignificant factor, became an interesting bit of information because it offered an explanation for Köhler's urgent need to leave Tenerife. Three independent accounts of Köhler's departure indicated that it was fast. Manuel González y García had emphasized that Köhler gave virtually no notice that he was going to leave for Germany, that his sudden departure came as a surprise. And although the minutes of the March 20 meeting of the Albert Samson Foundation indicated that health reasons may have accounted for Köhler's sudden return to Germany, Enrique Talg claimed that Köhler was sent from Tenerife by the Spanish government under "threat of force."

In view of the hostile feelings between British and German citizens, which did not end with the Allied victory over Germany in 1918, the weak Spanish government of that time may well have found it politically expedient to take the side of the winner and demonstrate its friendship and allegiance to Britain by following up on the long-standing accusations by the British residents of the island against German nationals. Certainly, in 1920, Britain had a stronger influence on the Spanish government than did Germany, especially at a time when the German government was unstable and the German mark was inflating rapidly. If the British did destroy Köhler's radio and thus expose him to the Spanish police, the government would have had no choice but to expel him or charge him with a criminal offense.

I began to speculate on how I might obtain information relative to this point, but judged that the probability of finding such records, if they did exist, was too slim to merit further exploration. Besides, hadn't I already answered the question? The essence of Manuel's story had been verified; all the proof I needed was already in my hands. While I might never find prima facie evidence—a letter or document proving beyond doubt that Köhler had been an agent of the German military—I had assembled a considerable amount of circumstantial evidence.

Even if Köhler's involvement in the war was not as great as I may have presumed initially, I was satisfied that he had served the cause of the German military through his part in building, maintaining, and operating a concealed radio for the purpose of communicating information that would contribute to the German war effort. I had come to learn, too, that Köhler's motivation may not have been complicated. In 1914, Germans were bound together by mores that dictated unquestioning obedience to parents and state. When the fatherland called, the good citizen answered.

Although I wasn't aware of it at that moment, my journey had come to an end. The day was January 23, the same date that three years earlier I first met Manuel and set out to verify his story. Yet, eventually I would learn that the story in itself was not the mystery. The mystery was Köhler. Köhler the spy was but one aspect of Köhler the man. Little by little, bits and pieces of information began to take the form of a mosaic, a mosaic from which a figure emerged. I knew the mosaic was incomplete, but, as is the case with mosaics, the likeness of the figure can be seen at a distance even though some of the pieces are missing. In fact, if one gets too close to a mosaic, so close that concentration centers on the individual bits and pieces, the whole figure is lost.

Brilliant as Köhler was—and my findings had done nothing to diminish my respect for his many accomplishments—he was not without flaws and failings. One might, in fact, surmise that it was Köhler's brilliance and single-minded devotion to his work that kept him from being a caring husband to Thekla and a loving father to the children, that in placing his career above his personal life, Köhler had lost touch with his family and had left behind a legacy of bitterness and regret. While there may be some merit to this idea, one cannot overlook other forces, not quite so grand, that may have contributed to Köhler's flawed family life and ultimate estrangement from Thekla and the children. To what extent had Claus and the circumstances that led to Köhler's marriage to Thekla colored their relationship? Might Köhler have harbored the suspicion throughout their years together that Thekla used the advent of Marianne's conception as the means for obtaining a father for Claus? Whatever the answer, the record shows that Köhler was in his mid-forties and at the

peak of his career in Germany when he left Thekla and the
children, married Lili, resigned his post at the University of
Berlin, and emigrated to the United States.

While Nazi control of the German academic establishment
was, no doubt, a factor in Köhler's decision to emigrate, it appears not to have been the only factor. Köhler wasn't so much
opposed to the politics of the Nazis as he was insulted by their
vulgarity, their crude methods, their strident voices, and their
disrespect for the established order, which meant disrespect for
him, an intolerable state for a proud man of prodigious achievement. When Köhler resigned his professorship and left Berlin for
Swarthmore, his professional life as well as his personal life were
in disarray.

What I had learned about Köhler would serve me well, but it
wasn't all that I had gained from my journey. I had come to
know a place and time as few know any place or time other than
their own. I had learned about Tenerife through its people, both
past and present, and the friends I had made were now a part of
my life. I had also come to know parts of the world that I
otherwise would never have come to know and had come to
meet people I otherwise would not have met.

Fields of psychology that require observations of behavior
independent of objective readings of meters are unique among
the sciences insofar as the psychologist is part of the subject
matter of the science. While all the sciences require strict adher-
ence to the rules of logic and evidence in the evaluation of
descriptive reports of observations, psychologists, because of the
nature of their subject, must exercise even greater care to avoid
allowing emotions to color observations. As one experimental
psychologist observing another, I could not help but admire
Köhler's ability to distance himself from his subject, but as one
human being observing another, I saw his detachment from personal ties as something less than admirable. While Köhler's cold
and distant qualities may have been key elements in his academic success, they led to emotional hardships that left indelible
marks on those close to him. Perhaps this is one of the costs of
achievement. If it is, after seeing the empty legacy left to his
children, I asked at what price?

Although my journey had enriched my life in many ways,
perhaps the single most important benefit was the opportunity it

had afforded me to assess my past and consider new directions for the future. I had set out on my odyssey at a time when I was just beginning to realize that my research in the psychology of memory no longer held a promise of rich discoveries. Through my journey to Tenerife and my desire to learn about Köhler, I had come to understand the fundamental nature of exploration. The rewarding experience of discovery can be known only by those who search. Skinner was right: "When you run onto something interesting, drop everything else and study it."

My reflections on the events of the past three years were interrupted by the passenger who sat in the seat next to me—a middle-aged woman who, during the period prior to takeoff, had expressed her anxieties about flying. Since anxiety is so commonly associated with flying, I wasn't alarmed by her remarks. But now her chest heaved rapidly as she sat, mouth wide open, gasping for air. In the moment before I turned to offer my help, I wondered if hyperventilation played a part in the initiation and maintenance of anxiety. Could it be that the effects of stress-induced hyperventilation were antecedents of anxiety as well as consequences? I wondered where this question would take me.

Index